CANOMA™ Visual Insight

Richard H. Schrand, Sr.

Canoma™ Visual Insight

The Coriolis Group, LLC
14455 North Hayden Road, Suite 220
Scottsdale, Arizona 85260

480/483-0192
FAX: 480/483-0193
http://www.coriolis.com

Library of Congress Cataloging-In-Publication Data
Schrand, Richard.
Canoma visual insight/ by Richard H. Schrand, Sr.
p. cm
Includes index.
ISBN 1-56710-626-8
1. Computer graphics. 2. Canoma (Computer file) I. Title.
T385.S352 2000
006.6'93--dc21 00-027942
CIP

Printed in the United States of America
10 9 8 7 6 5 4 3 2 1

President, CEO
Keith Weiskamp

Publisher
Steve Sayre

Acquisitions Editor
Beth Kohler

Marketing Specialist
Patti Davenport

Project Editor
Don Eamon

Technical Reviewer
Gary Shilling

Production Coordinator
Meg E. Turecek

Cover Designer
Jesse Dunn

Layout Designer
April Nielsen

Other Titles For The Creative Professional

3D Studio MAX R3 f/x and Design
By Jon Bell

3D Studio MAX R3 In Depth
By Rob Polevoi

After Effects 4 In Depth
By R. Shamms Mortier

Bryce 4 f/x and Design
By R. Shamms Mortier

Character Animation In Depth
By Doug Kelly

Digital Compositing In Depth
By Doug Kelly

Flash 4 Web Animation f/x and Design
By Ken Milburn and Janine Warner

Illustrator 8 f/x and Design
By Sherry London and T. Michael Clark

Painter 6 f/x and Design
By R. Shamms Mortier

Photoshop 5 In Depth
By David Xenakis and Sherry London

This book is dedicated to my wife, Sharon, my children, Cyndi, Courtney, Brandon, and Richard Jr., and my grandchildren, Samantha and Joseph. Thanks for putting up with me throughout this often-arduous and time-consuming project.

And to R. Shamms Mortier, fellow author and all-around good guy who violently goaded me into this line of work. Remember to always keep the company of trees, my friend.

❧

About The Author

Richard Schrand is a man who, over the course of almost three decades, has worn many hats. He spent over twenty-eight years in the broadcasting trenches as a writer, producer, reporter, news anchor, News Director, General Manager, and publicist. Throughout his career, he has interviewed everyone from the person next door to U.S. Presidents. He covered the attempted assassination of President Ronald Reagan from Washington, DC. As a publicist, he helped one of his clients be honored by then-President George Bush in a special White House ceremony. He also helped create a local television station in the Springfield/Branson, MO, market, and co-created and ran a highly successful international radio syndication company in Nashville, TN.

In 1998, he left this business that had garnered him two Emmy awards and numerous former-Broadcast Promotion and Marketing Executives Gold and Silver Awards, to follow his muse, which just happened to be computer design and writing. He just created his company, GRFX ByDesign, which specializes in 3D design and animation, corporate consultation, and Web design and is working feverishly to actually earn a living.

Richard is married, has two daughters and identical twin boys, two grandchildren, one son-in-law, three Macintosh computers, one incessantly barking, hyper-neurotic dog, and a house that is, to say the least, never quiet.

If you feel like giving the author a sympathetic pat on the back, you can e-mail him at **grfxprousa@netscape.net** or **grfxpro@mac.com**.

Acknowledgments

I need to thank so many people for helping in the creation of this book. As with any endeavor of this kind, trying to do it alone is impossible. Also, because this is the first book of what I hope will be many, I'm taking extra space to thank those responsible.

First, to the creative team of programmers, technicians, and beta testers who made sure Canoma became the program it is today: I wish you the best of luck.

To Robert Seidl and Mark Keohane: Great job guys! No matter what's happened, I'm anxiously waiting to see Canoma 2.0 in my mailbox soon.

To R. Shamms Mortier: a friend and co-author, who unselfishly shared his insights and knowledge, as well as guided me into this whole book-writing thing.

To all the people at Coriolis: Stephanie Walls who had faith in this untested person who said he could write a book; Don Eamon who helped guide what you have in your hands to become what you have in your hands; Beth Kohler, who hasn't heard the last of me yet; Meg Turecek, this book's production coordinator; April Nielsen, designer; Jesse Dunn, cover specialist; and Wendy Cutts, who was one of my first contacts at the company.

To David Fugate, my agent extraordinaire, who actually got me a contract within 30 days of my deciding to give book writing a shot.

To Gary Schilling: Thanks for the support and great work.

To everyone who supplied me with images, software, plug-ins, and equipment to produce this work, all I can say is I wish I had the money to buy all those nifty toys!

To my parents, Ed and Jane, who have always supported me no matter how wild my ideas may have seemed. Not that they necessarily understood me when I did them, but they supported me nonetheless.

Finally, to my wife, Sharon, and my children, Cyndi, Courtney, Richard Jr., and Brandon, I couldn't have done this without your love and support. The next project won't (I hope) take up so much of my time.

Contents At A Glance

Table Of Contents

Part II Projects

Foreword

I needed Canoma but it didn't exist yet. A couple of years ago, I was remodeling my kitchen—a major financial and time-consuming investment; one I would have to live with for a while. I needed to know what the project would look like and how it would work when it was finished. The problem was that the line drawings from the architect gave me no impression of the materials, textures, lighting, and *space* of the finished design.

I knew that it was possible to get a realistic 3D walk-through on current desktop PCs, and digital cameras were becoming affordable and were improving in quality. Why shouldn't I be able to take pictures of my current kitchen, quickly get a 3D model, and start rearranging—changing lighting, surface textures, and so on? I wanted a model that was reasonably realistic but not necessarily dimensionally accurate; the architect would supply that level of detail later anyway. Traditional "from scratch" modeling wouldn't be cost-effective here. It takes a lot of measurement and a solid knowledge of a CAD package, and you still don't get realistic textures. And then I thought, "Why not take it a step further?" Wouldn't it be great if you could browse Web sites of furniture and appliance manufacturers, go through their catalogs, and drag and drop the items you're interested in right into your kitchen model? This would make it easy to get a realistic impression and play with alternatives before you make the potentially costly decisions.

Well, that's exactly how Canoma was born. The idea behind Canoma is *image-assisted modeling,* which lets you work right on top of the images without ever seeing the typical multiple orthographic views, coordinate systems, and so on. Canoma is not quite automatic; you supply the level of detail at which things are modeled as well as the type of shapes used to approximate the real-world objects. On its own, Canoma figures out the dimensions, location, and orientation of the objects and the cameras, and *that* is a huge timesaver.

Originally conceived by two engineers, Canoma needed broader marketing and distribution support. We turned to MetaCreations, which was producing a stable of innovative 2D and 3D applications. Our team added two engineers working in France on the user interface, and we delivered the first version without ever physically meeting (thanks to the Internet and email).

We wanted to open the field of realistic 3D modeling to a wider audience of Web content and graphics professionals with a background in 2D tools such as Photoshop, Dreamweaver, Flash, GoLive, and so on. This is why Canoma makes it easy to edit textures in a flat "head-on" view that doesn't require users to think about perspective, even though the source image obviously had surfaces in perspective. To make it simple to put the resulting 3D models on the Web, we provided MetaStream output as well as ready-to-go Web pages.

But we also wanted to serve the 3D professionals who already use and like tools such as 3D Studio Max, Poser, Ray Dream, Carrara, Bryce, trueSpace, and so on. So Canoma can export a variety of file formats. In this way, you can integrate Canoma-generated models into new designs and animations, complete with texture and camera information. We shied away from loading down Canoma with modeling features that would duplicate these existing tools. Think of Canoma as a human-assisted 3D scanner program—one that is focused on output—rather than one to be used as a general-purpose modeler.

The initial response from users and reviewers has been very encouraging. Even though the program doesn't feel like any drawing tool they are used to, they enjoy its relative lack of complexity and good-looking output. Of course, users have suggested more features, and we are busily integrating many of them into the next versions of this program. Canoma 1 is the first step. With our users' help, we will get far more mileage out of the image-assisted modeling approach, perhaps one day moving to a more automated capturing method based on video footage rather than on still photographs.

For people who see it for the first time, Canoma has a certain "this is so easy, *I* can do this" feel. And they can do it! As with other tools, however, you'll find that learning tips and techniques from power users can increase your productivity and quality dramatically. That's why you will find this book a valuable resource. It complements and greatly extends the information in the manual. I recommend it to existing users who want to get more out of Canoma as well as to prospective buyers who just want to see what all the fuss is about.

—Robert Seidl

Introduction

It's fascinating where life can lead you. For over 28 years, I had pursued and gained recognition in one career. Here's the rundown on what happened next.

The Road To 3D

During the final ten years of my first career, I began to play with computers. Being the optimistic sort, I'd take up challenges I was uniquely unqualified to do at that time—designing newsletters and ads for clients that appeared in publications such as *Hollywood Reporter* and *Daily Variety*. I worked on a Mac Plus, with the first version of QuarkXPress and a handheld scanner that produced pictures at resolutions too low to be useful for anything. Always looking for new ways to show my stubbornness, I explored some of the low-end 3D programs available in the mid- to late-1980s and found them extremely frustrating.

Then came the Nineties. I graduated to faster and faster computers—always Macs because of their reputation for design prowess and because DOS and I didn't get along. I upgraded QuarkXPress, got Adobe Photoshop and Adobe Illustrator. Yet, I stayed away from 3D because it just didn't interest me. Then, a few years ago, I got a copy of Poser 2 by what is now MetaCreations. The ability to control humanoid and animal models without worrying about mesh form modeling and tweaking control vertices allowed me to delve into a whole new area that at that time was little more than a hobby.

This hobby began to possess me in ways I never could have imagined. I became a mesh-form junkie; Poser 2 became a drug that unerringly guided me into wanting to create my own 3D images. So, I searched the Internet and haunted software stores, looking for interesting programs that I could use. Bryce 3D was one. I tried Ray Dream 3D. I downloaded many demo programs in the unending quest for mesh satisfaction. Then I found a program named Pixels:3D, and my modeling prowess blossomed.

As I gravitated away from the business I had been such a part of for almost three decades, I decided it was time to create my own company. In 1999, GRFX ByDesign was born. My company specializes in 3D modeling, animation, and graphic design. I made contacts in the software industry—especially with MetaCreations and Pixels Animation Studios—and was contacted to help write tutorials for a book on Pixels:3D. I wrote how-to's and tutorials for various Web sites and other books. Then, in late 1999, I started to write this book.

Why Canoma?

This is a double-edged question. On the personal side, as I created more and more 3D models and worked on my mapping skills, I found that I would often use seamless photographic textures as image maps. If done correctly, they added a realism I was previously unable to attain. At that time, I had heard about Canoma, saw the ads for it, read reviews on it, but didn't really think much about it because I was becoming a Spline and Mesh snob. *A program that uses nothing but primitives*, I had thought. *No real modeling to be done*. It can't be a professional package, I reasoned, if I'm not pushing and pulling CV's! Then I received a copy and began to work with different photographs. I became enamored with the possibilities of how Canoma worked, and I quickly learned how wrong my initial impression was.

For those who have Canoma or are thinking about getting it, the program offers a value that goes beyond what you might expect. The ability to turn 2D photographs into fully-rendered and manipulable 3D images is fascinating. Canoma is on the cusp of a whole new modeling industry that will open the doors for professionals and novices alike to create images never before possible. The only limitation will come with your ability to take and scan quality photographs (see Chapter 3).

More Than Just A Pretty Box

One thing is missing from the MetaCreations/Canoma marketing machine—a well-rounded campaign that tells people about all the creative possibilities of this program. Prior to divesting its software interests, MetaCreations' marketing focus was on architectural structure creation, and it does this very well. However, little is discussed about the creative, often esoteric uses of Canoma. That's what this book is really about: opening the doors to creativity, with Canoma as a centerpiece to your work.

I hope to accomplish two things with this book:

- Through in-depth projects, I expand on the User Manual to help aspiring *Canomans* create the highest quality models possible. By working along with the various chapters, you should find your abilities growing stronger and stronger.
- To open your minds to the possibilities inherent in Canoma. It's more than an architectural enhancement package; it's a program of many possibilities for those who want to push the 3D envelope.

Defining The Canoman

What exactly is a *Canoman*? That can be a bit complicated. On the most abstract level, a Canoman is a person who uses the Canoma software to re-create reality through his or her art so that everyone, anywhere in the world, can experience and enjoy it. The Canoman turns something flat and two-dimensional, such as a photograph, into an interactive event, changing the way to view the world and giving a sense of the vast possibilities out there. Working with a photograph or a mixture of photography and blueprints, Canoma gives architects, graphic artists, and comic book artists—and even nonspecialists such as realtors and store owners—the capability to present their ideas in a unique and, until now, unexpected way. If you look at it in this way, Canoma is a bit of magic in a box.

To be able to place photographic textures on simple items such as boxes and triangles has long been the dream of many novices and professionals. With Canoma, artists no longer need to try to re-create reality through self-created textures, *bump maps* (images that are used to create bumpy or irregular surfaces on a 3D model), or *specularity maps* (images used to create the shine/light bounce off 3D models). Therefore, a Canoman is a person who embraces 3D technology for the sake of art and places him or herself on the threshold of digital image creation.

The Novice

Each chapter in this book builds upon the techniques you learned in previous chapters. Sometimes, the chapters will review modeling techniques learned earlier, but this is a good thing. Refreshing your skills can only prepare you for more challenging work. Ultimately, this book takes you to Asheville, NC and helps you to recreate the city in full 3D splendor.

The Intermediate To Advanced User

I'll take you through integrating your Canoma models into other 3D applications to create realistic and otherworldly imagery. You'll work with Bryce 4, Poser 4, and 2D image programs such as Adobe Photoshop to achieve the look you want, and again, hopefully open your eyes to the potential within Canoma's basic code. I also hope to show just how fun Canoma can be and how you can bypass its inherent limitations to build the image you want or need.

The Professional

So many professions can make use of Canoma that listing them all is difficult:

- The Web and/or graphic designer can use Canoma to create easily loaded interactive imagery and stills for clients' Web sites. It also adds unique visual capabilities for creating print advertisements.
- The Architect and City Planner can use Canoma to place building designs into the actual location where construction will take place, so you can truly visualize photographically how it will interact with surrounding structures.
- The 3D artist will find that Canoma offers a solid addition to his or her arsenal for creating intriguing visuals in half the usual time.
- Traditional artists interested in 3D, but uninterested in learning a whole new technical procedure will find that Canoma gives them the freedom to create that next generation of artwork—one that incorporates photorealistic 3D combined with pens, brushes, and chalk.

The preceding list shows only a few of many professionals who can benefit from Canoma and who will want this book handy for reference.

How This Book Is Laid Out

As mentioned previously, this book takes you through a range of modeling assignments, from simple to complex, to match your learning curve. Each chapter delves into new areas of modeling. Each project has a definite purpose, whether obvious or not, to help you become a Canoma expert. In later chapters, you deal with some daring and complex assignments, such as using Canoma to create 3D comic books, and—as I also stated previously—building the city of Asheville, NC. *Canoma Visual Insight* is not meant to replace the User Manual; which contains valuable information that gives you some of the basics upon which this book builds. Read the documentation; a strong starting foundation will help you as you move through this book. Although I do review these basic skills, the User Manual is a wonderful resource. I look at the learning process like a serialized movie, and *Canoma Visual Insight* as the culmination of the series.

Getting To The Files

You'll notice that no CD-ROM is included. Fear not; you can access an FTP site to download chapter images that you will work on, and other software supplied by vendors such as Dynamic Graphics, Extensis, ClickArt, and MetaCreations. So armed, you can practice long into the night. You can access these files at the FTP site at: **ftp.coriolis.com**, in the **Canoma_Visual_Insight** folder. Demo copies of Bryce 4 and other MetaCreations software, fully-functional but time-limited Extensis PhotoFrame, and PhotoGraphics filters for Photoshop and Painter are included on this site. Although no demo version of Poser 4 was available at the time of writing, you can check the MetaCreations site at **www.metacreations.com** to see if one becomes available.

The Future Of Canoma

During the course of writing this book, MetaCreations went through a major shakeup, and is in the process of divesting itself of all its software, including Canoma, to focus on its MetaStream technology. This doesn't mean your investment in Canoma is in jeopardy. After a home is found for it, you'll see some additions that will help you create models that are even more stunning.

A furor ensued when MetaCreations made this decision to get rid of its software division to focus on MetaStream. The backlash from it has yet to be truly felt. The user base for their products—Canoma, Bryce, Poser, Ray Dream, Carrara, and others—is so vast, however, you can expect them to be quickly purchased and distributed under another company's banner. Until then, all the programs mentioned above will be available for purchase from your favorite software vendor.

Carry On Intrepid Canoman

Now let's begin your journey into Canoma. Thank you for purchasing *Canoma Visual Insight*, and I hope you enjoy reading it as much as I enjoyed putting it together. If you have questions or comments, please feel free to e-mail the author at **grfxprousa@netscape.net** or **grfxpro@mac.com**.

Part I

Techniques And Tasks

Chapter 1
Becoming A Canoman

- Become familiar with the basic tools
- Create and texture basic primitives
- Work with the Table and Stair primitives

Exploring Your Workspace

Open Canoma. The screen looks plain compared with other MetaCreations programs, doesn't it? Canoma's apparent simplicity belies what the program can do.

Start by creating a special folder where you will put all the project images. Canoma doesn't allow you to save images outside the folder from which you started.

The Opening Screen

The nice thing about Canoma is that it stays with the same look and feel of its sister products—Bryce and Poser—so if you're familiar with them, you'll feel at home here. Also, as with other MetaCreations products, you can click and drag the major control groups so that they're positioned where you want them.

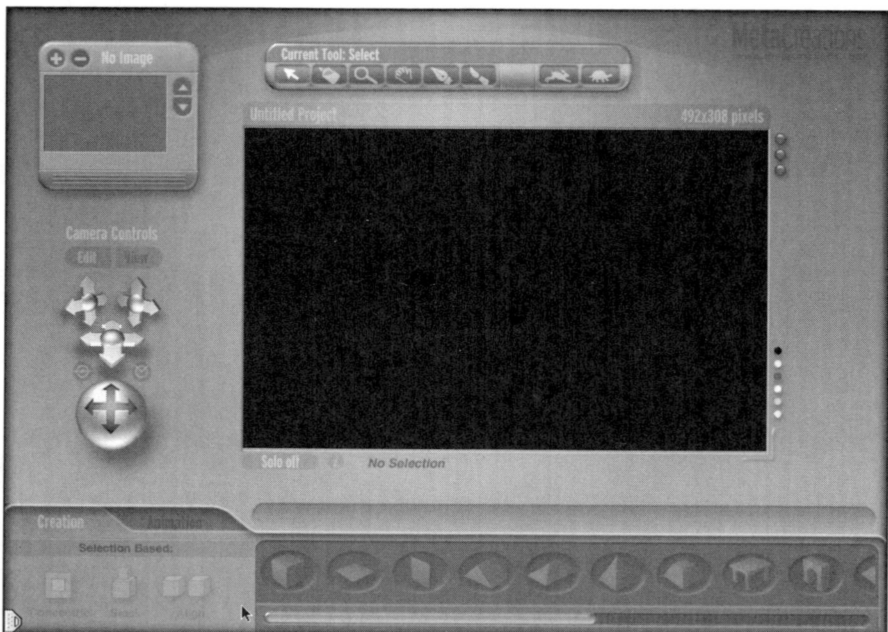

Setting Your Preferences, Part 1

Now set up your preferences so that you don't have to worry about them later. First, go to File|Preferences. The Preferences Menu will appear.

Setting Your Preferences, Part 2

You'll probably want to have the program open to the same format each time, so select Maintain Workspace. If you're new to the program, select Choose Active Guide to get extra on-screen help as you're working. Now here's a wonderful element of Canoma: You can set a helper application to use for modifying your working image without leaving the program. (You learn more about this feature in Chapter 4).

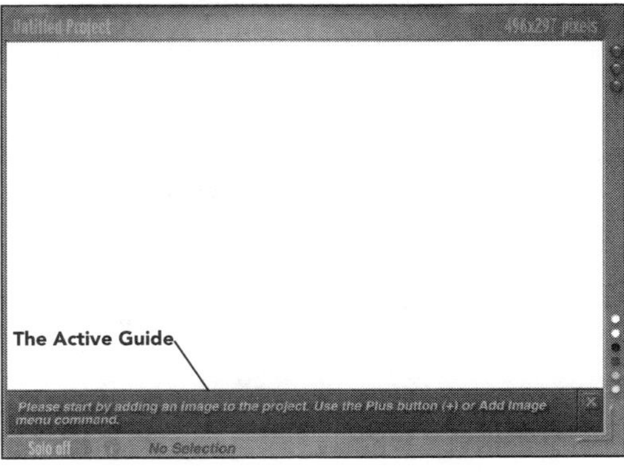

Assign A Helper Application

A helper application comes in handy in many ways as you create images for clients, family, friends, or for your own purposes. Select your image-editing program (such as Adobe Photoshop or CorelDRAW) by clicking on Browse. After you assign the program, select the format to save the image in PICT, JPEG, or TIFF format and then click on OK.

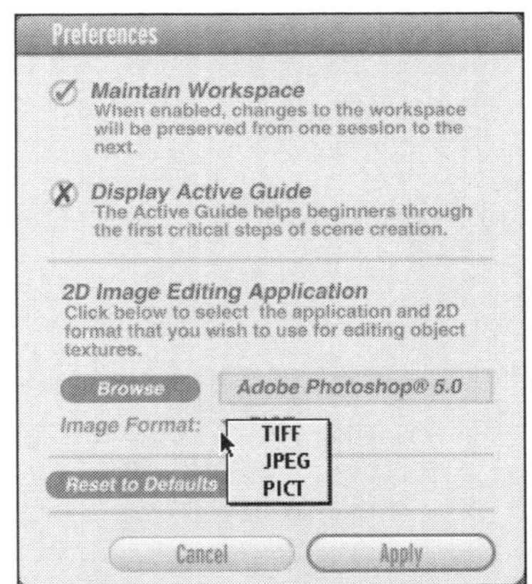

The 2D Image Palette

Examine the workspace starting in the upper-left corner and the 2D Image Palette. Here, you import photos—JPEGs, PICTs, or TIFFs. Your import capability is limited only by your computer's memory, based on how much memory you allocated to Canoma. The plus sign button opens the selection screen, and the minus sign button deletes an image from the viewer. As you add images, scroll through them using the up and down buttons (right). Obviously, you can preview pictures in the Image Palette window.

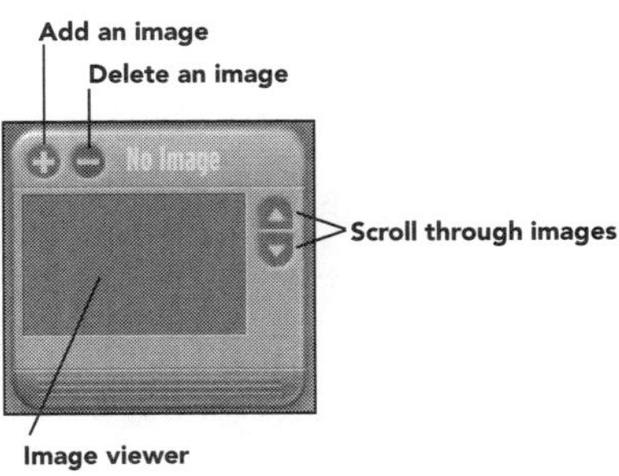

If you're working on a Macintosh and don't know how to allocate memory to a program, consult your system software's user manual.

More Than One Image

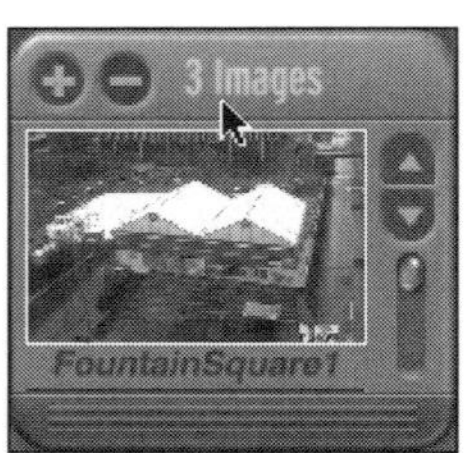

Why would you need more than one image? By using different angles, you can re-create the scene in more detail. You can also work originally in low resolution to build your *model* (the 3D image object that you and Canoma generate) and then remap a higher-resolution image for print after the model is complete. Chapter 3 explores the best ways of shooting photographs for use in Canoma.

Camera Controls

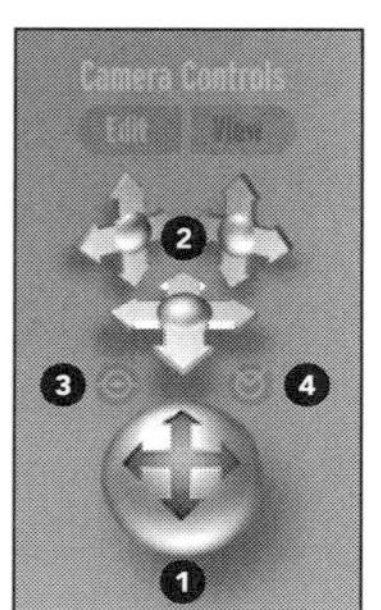

Just below the Image Palette is the Camera Controls panel. Like other MetaCreations programs, the controls consist of the following:

1. A trackball
2. Directional arrows
3. Camera Banking—Manipulates the camera "body," swiveling it to various angles.
4. Field Of View—Acts just like the lens of a camera, increasing or decreasing the depth of field so your rendered image focuses on the desired object.

The Tool Palette

To the immediate right of the 2D Image Palette is the Tool Palette. It holds the basic controls you use to accomplish your tasks. As you move through the projects in Part II, you learn about these controls in greater detail. From left to right, these tools are as follows:

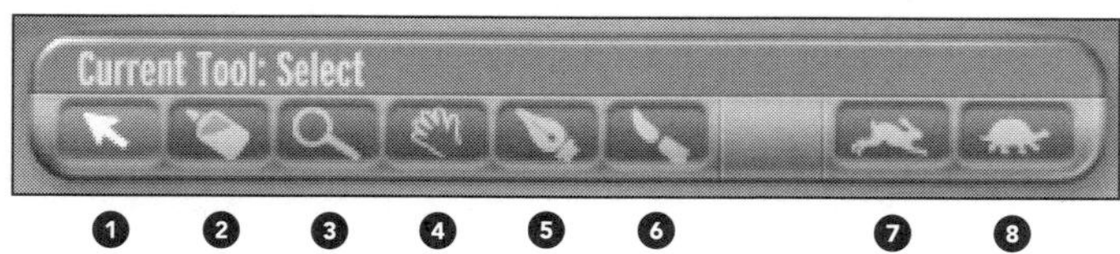

1 2 3 4 5 6 7 8

1. *Select (the Arrow icon)*—Used to select the primitive (the tools you'll use to create your 3D images) you want to work with. This is your main tool.
2. *Glue (the Glue bottle icon)*—Used to glue a point of one primitive to the points or edge of another primitive.
3. *Zoom (the Magnifying Glass icon)*—Used to zoom in or out to tweak your model.
4. *Pan (the Hand icon)*—Used to move the image around to work on different areas of your model.
5. *Point Pen (the Pen icon)*—Used to add or delete polyline contour points—the Translation Sweep, Polygon, and Curtain objects.
6. *Texture Brush (the Paintbrush icon)*—Used to edit using the Helper Application you've selected.
7. *Quick Texture (the Rabbit icon)*—Gives a rough approximation of how the texture looks on your primitive(s).
8. *Quality Texture (the Turtle icon)*—Maps the cleanest texturing on your primitives. Using this tool takes a little more time to render, and it should be used for your final renderings.

The Main Workspace

The main screen is where you do all your work. It's fairly self-explanatory except for the two sets of buttons on the right, which are described next.

The Display Buttons

From the top, the buttons are as follows:

1. *Shadows On/Off*—This feature helps when you're placing one primitive on top of another. It projects a "shadow" that shows the proximity of the two objects.
2. *Background On/Off*—When this option is on, you can view your textured model superimposed over your full image. This gives you a good idea of how your model is laid out in conjunction with the image. When this button is turned off, you see only the textured primitive(s) over black (or whatever background color you've chosen).
3. *Stress Display On/Off*—As you're positioning a primitive, the stress display projects a white outline. This outline either conforms to the primitive or shows how the primitive is being stretched in a manner that will produce uneven results when textured. This option is great for determining where problem spots may lie.
4. *Change Background Color*—If you don't like working with a black background, you can use this button to change the color. Colors are based on your computer system.
5. *Change Highlight Color*—This changes the color of the primitive outline you're working with. The default color is red.
6. *Change Unselected Highlight Color*—Here you can determine the color of a placed primitive that is not *active*. An active primitive is the one you are working on; so the inactive primitives are the ones you have already manipulated and are deselected. The default color is yellow.
7. *Change Stress Display Highlight Color*—Again, this allows you to change the color of the Stress Display. The default is light gray.
8. *Change Shadow Color*—Change from the default color (white).
9. *Change Object Constraint Color*—As you move your cursor along a primitive, *beads* (one of the basic Canoma control elements that you'll use to manipulate your model) and *glue points* (another control element) show up as cyan (blue). You can change the default color here.

The Building Blocks

Here, you see where all the primitives are located. Notice that there is no circular primitive (other than the Arch, which has a rounded interior). The mathematical equations are too complicated at this juncture to provide quality circular images. There are workarounds for this, and you'll learn about them in Chapter 4. The primitives' names are as follows:

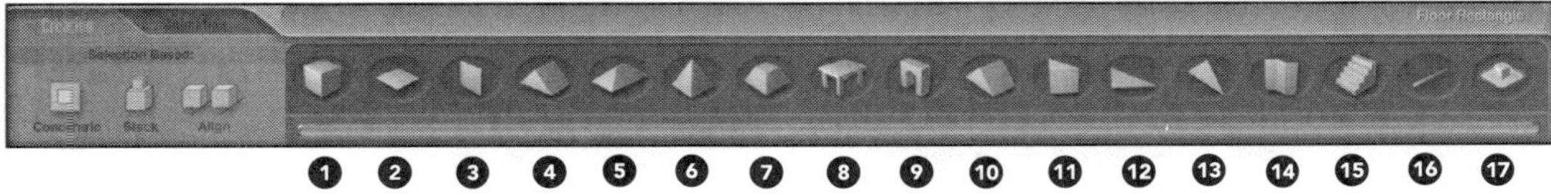

1. Box
2. Horizontal Rectangle
3. Vertical Rectangle
4. Roof
5. Slanted Roof
6. Pyramid
7. Truncated Pyramid
8. Table
9. Arch
10. Horizontal Translation Sweep
11. Vertical Translation Sweep
12. Horizontal Polygon
13. Vertical Polygon
14. Curtain
15. Stairs
16. Line
17. Floor Rectangle

The Creation Tab

On the left of this area are two tabs—Creation and Animation. As you create an image, you'll use the tools in the Creation screen.

Accessing The Animation Controls

Animation works as a series of *keyframes*, allowing you to save images and have Canoma fill the in-betweens. Look at this as setting up the "key," or main, transition points (i.e., wide-angle and close-up shots on a specific portion of your model) and allowing Canoma to figure out how to smoothly move between each. Keyframes are a standard tool in most 3D modeling and animation programs. You can then save your animations in various formats, which we discuss later.

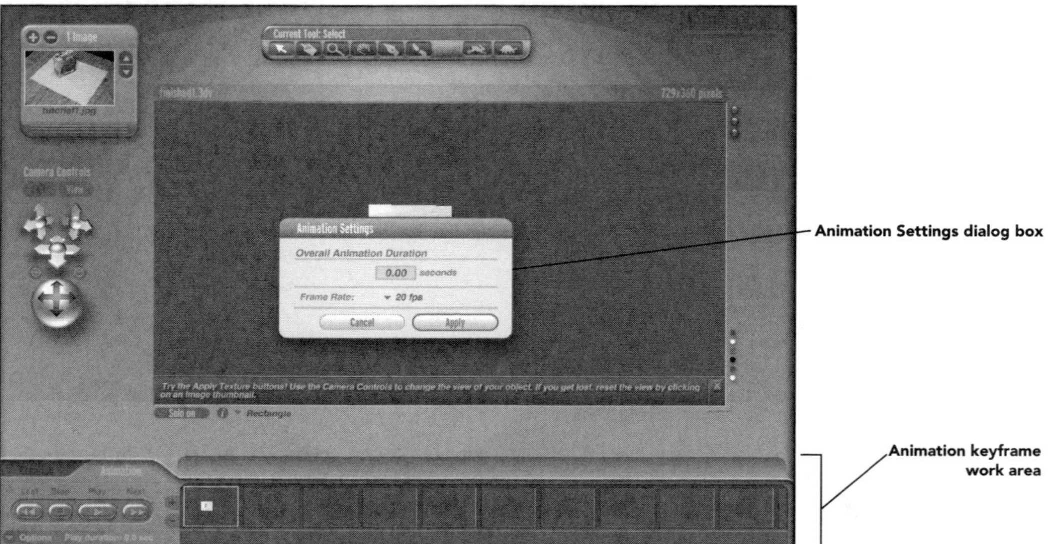

Getting Boxed In

Now that you know where everything is located, let's create a rudimentary model so that you can get a feel for working with Canoma. The first step is to create a section of a building. Then you add and align a second portion along the same plane.

Your First Subject

Make sure that the Select tool is chosen, and click on the Creation tab in the lower-left corner of the screen. Then select the Box primitive.

The Primitive's Outline

An outline of the primitive is overlaid on the image. When you click on the primitive, it always appears in the center of the workspace.

Build From The Ground Up

Always begin building your model from the ground up. Creating it from the top down is like laying bricks starting at the top of a structure rather than at the bottom; there's no base from which Canoma can build, just as there's no base for the bricks. So click and drag the lower-left corner of the primitive to the lower-left corner of the building.

Zoom And Tweak

Use the Zoom tool to move in on your model to tweak it. As you zoom in, you lose some definition in the photograph and, depending on how far in you zoom, the edges of your subject will become more and more jagged—which is called *pixelation*. Just keep the primitive's outline along the edge of those areas, and don't worry about the jaggedness.

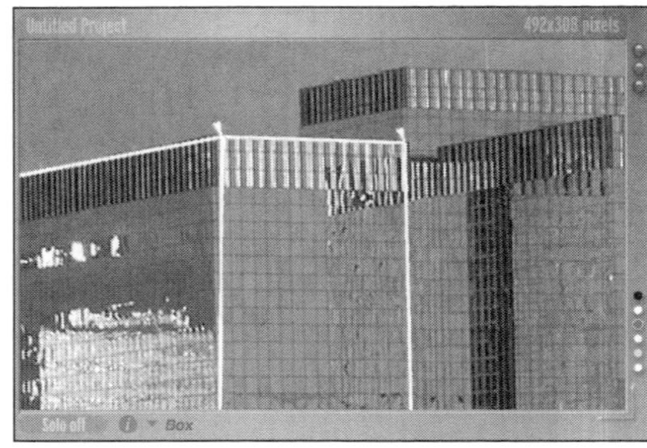

Pinning Your Primitive

When you release the mouse button, it's like placing a pin in the picture. You've *pinned* that point to this position, effectively locking the point in place so it doesn't continue to move around. Just because it's assigned a position on the workspace, however, doesn't mean you can't move it later.

Continue Pinning

Now move the other two visible bottom corners to their respective corners on the building.

It's always a good idea to build from the bottom up, working from the visible back point of the image. Often, if you don't do it this way, the primitive will move in such a way as to hide its dimensions, which makes it very difficult to select the appropriate corner of your primitive.

Finish Pinning

Next, drag the upper corners to fit with the building's upper corners. To move around in the image, hold down the spacebar. When you do this, the cursor turns into a hand icon. While in this mode, you can move the image around freely.

Fine-Tune The Alignment

To check the alignment, click on the View button above the camera controls. Doing so shows how the primitives look with none of the image mapped onto them so you can see how the primitives line up with each other. You also can double-click on the Magnifying Glass icon on the toolbar to return to the full-screen view of the image.

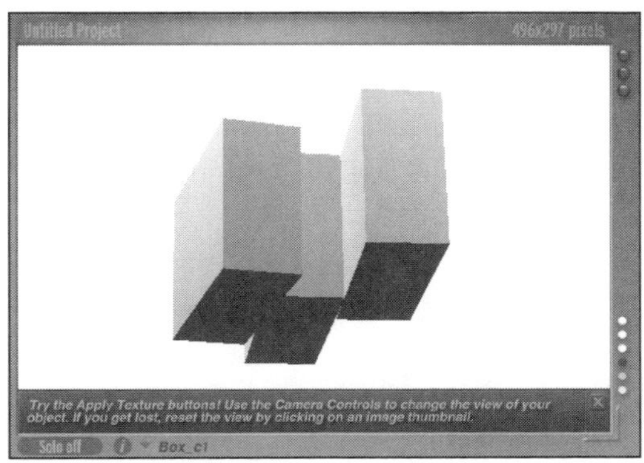

When Zoom is selected, hold down Alt to zoom out. While holding down the mouse button, drag the Zoom tool across the area you want to zoom.

Mapping The Image

Click on the Rabbit icon and then use the Trackball to admire your creation. I used the Quick Texture method here because it's faster, and it gives a good idea of how the image is mapping onto the primitives. This is always a good feature to use when building your model because you can quickly see the results.

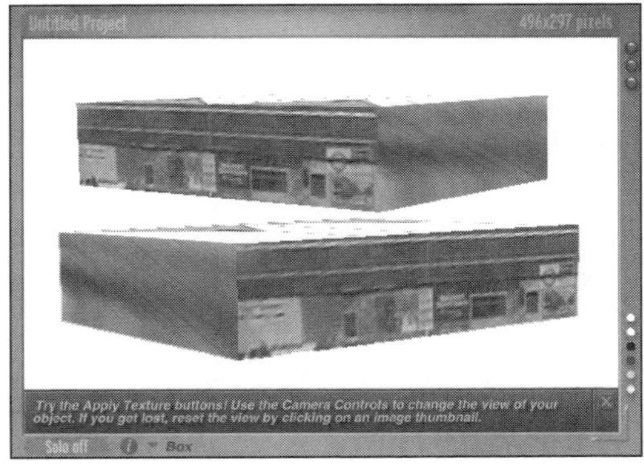

Mapping Images On All Sides

If you chose to mirror your textures (Textures|Mirror Textures), Canoma places the image on all four sides of the box—as MetaCreations likes to say, it "steals" textures.

Mapping Images To Only One Side

If you didn't choose Mirror Textures, as you rotate around the model, the rear sides will have a flat color. Don't worry about this—it's the function you want to use when you have multiple images showing the various sides of a subject. If you have only one image to work from, use the Mirror Textures function so that all sides have an assigned image.

Duplicating Existing Primitives

Many images are made up of basic shapes that are repeated. In the picture you just worked on, for example, notice that the base of the building can be seen as three rudimentary boxes: the front (which you've created), the back (which you're about to create), and the inset center.

Duplicate Your Primitive

At times, it will be easier to duplicate an existing primitive rather than create a whole new one. In the case of this picture, it will be quicker to make a copy of the Box primitive rather than create a new one and shape it to fit.

Duplicate The Box

Duplicate the box (Command/Option+D or Edit|Duplicate) and move it into position by clicking on the lower-right corner and dragging it to the rear portion of the building.

Tweak To Fit, Dupe Again

This section isn't as deep as the duplicated primitive, so you must tweak it to fit. Again duplicate the shape and place it between the existing boxes.

Check Alignment

Many times, as here, you can't see all the elements in their entirety; often you must guess to position the primitives correctly. So modify the new center primitive and click and drag on the camera trackball to see how the elements are lining up.

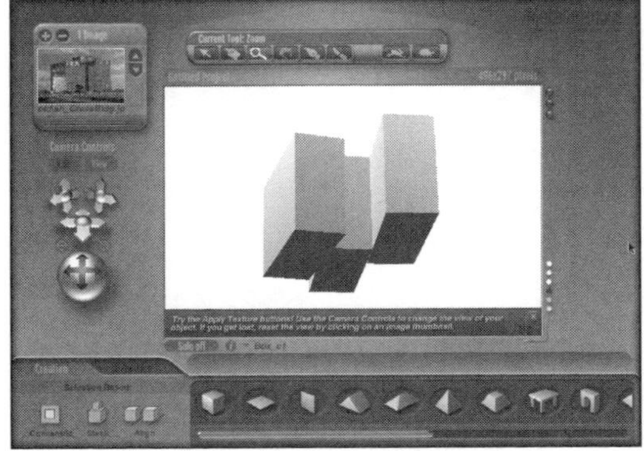

Save The File

When you're happy with the model, you can save the file (Command/Ctrl+S or File|Save) if you'd like. Saving is not imperative, but you might like to keep a record of your progress.

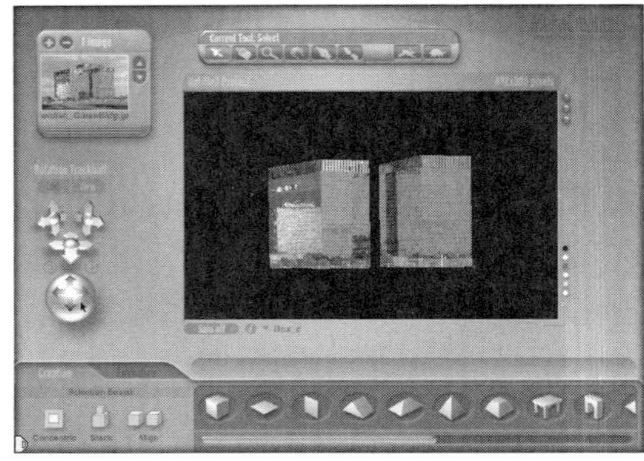

Using The Odd-Shaped Primitives

Canoma's collection of interesting shapes can help you create models. (You might think it's easy to put together, for example, a table using box primitives; it's hard.) You have to ensure each box is aligned precisely. So, Canoma has a prefabricated table primitive to take care of this detail. A price, however, is paid: As you pin the tabletop primitive to the table, the legs expand, separate, and otherwise behave strangely. Still, let's try it. To get these images, download the files from the **ftp.coriolis.com\Canoma_Visual_Insight** folder. For the following exercises, you need to download only the Chapter 1 materials.

The Table Primitive

From the Chapter 1 folder, open the file named CornerTable.jpg. This is a low-resolution image, so don't expect to use it for your portfolio.

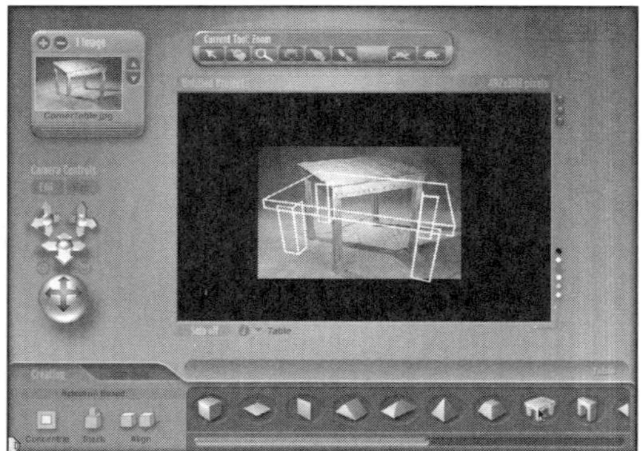

Select The Table Primitive

Scroll through the Primitives selections until you get to the Table primitive. Click on the Creation tab and then click on the Table primitive, and you'll see something similar to this.

Start At The Top Here

You model from the top down because, with this primitive, it's best to set the table dimensions first. This is a rare instance where it truly is better to start from the top because the table portion itself is the main part of the primitive, with the legs acting as additions to it.

Begin To Pin

Now select the upper-left corner and drag it into place. Now start pinning the other three visible corners. For the right-rear corner, you'll need to estimate it's placement.

Don't Worry About Your Legs

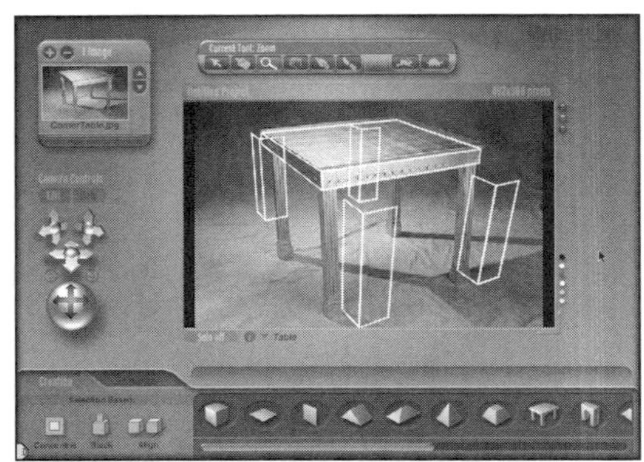

Now you can see what we meant about the legs! They've gone all askew. Fear not, intrepid almost-Canoman, because you're about to learn how to fix this.

Fixing The Legs

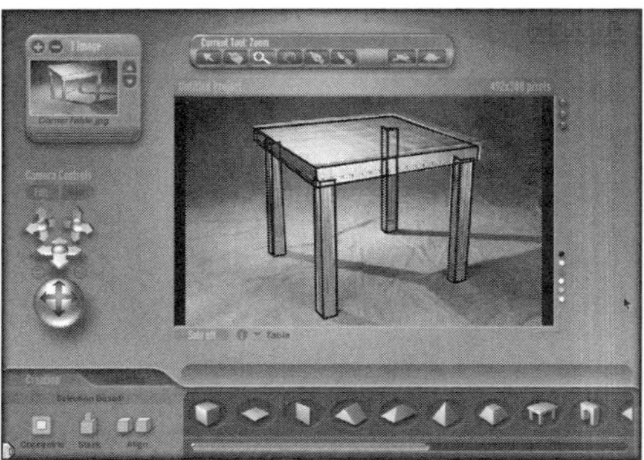

If you zoomed in to do your tweaking of the primitive, zoom out and begin work on the left rear leg of the table, starting with the lower-right corner. Notice that the legs in the image are round but those on the primitive are rectangular. Sometimes, you must make trade-offs when you use the basic primitives to build objects.

Final Steps

With this table—unless you save the image as a MetaStream file and someone zooms in really close—the small areas where the background shows through won't matter. (This image was modified to better show where the bleed-through occurred.) Also, as you begin working on the legs, you'll notice the other legs responding to the reshaping. Don't worry; as you move from leg to leg pinning the corners, each finished leg will remain in the position you set.

A Master Canoman

When you have all the table legs positioned as you want them, do a fast render and enjoy your handiwork. Now that you've mastered the table, it's time to place it in a dining room that has a staircase leading to the second floor. From the Chapter 1 ftp folder, open the Staircase.jpg low-resolution file.

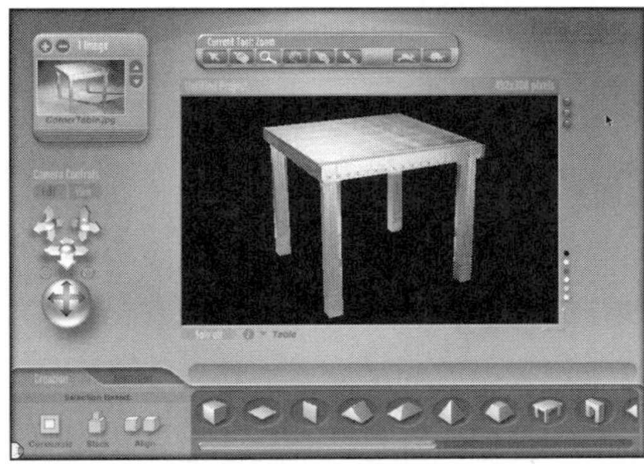

Creating Stairs

In this example, you'll model only the bottom flight. When you're working on a scene of a house interior, you sometimes have to deal with staircases. Creating stairs by stacking Box primitives can be tedious. Luckily, Canoma provides a wonderful tool that makes short work out of staircases. Click on the Creation tab and locate and select the Staircase primitive.

Step Options

When you first select the Staircase primitive, you have the option of having Canoma create up to five steps. If you need more than five, you can set your own number. You're working on the bottom landing—which has four stair steps—so select that number. Then pin the lower-left corner as close as you can to the top of the landing.

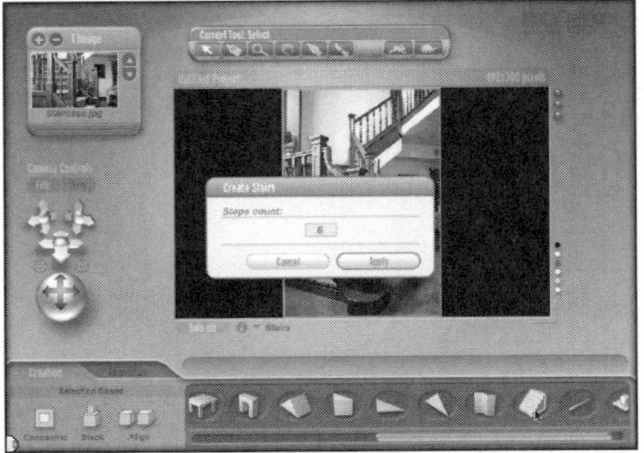

Fixing Your Wild Stairs

But wait—now the staircase points the wrong way, and it's more trouble than it's worth to try to position the staircase correctly. Go ahead—try it.

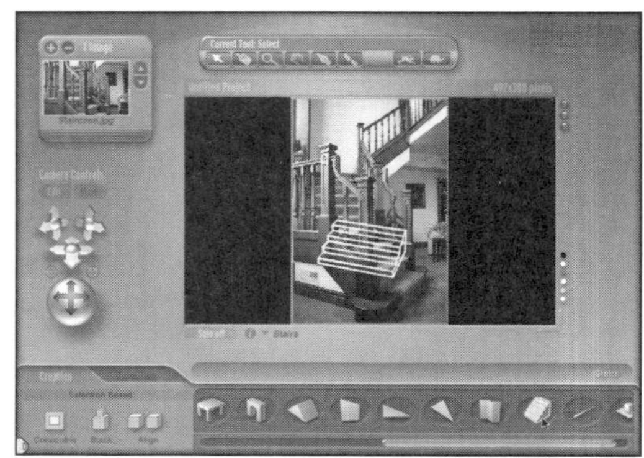

Unstable Staircase

The primitive does some weird and nasty things. Let's fix this. Undo your preceding actions by pressing Command/Ctrl+Z until the primitive is back to its original form. Alternatively, you can press Delete and select the Staircase primitive again.

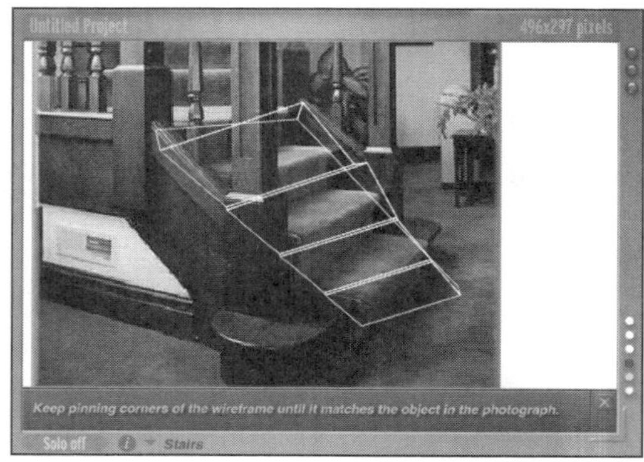

How To Rotate Primitives

With the primitive selected, click on Create|Rotate 90 Degrees On The Y. This rotates the primitive so that the staircase is pointing the right way.

Build Staircases

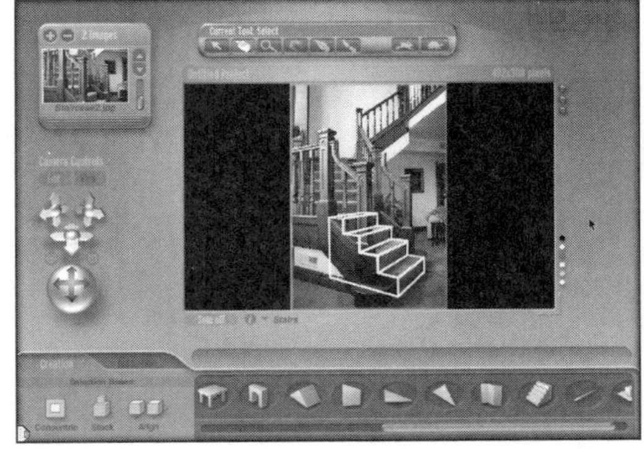

Repeat the pinning process starting from the lower-left corner and moving to the lower-right corner. Zoom in to the various stairsteps and pin the far right side to each corresponding step until you have them all blocked in.

Removing Stress

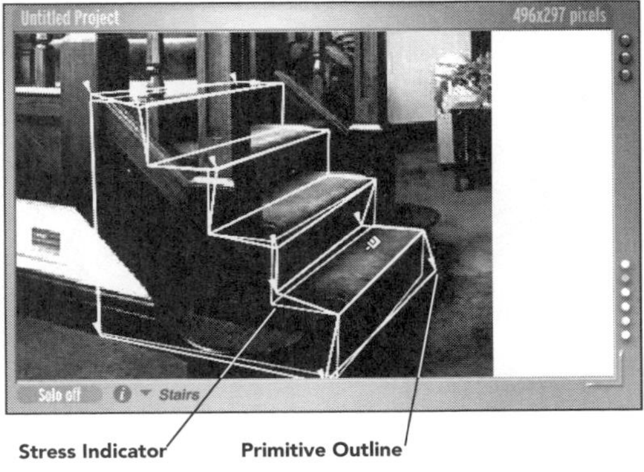

Take your time and make sure you have the Stress option turned on; with a primitive that has many corners, you must make certain that there is little or no stress on the model. Remember, unless you modified the color of the Stress outlines, you'll see the stress points as light gray lines.

Mapping Anomaly

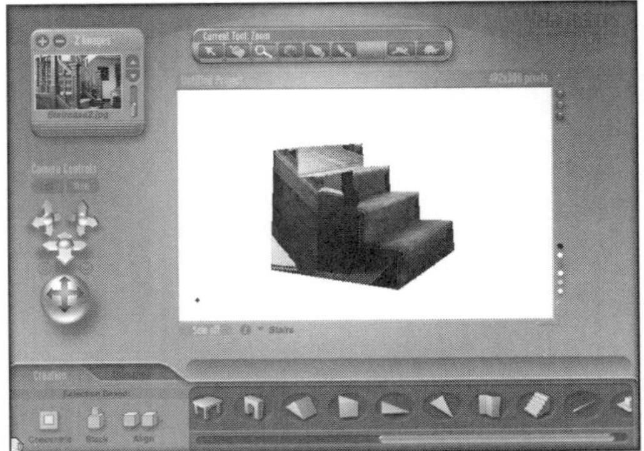

Now do another Quick Render. This example shows the one bad thing about the staircase image and demonstrates the care you must use when photographing elements like this. The top step of the staircase is so "busy" (many items to map in a small area: carpet, shadow, curved lip, and wooden post), that Canoma has trouble rendering it. Usually, you build the staircase encased by primitives on either side, but this instance gives you an idea of things to watch for when you work from photographs. (In Chapter 3, you explore photography for Canoma in more detail.)

Looking To The Future

Since I began writing this book, a number of changes have occurred in Canoma and the MetaStream technology. In late 1999, MetaCreations decided to close its software division and sell all its programs. As I completed work on this book, it was announced that Adobe has purchased Canoma. When the upgrade arrives—as we know it will—it will be under the Adobe banner.

A MetaStream Upgrade

Meanwhile, MetaCreations upgraded MetaStream from version 2 to 3 as this book went to print. The new plug-in and development software will not be backward-compatible with MetaStream 2.

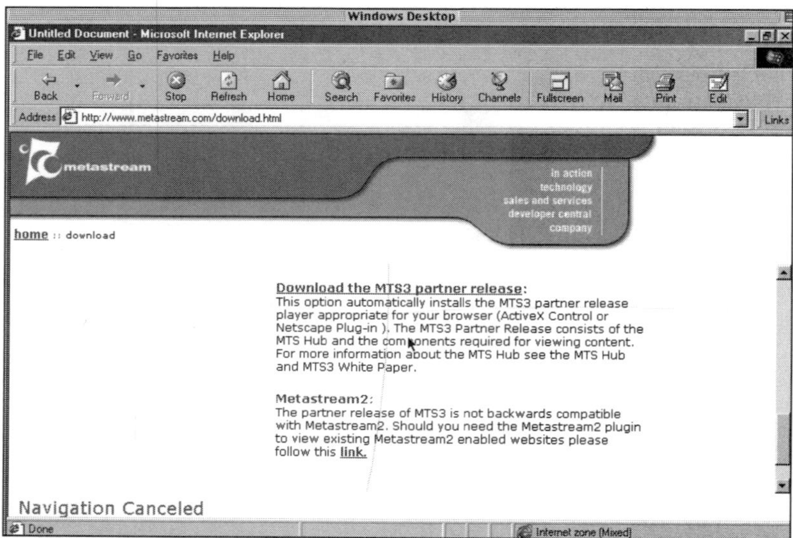

License Changes

There are also some changes in the licensing of MetaStream for use on the Web. In some cases, this will affect how you can and cannot use images. To get the latest information on using MetaStream for personal and professional use, go to **www.metastream.com**.

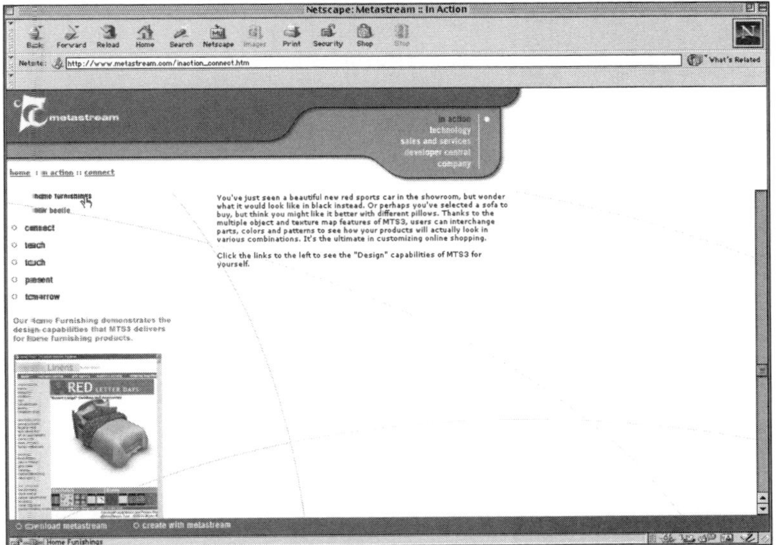

Pick A Color, Any Color

One of the most important changes in the MetaStream format is that it now lets you set up your files so that viewers can do things such as change the color of an object—such as a car—just to see what it will look like.

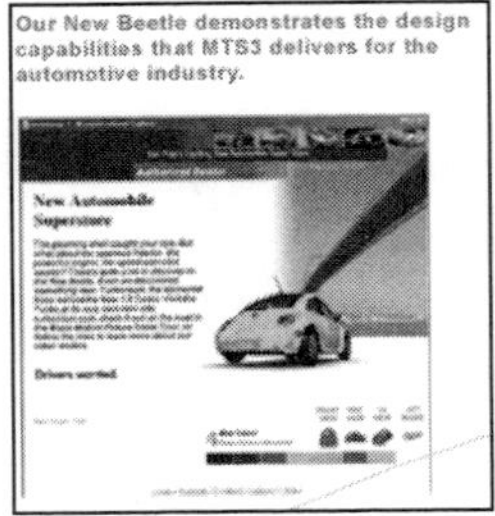

On Your Mark

With these changes, new possibilities for creating bigger, more intricate models will open up for you, the Canoman—and you'll be ready to take full advantage of them. You now have a good handle on this remarkable program, and you're a lap ahead of the competition when it comes to maximizing Canoma's amazing capabilities.

Chapter 2
The Intermediate Canoman

- Align primitives to create an entire model
- Work with odd-shaped primitives
- Stack primitives to create multilevel structures

Alignment Basics

As you become more comfortable with how Canoma works, you'll find yourself looking for new and more intricate models to create. You'll notice multilevel homes with front dormers, apartment buildings with cantilevered balconies, interesting streets with turn-of-the-century row houses, and gothic mansions reminiscent of Notre Dame. Remember, however, that you can use Canoma for more than rendering buildings. When you are learning the program, however, using larger subjects such as houses and office buildings gives you a good feel for how the different primitives work and interact. This approach makes it much easier when you move on to smaller or more intricate pieces.

Before you begin, create a folder on your computer named Chapter 2 (or use another impressive and creative name) and—if you haven't done so already—download the files from the Canoma folder on the **ftp.coriolis.com** FTP site into your folder. You can save this chapter's projects in your new folder.

A Study In Alignment

Aligning objects so they lay against each other may seem like a simple enough task; you just create a couple of primitives, match them up to the photograph, and voila! Right? Not really. The following few sections describe how to align objects in Canoma.

Create A Primitive

We're going to use our favorite file—Goldish_GlassBldg.jpg (the Glass Office Building). Create your first primitive, as you learned in the Chapter 1.

Photographs used throughout this chapter are from the ClickArt CD collection. Used by permission.

Create A Second Primitive

Now create a second primitive (remember to click on the Creation tab prior to selecting a new Box) and line it up with the center portion of the building. Looks pretty good, doesn't it?

Check It Out

Try rotating the image and take a look at how the two primitives align with each other. Why did the two primitives separate? To put it in its simplest terms, there was no reference point for the second primitive to align itself to. So, although it appears that the two primitives should align, you only created two separate boxes, and each box had very different coordinates.

Start Over

This time, work your way forward. Get rid of all the primitives (if you haven't already) and create another one to act as your base primitive.

Start By Creating The Base Building

Start with the lowest visible corner and pin it to the back section of the building. The *pinning* process is simple—you only need to pull each of the corners to the spot you want. The pinning takes place automatically.

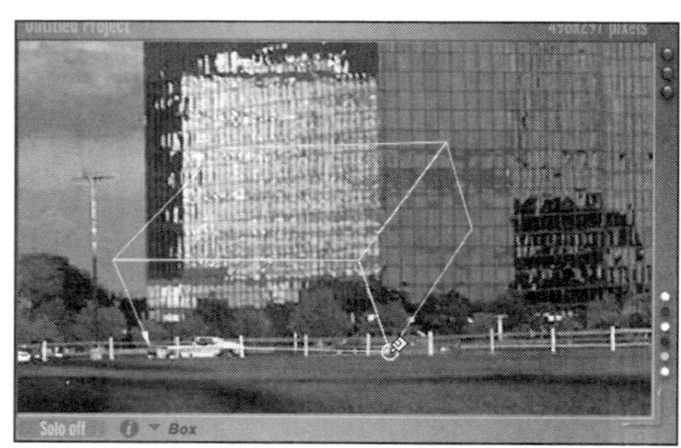

In the image, notice that instead of the standard cursor arrow, you see a glue-bottle cursor. On the Mac, screen captures are created by using Command+Shift+3. The Command key on the Mac and the Ctrl key on the PC are shortcut keys that allow you to Glue "on the fly." Because of this, you'll see the bottle-shaped cursor in many of the images in this book.

Make The Primitive Fit More Exactly

Although you've pinned the corners, you can still modify the primitives. Consider the initial placement of primitives as a rough draft; you need to tweak the corners so they fit the model more precisely. Use the Magnifying Glass to zoom in on your image (don't worry about zooming in too close—the closer the better when tweaking), and place your corners more exactly so the primitive outlines the building's edges as closely as possible.

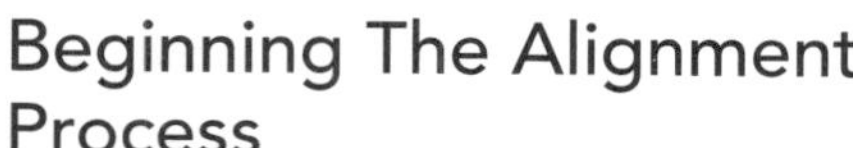

Beginning The Alignment Process

After you've finished creating the initial portion of the building (or you could call it the base primitive), make sure it's active and click on the Creation tab. Then click on Align.

How To Know You're Ready To Align

A checkmark appears over your placement selection (in this case, Align), letting you know the program is ready to do its thing. Create a new box and pin it to the center section of the building.

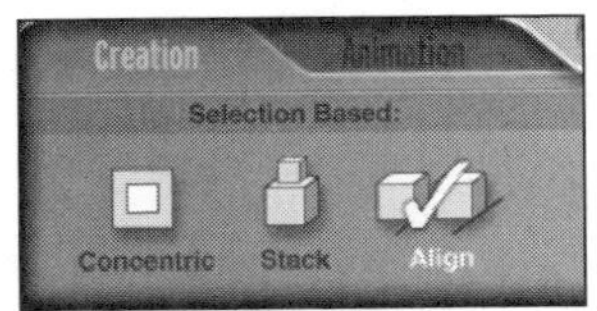

Gluing The Elements

After your primitives are in place and you've tweaked them to your satisfaction, select the Glue Bottle and glue a corner or intersection of your new primitive to the first primitive. Call this your safety net; by gluing at least one corner or intersection of the new primitive to the first guarantees the two will align properly.

How To Know When The Glue Sets

When you glue one element to another, a circle appears around the glued point to let you know the gluing was completed.

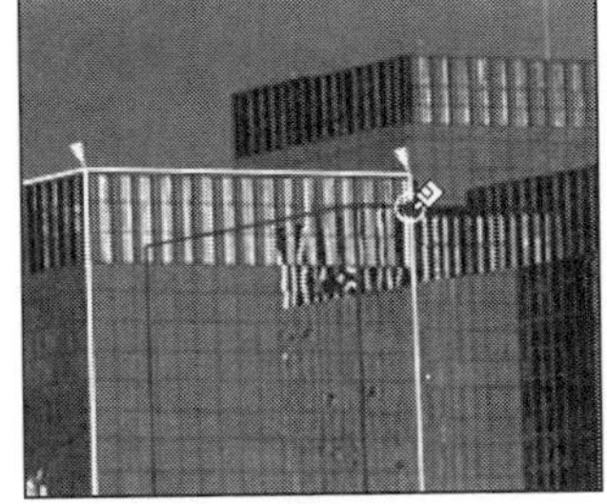

Check Out Your Work

It looks much better, doesn't it? That's because you told Canoma to work with your existing primitive, which helped the program figure out the relationship between the two structures.

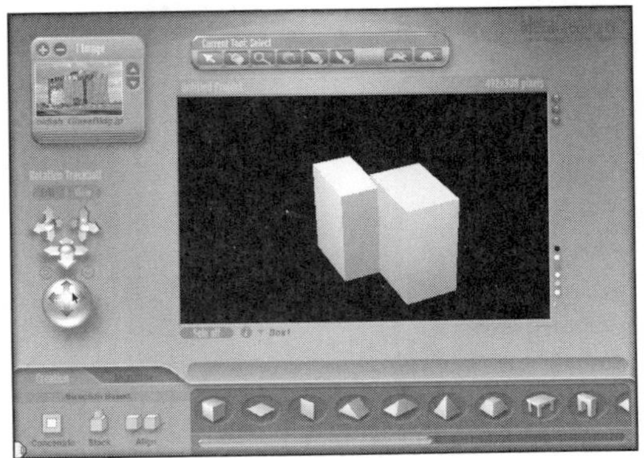

Repeat The Process

Repeat the preceding actions to add the front of the building to your model. Again, make sure that you have the existing primitive you want to use as your base is selected, and then choose Create|Align and the Box primitive.

Fitting In

Modify the primitive to fit the subject area of the image, conduct the gluing process again, and then do a Quick Render. You'll see that, again, the elements are properly aligned and placed. You can modify any of the primitives again if you need them to fit the subject's layout more correctly.

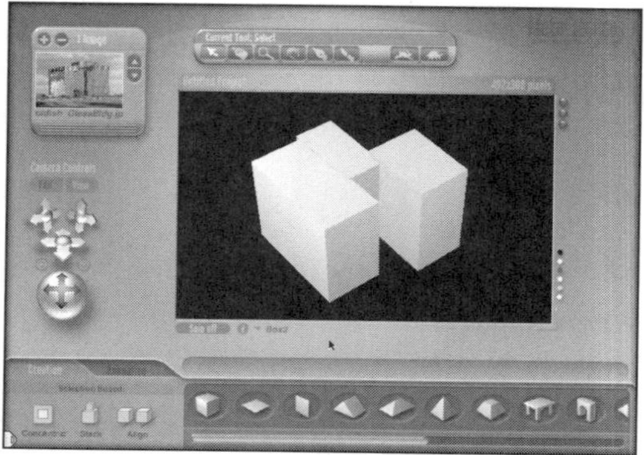

The Back Portion

Now, all you need to do is add one more box to create the taller portion of the building. In this case, you should use Align in conjunction with the center primitive.

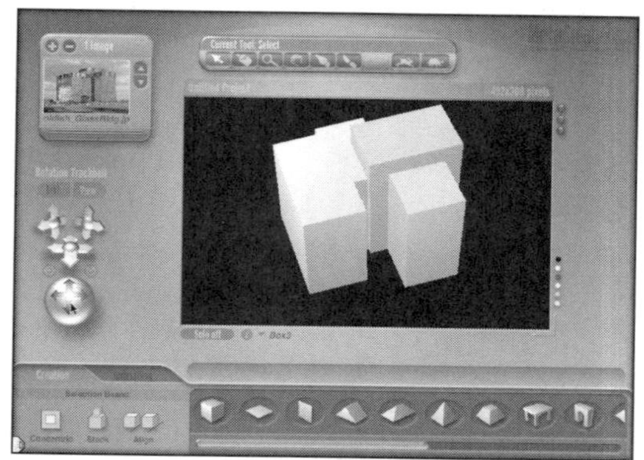

Violate Your Existing Primitives

Make sure that the edges of the new box violate the boxes it interacts with. In this way—because you don't have an aerial view to set the perspective by—you can guarantee that the new box will attach to the others.

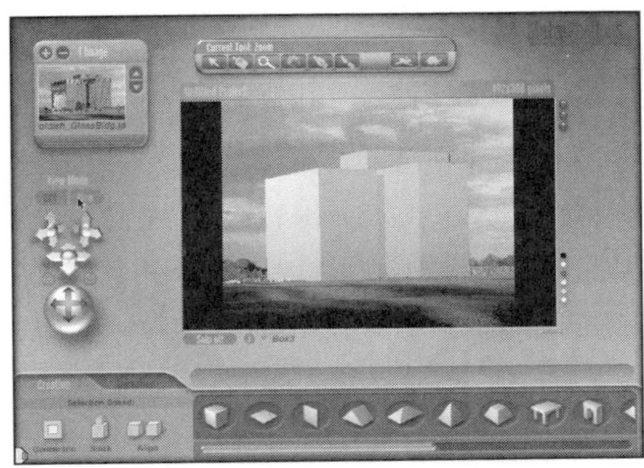

View The Difference Between Renders

Now do a Quick Render by pressing on the Rabbit icon in the toolbar. Quick Renders are perfect to use when you just need to make sure that the primitive is mapping correctly.

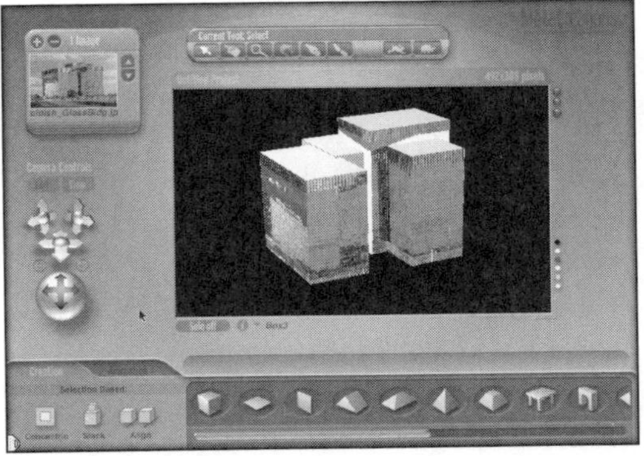

What Are These Rips Doing Here?

You'll see "rips" at various edges and intersections of your model because the program isn't wasting time doing a clean mapping job. Don't worry. When you do a Quality Render these rips in the mapping won't be there.

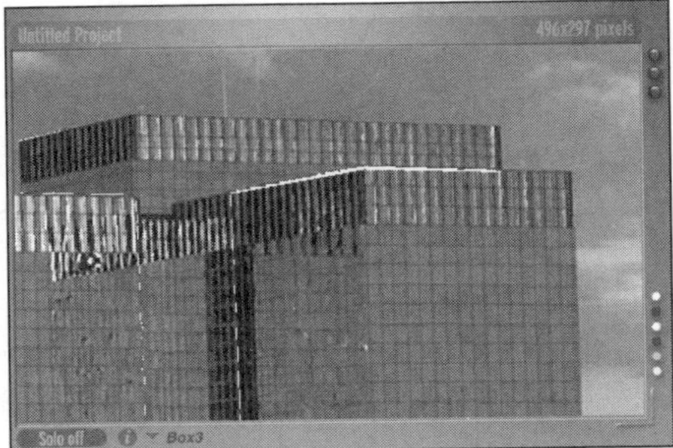

The Quality Render

Click the Turtle icon in the toolbar. Here's your model, as clean as it will get. Depending on the size of the file, it can take a few seconds to do the Quality Render, but it's worth it when you really want a good feel for how your pieces are coming together.

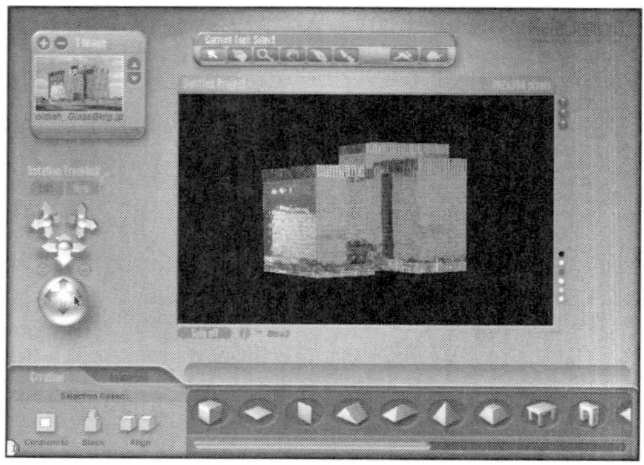

Model Those Odd-Shaped Structures

Architects love to design interesting and offbeat structures to add life to a building or to the surrounding area. Interesting lines, strange shapes, unexpected curves—buildings with these types of features add extra interest for the Canoman who enjoys a true challenge. Just as in most aspects of life, there is more than one way to skin a cat with Canoma.

An Odd-Modeling Example

Start a new file (Command+N on the Mac, or Ctrl+N or File|New in Windows), and import the OddShapedBldg.jpg photograph from the Chapter 2 folder.

Choosing A Primitive Shape

At first glance, you might consider using a well-stretched box primitive for this building. But look closely. The building is *pyramidal* in shape (a technical term used by architects), lending itself to your using one of the Pyramid primitives—namely, the Truncated Pyramid (the flat-topped one). You're going to use the flat top as the side of the building facing you.

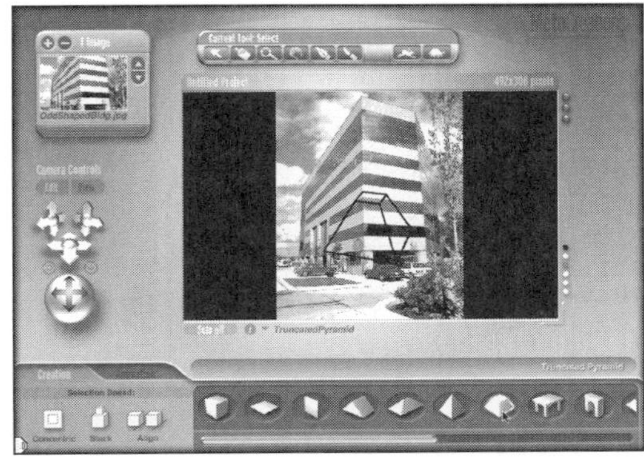

Setting The Corners Of The Shape

Starting with the bottom-left corner, pin the back corners of the building. Here, you are pinning the bottom corners to set your base.

Handling Stress

Things are going to become stressed as you pin the corners to the image. This is because, although the building seems to be facing you fairly squarely, it isn't. The right side isn't as distinctive as the left. Here, you will play with this to show that you can work around a "stressful situation" and make the best of it.

A Work-A-Round

Let's add something to help you out. Using the Vertical Rectangle as a backdrop, position and pin this primitive to the edges of the photo. When you do add your texture, this rectangle will act as a screen, mapping the sky behind the building and giving you what you need to make a stressed-primitive situation like this work.

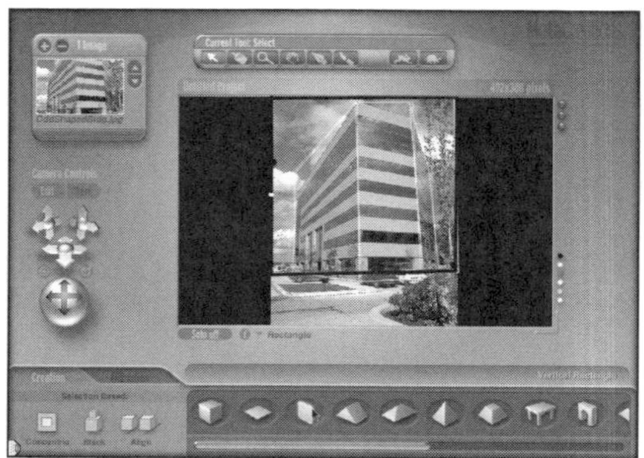

Mapping The Sky

Line up the Truncated Pyramid primitive with the stress lines now. Yes, the sky will be mapped to the TP, but if you're careful with the way you display your finished piece, this won't be a problem. You're gonna fool the viewer, fake 'em out, practice some pixelated prestidigitation. You're going to cheat.

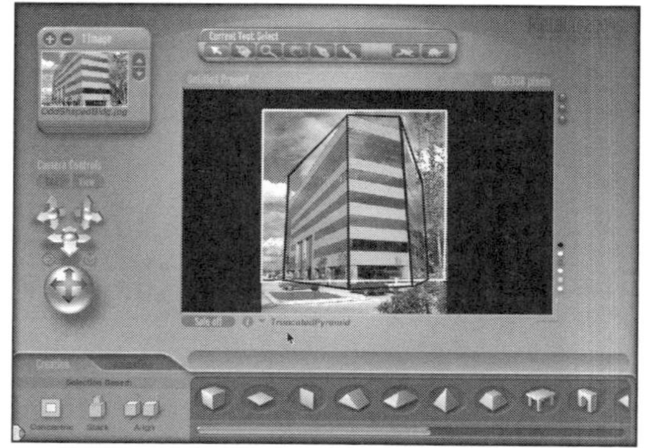

Check It Out

After you have everything in place and the stress is gone from the TP (or Truncated Pyramid), do a Quality Render by clicking on the turtle icon.

How Far Can We Go?

After the photo is mapped, use the Camera Trackball to see how far you can circle around the image before you notice your little bit of electronic magic.

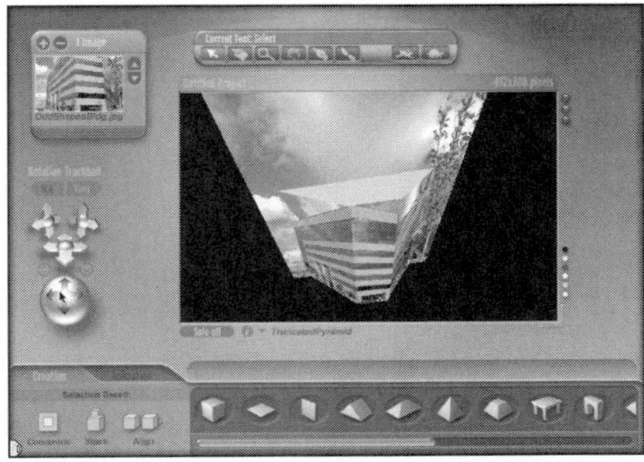

Stacking: Advanced Primitive Handling

By Steve Shanks

So far, you haven't done much except place some primitives side by side and looked at alternative primitives to complete tasks. Frequently, you're not only going to use alternative primitives, but you'll also have to stack them. Stacking is an important part of Canoma. By using the Stack command, you can save time that you would otherwise spend positioning the primitives correctly.

The Washington Monument

You can consider this series of images both a Stacking Primer and another chance to practice on an odd, albeit famous, shape. For this, you'll use a picture of the Washington Monument and two different primitives (located on the ftp site, in the Chapter 2 folder).

Begin With A Truncated Pyramid

First, start a new file, import Washington-Monument.jpg from the Chapter 2 folder, and then zoom in on the tower. Notice that when you zoom in, the Monument has two basic shapes. Due to the angle of this shot, one is a TP, the other a regular triangle. Start by adding a Truncated Pyramid and select the bottom-left corner. Drag the pyramid into place on the lowest visible left part of the tower.

Form The Body

Grab the right front; attach it to the corresponding portion of the tower. Before you zoom in to tweak the primitive, position the back-right corner, making sure Show Stress is on (View|Show Stress), and then drag the corner into place. Notice that the leftmost edge of the Truncated Pyramid aligns with the edge of the tower. Using these edges as guides, adjust the corner from side to side until they align.

Pin The Top

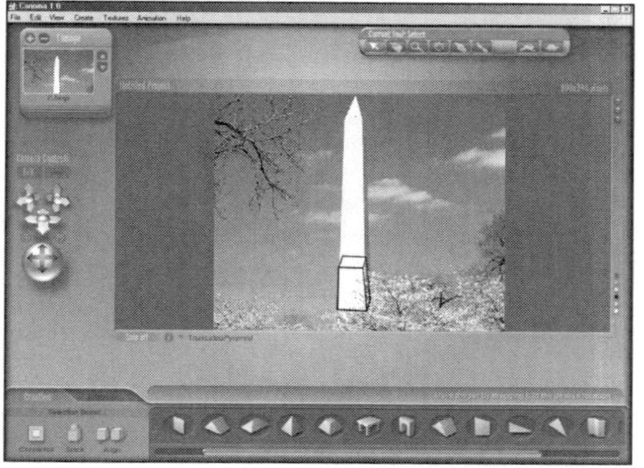

Next, pin the top. Now that you have the bottom lined up, it's time to pin the top corners. Select the top left corner. (We use this one because it's the most visible and accurate part of the image.)

Pinning, Continued

Take the back-right corner and pull it into place, followed by the front right. If you miss, the stress lines will show. This occurs because you have the bottom out of line (the bushes were in the way).

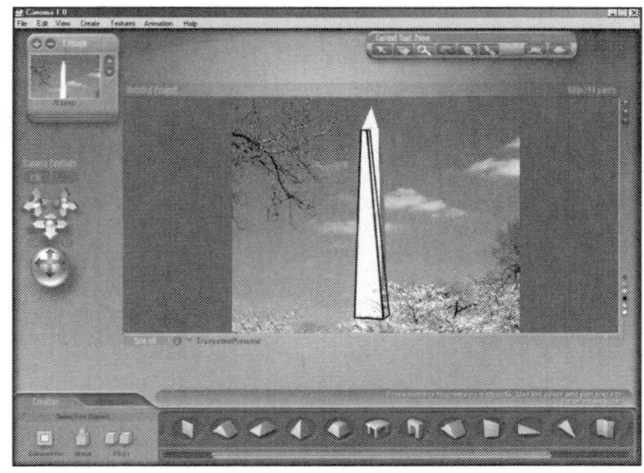

Relieving Stress

You correct the stress by zooming in on the Monument base and adjusting corners until the stress lines disappear. It's a good idea to have the Show Stress option turned on so that you know if something is misaligned. It saves time down the road because if you have put together a complex model, fixing the problem can cause a lot more problems in the end.

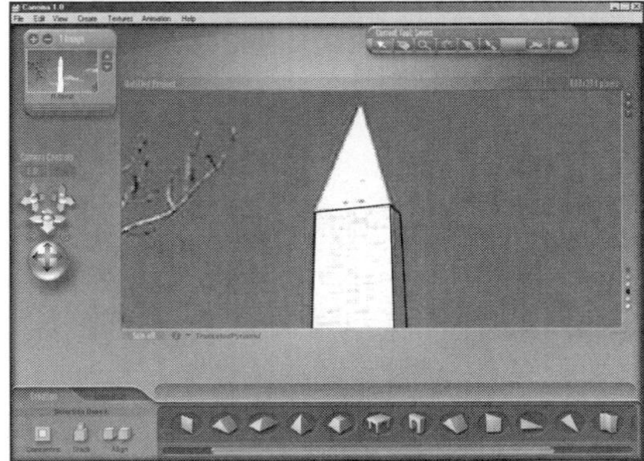

Cap It All Off

Make sure that the primitive you just worked on is selected, click on the Creation tab, and then click on the Stack icon. You'll know Stack is activated when a checkmark appears over the icon. Next, click on the Pyramid selection, and it will appear on top of the Truncated Pyramid. Zoom in to the point on the tower.

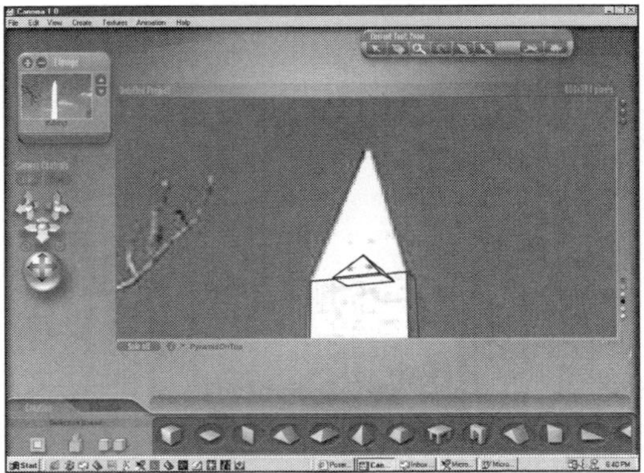

Complete The Pinning

Finally, pin the front-left corner, and then pin the back-right corners. If you're lucky, the front right falls into place. Check for stress. I noticed that you could be fooled into seeing objects in less depth than they really have. This is a good example. So, if your pyramid shows stress, return to the Truncated Pyramid and verify that you have enough depth at the top.

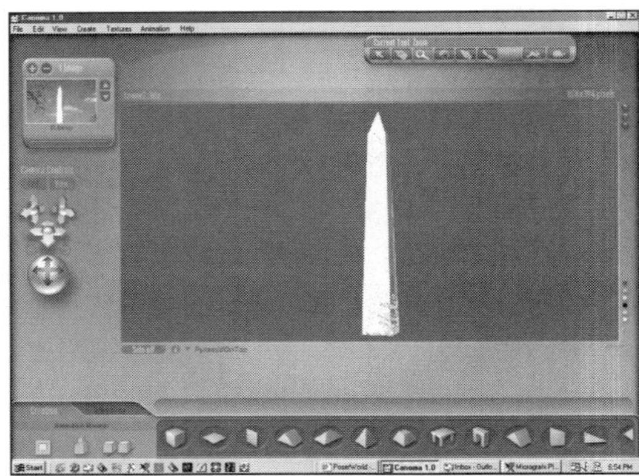

Verifying A Primitive's Depth

A good way to check depth: Click on the Edit button and rotate the object. The sides should be equal in depth. If they aren't, that's the "stress" problem.

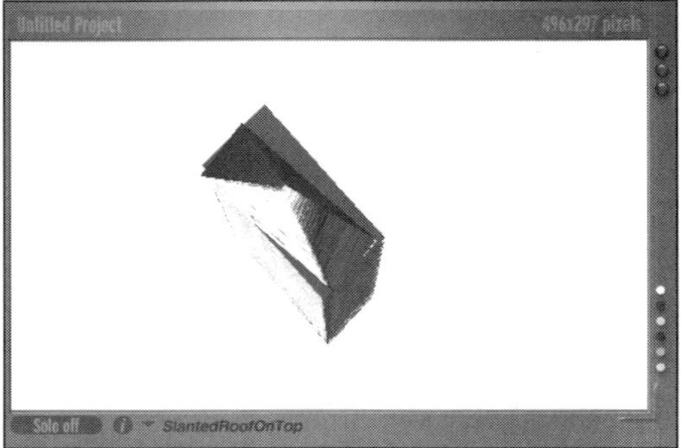

Discover The Arch Primitive

Now that you've re-created an historic location by using primitives other than a box, look at what's probably the most interesting and complex of the primitives—the Arch. When I first saw this primitive, the Arc de Triomphe came to mind. There are so many uses for this jewel, especially with architectural structures, that I had to find a photograph quickly just so I could try this out.

The Guinea Pig

We found this little jewel in the ClickART CD-ROM collection. For lack of a better name, I called it Storefront.jpg. Download from **ftp.coriolis.com** and place it in your working Chapter 2 folder. With its arched doorways, this image makes the perfect guinea pig.

Create The First Archway

Create the archway by scrolling through and selecting it from the list. Once again, as with the examples in Chapter 1, you'll see it comes in facing the wrong way.

Flip And Place

Rotate it 90 degrees (Create|Rotate 90-Degrees On Y Axis). Next, drag the primitive by the lower-left corner to the far left archway in the picture. From there, pin the primitive into place, but don't worry about the arch yet. Position the primitive with the right side ending about the center of the two arches. This method allows you to use Align and, with a second Arch primitive, create a model with a seamless texture.

The Beauty Of The Arch

This is a great primitive because the Z- or depth-coordinate is revealed in the complementary part of the arch. Notice the various lines along the curve connecting the front to back, and the sharper corners of the near portion of the arch. Each line and corner are separate edit points. You can control where the left and right curvatures start and end their angle of curvature.

Create The Arch

Zoom in to align the archway. Select as many points around the arched area as needed, pushing and pulling them until you align it as perfectly as you can. Select Quick Render.

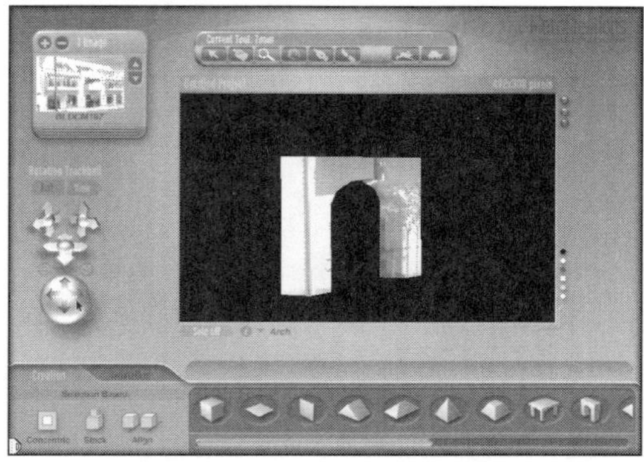

"See" Through The Pole

As this example shows, a telephone pole runs up the middle of the doorway. You can create another primitive to map this onto, which you would usually do when creating a full street scene. You can also configure Canoma to "see" the telephone pole as a separate object and, when mapping the building onto the Arch primitive, to continue the wall's texture through that area (discussed in Part II).

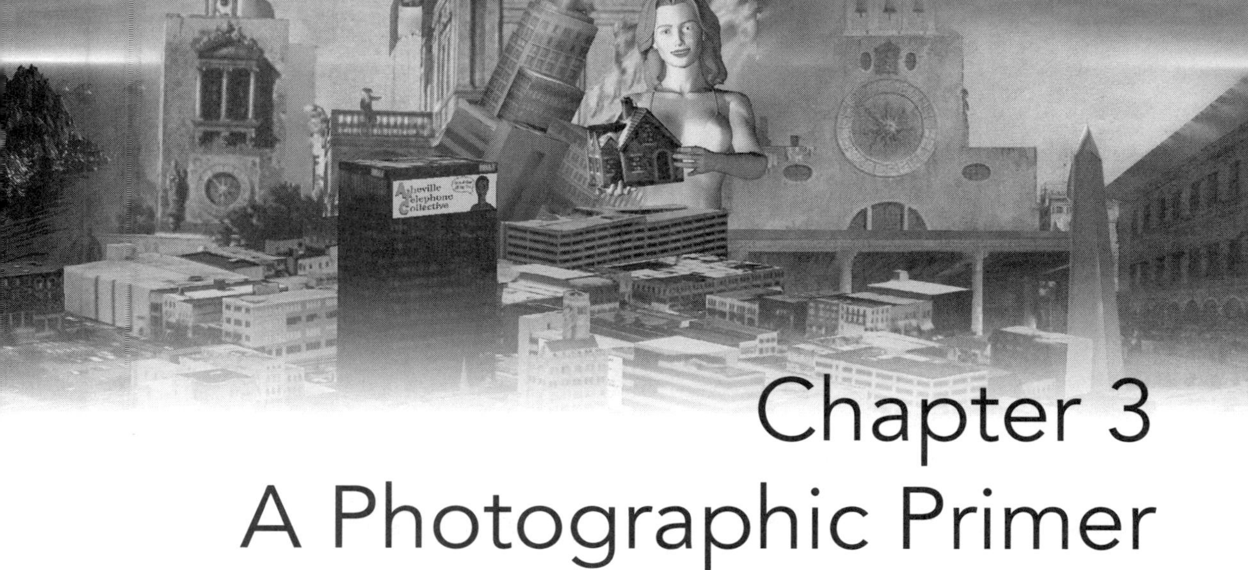

Chapter 3
A Photographic Primer

- Create a workable image
- Scan images: A short course in advanced image manipulation
- Learn about your film and digital photographic choices
- Understand film versus digital versus video
- Estimate the costs

Creating Workable Images

Before you start shooting, review what you *should* do when taking photographs for Canoma and what equipment you should use. Remember, your goal is to ensure that, if needed, you take accurate fronts, sides, and backs. Success at interactive creation depends on your ability to shoot digital images or to scan photographs.

There's More To It Than Pressing A Shutter Button

It's not just a matter of heading out with a single-lens reflex (SLR) or digital camera, and shooting an exterior as shown here. Retrain your mind's eye to mentally replace real objects in the scene with primitives. You'll often need to use various angles to get a true rendering of your subject; don't use mirror texuring on every model you make.

Envision Your Shots

You can't simply shoot an interior either. True Canomans see all subject matter as primitives, waiting to be texturized from all angles. As with every 3D program, you need to see the world as collections of primitives, no matter how advanced your tools are.

Look At All Sides Of The Subject

Take a closer look at this photograph of the Bell South Building in Nashville, TN (referred to by the locals as "The Batman Building"). It's a fascinating structure and very "primitive" in its design.

Gotta Love This Kind Of Structure

You can easily shoot buildings like this: It's the same from both front and back. It's still a difficult shoot. Unless you use a costly perspective-control (PC) lens on a 35mm (or an expensive view) camera, use a normal-to-moderate telephoto lens or zoom setting and to get enough distance from your subject to keep it as vertically level as possible.

With a good 35mm SLR camera system, you can change lenses to fit your needs, from wide angle to macro. As was mentioned previously, PC lenses, (which help you "pre-correct" many parallax problems) are also available for some high-end SLRs. Your overall photographic choices are very flexible. Also, some of the high-end digital cameras feature interchangeable lenses.

Looking Beyond The Subject Matter

Notice the buildings that inhabit the bottom of the shot. This photograph of Broadway Street shows the tourist area just below the Bell South Tower building. In later chapters, you'll remove the Bell South Tower and place Broadway Street into some very different scenes.

A More Complicated Subject

A building you can shoot from one side and use that single image to map both sides of the model is rare, but how do you shoot buildings that differ on all sides? This stone house (an empty store in Nashville's tourist attraction area, Music Row) has possibilities, but you can't texture this model correctly using Mirror Texture. You need to shoot it from various sides.

Be Careful When Lining Up Your Shots

When you must shoot an object from all sides, you usually have to be careful when lining up the shots. If you compare this example with the preceding figure, you'll have a better idea of what I mean. Here, I tried to line up at the same angle to each respective front corner. In this way, I have an even perspective to perform the Canoma mapping.

Mistakes Happen

You'll also notice that, unfortunately, the top of the building in the second image is cut off. There are ways around this problem, which I'll discuss in later chapters, but it's best to be more careful when you align your shots.

The Back Of The Building

I'm not worried about shooting both sides of the fence; viewers will believe both sides can be the same. I have the texture for the far side of the building. (Refer to the section, "Be Careful When Lining Up Your Shots.") By closely aligning the top and bottom of the house with the front shots, I produced an entire image series from which a model can be created.

The care you put into aligning shots will pay off. Don't spend hours on a shoot, not have the pictures turn out, and have to return (at your expense) to reshoot. If it's a local shoot, your expense is nominal; if you have to travel, it's a monetary disaster. Get it right the first time—shoot a lot of images!

Shooting Tall Buildings

To create a city scene or to make an area model, you need an aerial shot. Aerial shots, however, are difficult to obtain. Airplanes (or blimps) are expensive to rent; unless an observation area exists, many companies' insurance policies preclude access to rooftops. Check your library or the Internet for shots of your city, but follow all applicable copyright restrictions. In hilly areas, shooting is easy. If you have friends in high-rise apartments, you're set. You need to work through the inherent problems.

Scanning—Film And The Digital Darkroom

Now that you've become the Ansel Adams of non-nature and non-scenic color photography, you need to take a long look at the hardware used to get your shots into your computer.

Print To Scan

First, film is not dead! Digital is great because it gives immediate feedback. However, film—its smell, feel, texture, and quality—is hard to surpass when you take pictures. Use care, however; you can have the most beautiful shot in the world, but it won't mean diddly if it's printed on the wrong surface.

Paper Selection

By wrong, I mean printing your shot on paper that doesn't scan properly. Are the photos printed on matte stock? Glossy paper, while nice to look at, reflects light from the scanner bed and can cause unwanted glare or discoloration (see lower right insert). So, if you will scan the image, demand matte stock when you have the film processed.

Many Resolutions

Shooting pictures on film gives options you don't necessarily have with a digital camera. You can scan photographs at any resolution you need, allowing you to manipulate their size more thoroughly. For print, you don't need to go above 300dpi (unless you're illustrating a book or other large-format piece); modern scanners can import a picture at high pixel ratios, which then allows you to downsize to a higher quality.

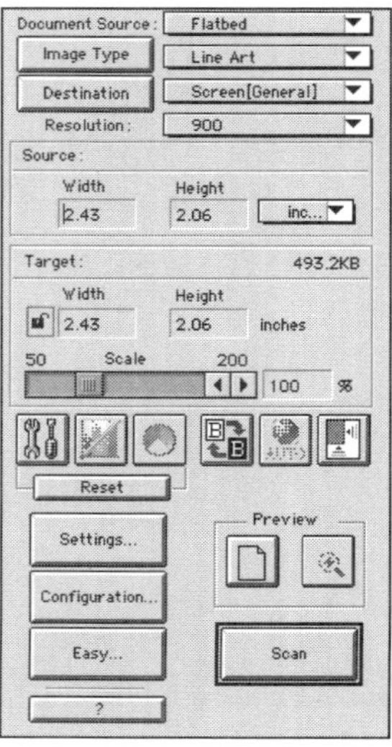

Size Matters

If you scan a picture at, for example, a screen resolution (such as 72dpi), you can downsize the image but you can't make it larger without losing quality.

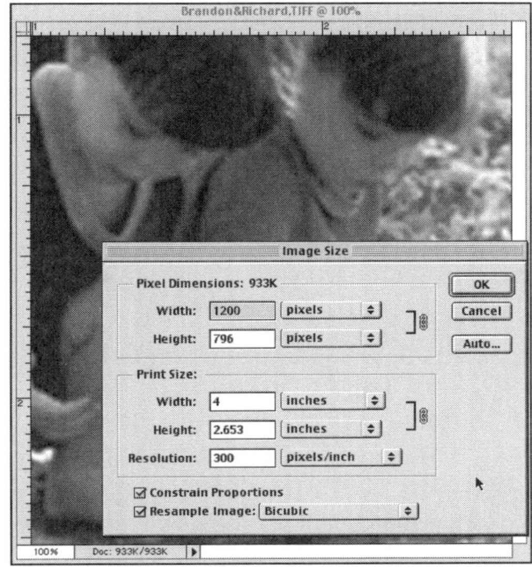

High Resolution

A 4×5-inch picture scanned at 72dpi is 360×288 pixels. Scan this image at 300dpi, and you'll have a 1,500×1,200-pixel ratio. If you take that 300dpi image, turn off resampling, and resize it to 72dpi, you will get an increased image size of 21×14 inches.

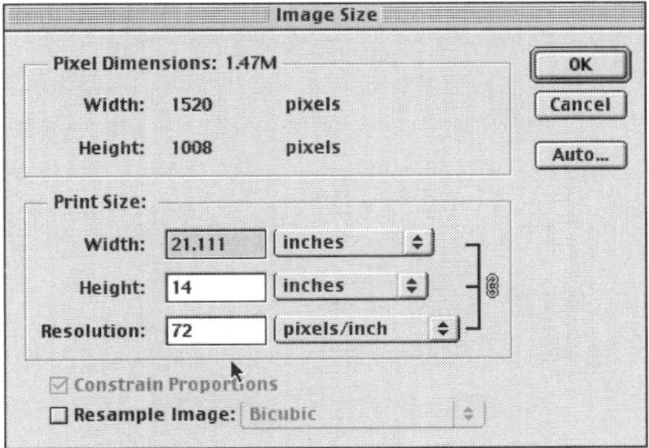

Low Resolution

Subsequently, if you have a photo that is 72dpi and 11×19 inches and want to increase the quality to 300dpi, turn off resampling, and you'll get a high-resolution image of 2.85×4.7 inches.

All Resolutions

The more you manipulate images, the easier it becomes to understand this process. You can turn a wallet-size photo into a poster by scanning at extreme resolution (your scanner's highest setting), then downsizing the image to enlarge it. Digital cameras can shoot only to their maximum pixel depth; you can't resize a photo beyond that point—unless you print, scan at higher resolution, and then enlarge it again. This, however, isn't recommended.

Digital Photography

Now I'll praise digital photography. I took most of the shots in this book with a Kodak DCS-315 digital camera with a pixel ratio of 1528 × 1016 (you can buy cameras with higher pixel ratios). Your choice depends on your needs; the higher the pixel ratio, the larger the image when you downsize within your photo manipulation program.

Low-Cost Equipment

Many inexpensive cameras ($400 to $1,000) have fixed, non-zoom lenses; some, however, have zoom or macro lenses for extreme close-ups. Sony's Mavica series lets you store images on floppy disks. The pixel ratios of the inexpensive cameras run from the middle hundreds to the low thousands and are suitable for creating images only for the Web and not for translating images for print.

High-End Equipment

If you decide digital is the way to go and you plan on shooting photographs for both the Web and print, you need a higher-cost unit that shoots at higher pixel ratios.

Many expensive digital cameras let you use interchangeable 35mm lenses. With research, you may find a digital camera that uses lenses you already own. For these features, plan on spending from $2,000 to $7,000. For information, go to the ***ftp.coriolis.com*** *ftp site and download the PDF files from the* ***\Canoma_Visual_Insight\Chapter03*** *folder.*

Still And Motion Cameras

Some expensive cameras give you far greater flexibility than just shooting stills. Several high-end models take either video or still-images. With these cameras, you can shoot full-motion video and then grab the best still frames to use. This capability gives you advanced modeling options that go far beyond building a Canoma model (which I'll cover in detail later in this book).

What About VHS Video Captures?

If you want to go into digital videography, you can get a good start with a home camcorder, but I don't advise trying to put together any type of quality presentation by using VHS equipment.

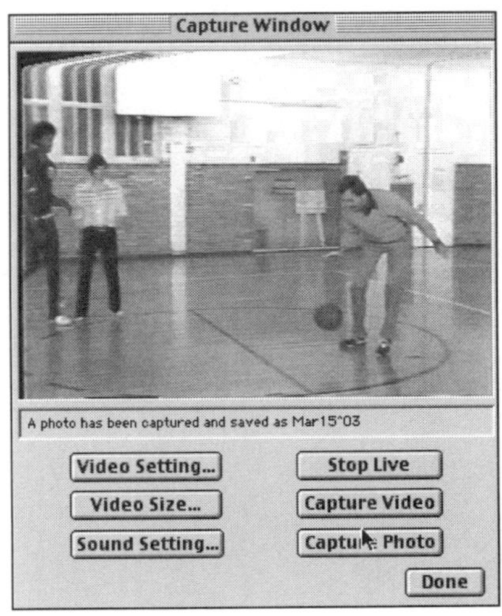

Evolving Formats

VHS is doomed, and High Definition Television (HDTV) format is on the way. VHS is designed to capture family special moments; its quality is low, and VHS is unusable for broadcast use. If you've seen those home videos of tornadoes or watched home video shows, you know the quality difference between VHS and professional Beta that broadcast facilities use—it's night and day.

Cleaning Up Your Video

If you must use VHS for video or still captures, use it only for rough cut presentations, not for final format. You can digitally clean up VHS video or frame captures from programs such as AfterEffects, Photoshop, and Photo Paint, but it's a lot of work and expense to get a good-looking three-to-five-second clip.

The Investment

As with anything, look at the long-term cost associated with any equipment you buy. This table presents a very simplistic chart to give you a start on your calculations.

A Canoma Hardware Comparison Chart

Camera Type	Number Of Shots	Review Time	Cost/Shot
35mm SLR	36	1 Hour[1]	$9–$15/roll[2]
Digital Camera	100's[3]	Instant	Cost of card
Digital Camcorder	1,000's	Instant	Cost of tape/card
VHS Camcorder	1,000's[4]	Minutes	Cost of tape

1. Not including drive time to and from photo developer.
2. Depending on processing costs and number of usable shots.
3. Depending on the size (in megabytes) of the card used.
4. Between 24 and 30 frames per second × up to 6 hours.

Decisions, Decisions

There's much to consider. Most people have some type of 35mm camera. You may have a VHS camcorder; but if possible, invest in a *digital camera* (or *digicam*, as they are often called). In the end, you'll save on film-development cost, which will eventually offset the cost of the camera. The capability to immediately view, save and/or erase, and reshoot is worth the added cost.

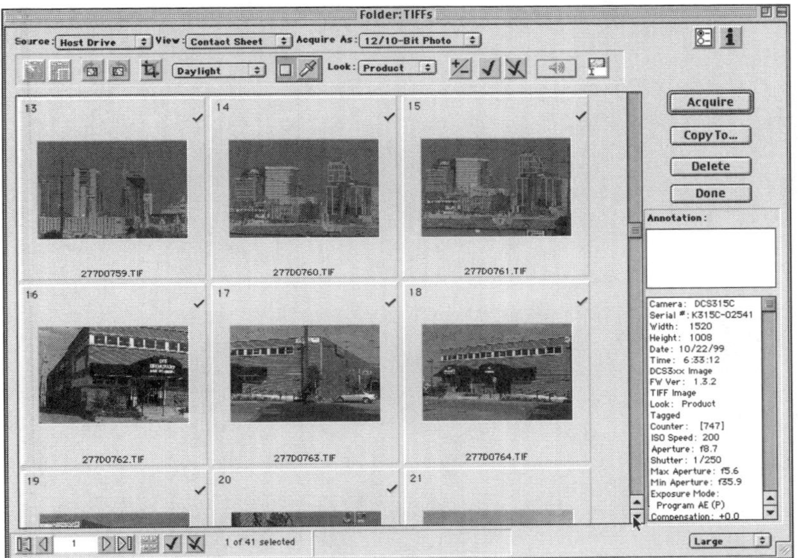

Remember Your Final Destination

No matter which format you use, learn the pixel-to-inch conversion ratios so that you can create the highest quality image possible for the work you produce. A 72dpi image is perfect for anything that will be viewed on the computer monitor. A 300dpi image is generally the highest you'll really need for print.

Canoma High And Low

When working with Canoma, you should build models with images saved at 72dpi, but have a high-resolution copy in the wings. This way, if you're using your model for print, just remap the model with the higher-resolution image. With Canoma, more is better; the more shots you take from different angles, the better your final model will be.

Chapter 4
The Expert Canoman

- Learn to use the Sweep tools
- Access helper applications within Canoma
- Create QuickTime and AVI videos
- Export models for use in other programs

Tools And Applications

Before you can create interactive 3D worlds from photographs, you need to explore some areas. Because of the angular setup of almost all primitives, it's difficult to create complicated objects. Sweep objects let you create human and other odd-shaped figures. Using Horizontal or Vertical Sweeps with Add Points opens endless possibilities.

Objects That Don't Fit In

Whenever you shoot a street picture, it will probably include parked cars, people, or other objects that aren't easily built using the standard primitives. This is when the Free-Form Primitive tools come in handy.

Vehicular Variations

As you can see in the close-up, this shot has a lot of vehicular "debris." Again, you could use the standard primitives, but you will quickly discover the limits of these tools.

Primitive Result

If you do use standard primitives, you'll see something like this. You can do this quickly by using the Box primitive, but it creates problems. First, note the way the buildings behind the vehicles are mapped onto the car primitives. This mapping causes problems if you're trying to build a street scene in which the viewer can move around.

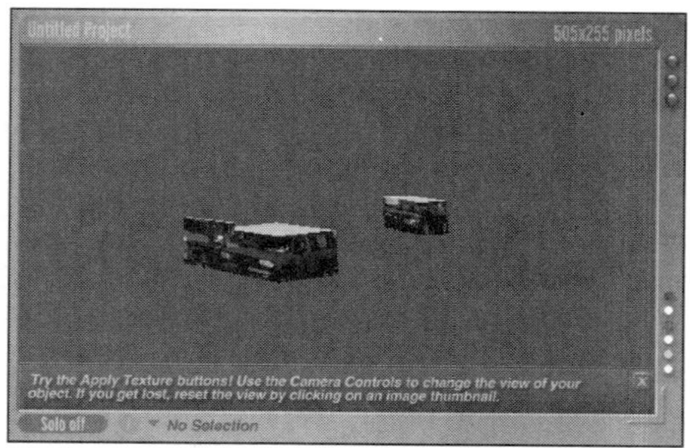

Stacking Instead

Another vehicle solution is to use the Stack option, which is a better choice than using a single standard primitive. In this way, you can gain more control over how Canoma maps the image onto the model.

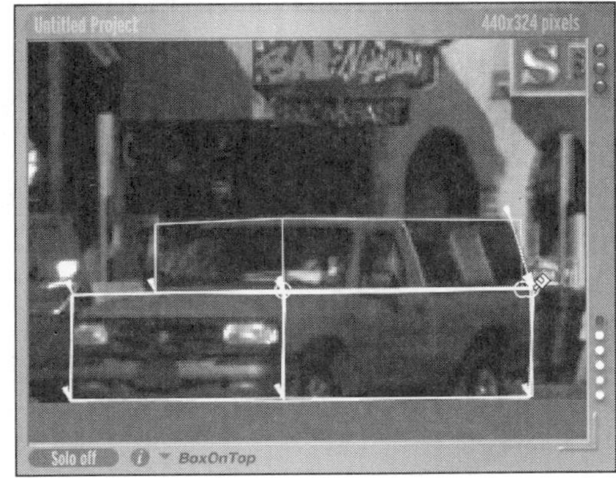

How To Stack

After you place your initial primitive, make sure it is active (selected). Go to the Creation palette and select the Stack option followed by the type of primitive you want to use—in this case, another Box.

The Stacked Primitive

This new primitive appears over the original Box primitive you created. By using different primitives to build your model, you eliminate most or all of the extraneous background elements that may hinder the quality of your work.

To keep the orientation and give yourself less to worry about as you model, hold down Shift when aligning or stacking onto a basic primitive.

The Translation Sweep Option

For best results, you can use one of Canoma's most powerful tools, Translation Sweeps, to create rounder edges. Translation Sweeps add control over your modeling because you aren't working under set parameters—such as forcing a Box primitive to map an object with a circular top.

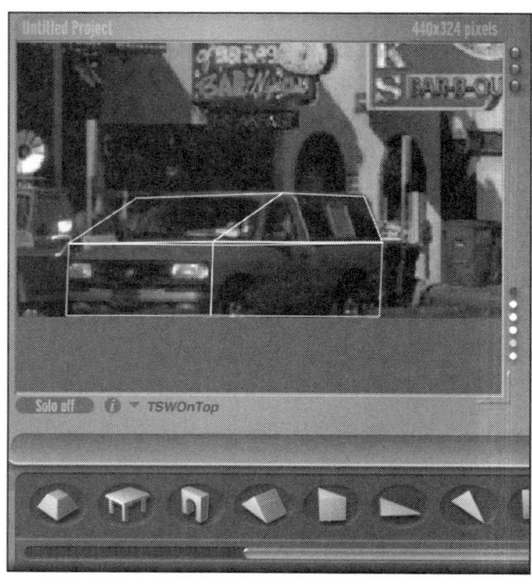

Using The Translation Sweep Tools

First, you determine whether to use a Horizontal or a Vertical Sweep. For these cars, Horizontal was chosen because the cars are longer than they are tall.

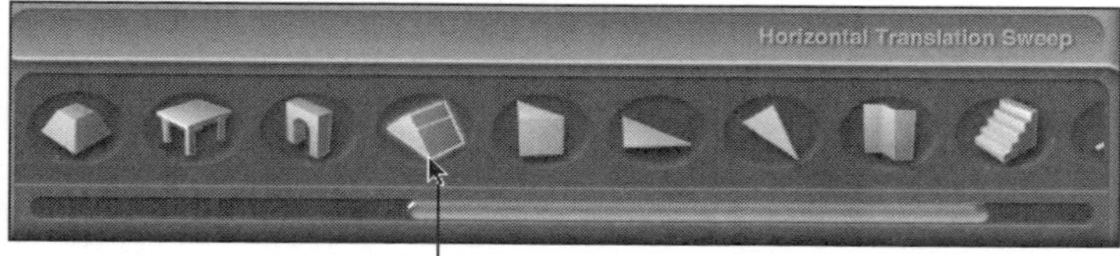

Horizontal Translation Sweep primitive

Don't begin with a Translation Sweep when creating a model. First create a basic primitive and build your Sweep onto it. This approach helps with overall alignment and orientation.

The Translation Sweep In Action

Here's an example of the Horizontal Translation Sweep used to model the top half of the truck. This is the unmodified HTS, stacked on top of the base Box primitive.

Power To The Modeler

Here's a look at the HTS in its modified form. As you see here, the power of the Translation Sweep tools lies in the capability to add modification points, thus giving you complete control over the HTS primitive's shape.

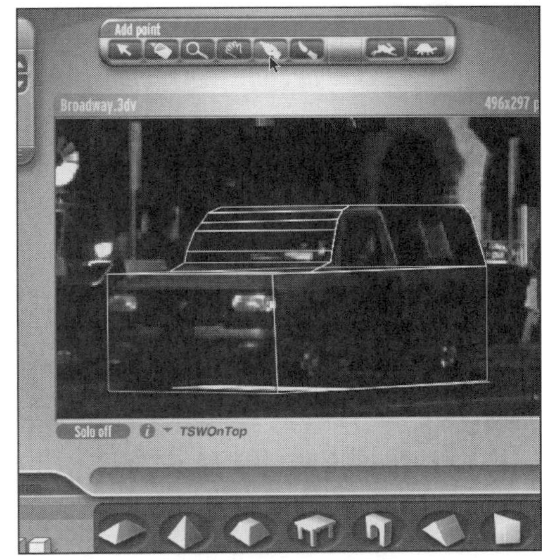

Precision Placement

Now it's your turn. You don't have to be overly precise with Sweeps. You'll be approximating circular paths, and you'll have to accept some limitations. Just take your time and carefully make the Sweep fit the outline of the image.

One main complaint about Canoma is about a lack of circular primitives. Sweeps help alleviate this problem, although not completely.

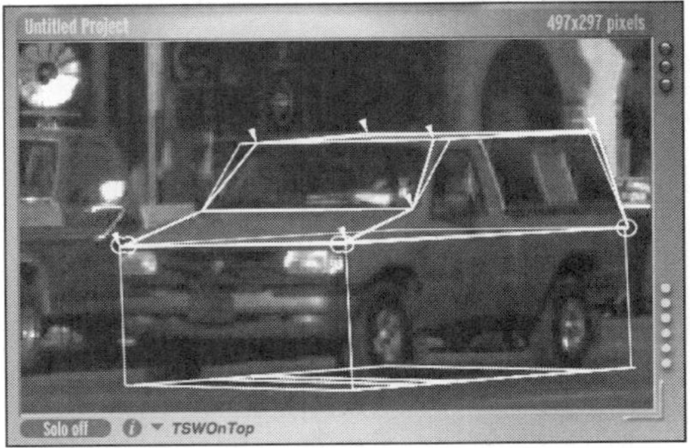

Adding Points

Add points by selecting the Add Point tool (fifth from the left in the toolbar). This lets you modify the shape to better fit the image. It's also a wonderful tool when using modifiable primitives, which is discussed in later chapters.

By adding extra points, you can enhance the smoothness of a curve.

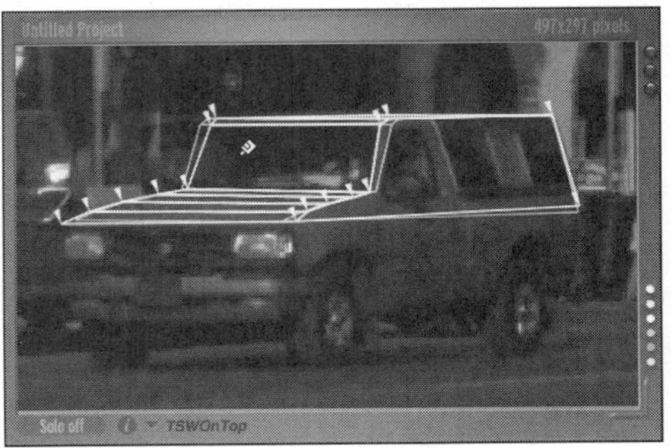

Using Other Sweep Tools

Here, two children are playing in the leaves. To work with this image, select the Horizontal Polygon tool.

Set The Points

To set the points accurately, it's often best to pin the lower-left and then the topmost point. This gives Canoma the starting parameters of the element that you want to create and simply generates fewer headaches when trying to initially surround your subject.

The Add Points Tool

Using Add Points, again add points where needed to shape the Horizontal Polygon tool to match the object. If, for example, you want to modify the area around the arm, create a point between hand and shoulder, move the point into position, and then add points between the originals and the points you just created.

Create A Leaf

Now do the same to create the large leaf to the left. Note that you need to zoom in close to make sure that you matched the contours as closely as possible. This is why you have some pixelation.

Images are created from square pixels. Software "blurs" edges, creating an illusion of smoothness; when you zoom in, the illusion disappears. So, as you zoom in on the image, you see jagged edges (or pixelation).

Now Do A Quality Render

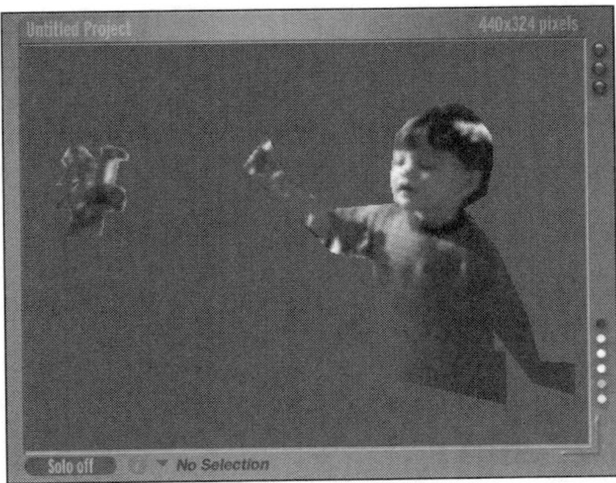

To see how your Sweeps worked, perform a Quality Render to get a good idea of how the Sweep interacts with the photograph. You'll get a better look at where unwanted areas of the image are being included with your Sweep, and then you can more precisely add and manipulate points.

Sweeping, which creates a cutout look, is perfect for both interior and outdoor shots. The cutout look—for people, mannequins, or leaves—adds an interesting, unexpected slant to your work. Remember, with Canoma layouts, rules can be broken. By creating the unexpected, you may pioneer the next hot look in design.

Helper Applications

Sometimes when you're modeling within Canoma, you need to edit a part of your image, perhaps deleting a sign or changing some packaging text. You can use helper applications without leaving Canoma.

Advanced Photo Manipulation

Usually, you have to quit the program you're working in, open a 2D program (such as Photoshop or Painter) to make the changes, and then re-import the edited picture. Canoma offers a shortcut that automatically opens your 2D editing program and lets you make the changes, instantly seeing the results.

Select Your Helper Application

Open File|Preferences|2D Image Editing Aplication, click on Browse, and select the application. This lets you modify images without leaving Canoma. You can also choose the format in which to save the modified files.

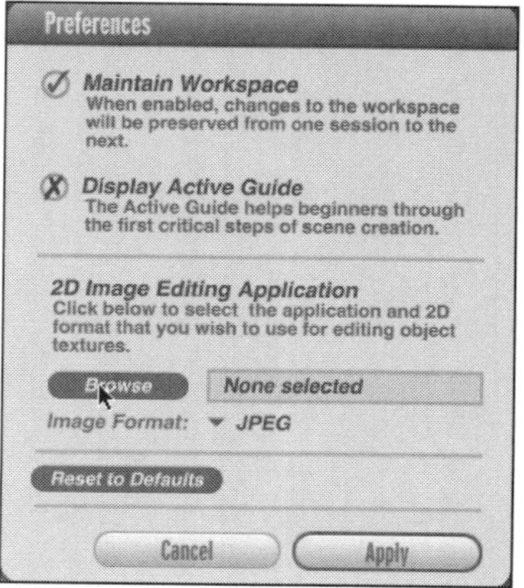

Choose The Format

In this case, Photoshop is my editor, and I selected the JPEG format as the format in which the files will be saved. You can also save the file as a PICT or TIFF image.

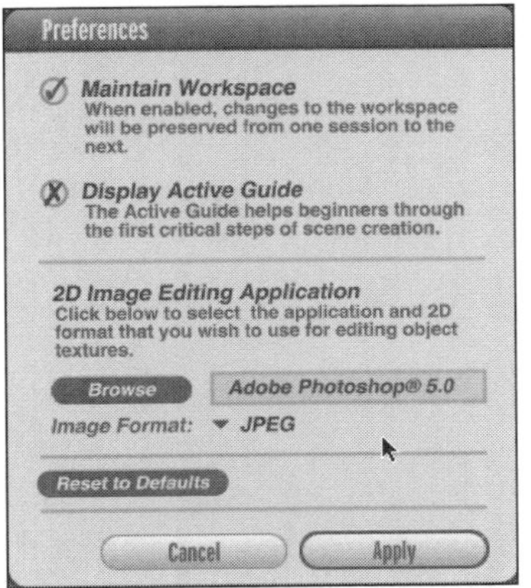

Do A Quick Render

First, ensure that you mapped the area you want to modify onto a primitive. Then click on Quick Texture (the Rabbit icon). Depending on image size and the number of primitives already in the picture—as well as your computer's speed and RAM—this may take from one or two seconds to a couple of minutes.

Use The Helper

Next, select the Brush tool in the toolbar and click once on the area you want to modify. This opens the editing application you selected.

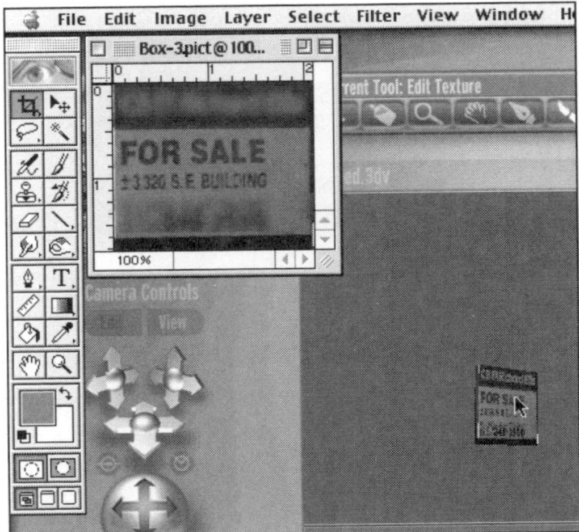

Final Modifications

Here, I modified another part of the image and used the PhotoGraphics filter set by Extensis. This plug-in provides options for control over text that are otherwise unavailable in Adobe Photoshop. Because MetaCreations Painter accepts Photoshop plug-ins, you can also use PhotoGraphics in Painter.

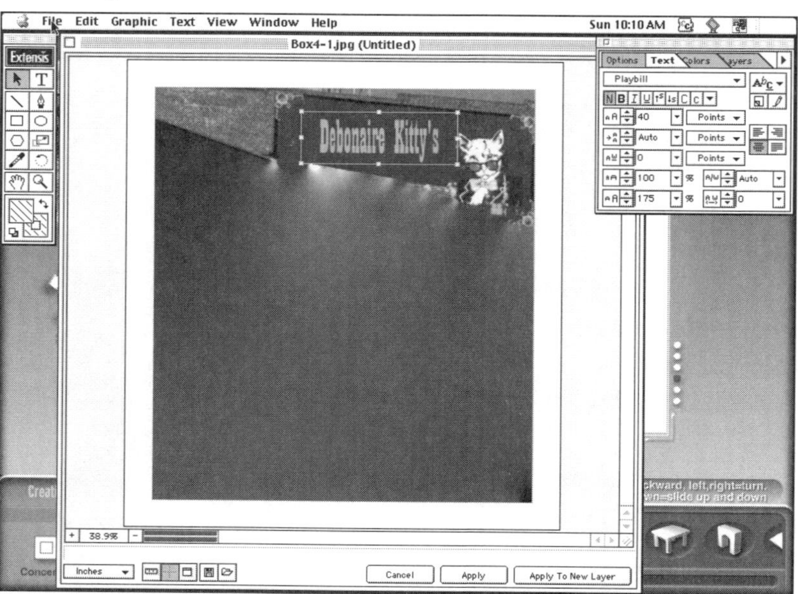

You can download a fully functional, time-limited version of PhotoGraphics from the Extensis site: ***www.extensis.com*** *or* ***www.creativepro.com****.*

Instant Gratification, Part 1

When you've completed the editing work (not covered here), the image is automatically updated on your model. Also notice that the file opened in your 2D software is given a specific name. When you close the file, save it in your model's folder so that you can access the information. (Canoma doesn't allow you to save the file anywhere else.) Don't rename it; just click on OK.

Instant Gratification, Part 2

You can edit as many objects on your model as you want, instantly seeing what the final model looks like after you build it. This technique is useful when you create product models.

How This Can Work

Let's use the TomKat's sign on the face of the building. Suppose that the client supplied this image but now has decided to change the company's name. You can re-create and edit the logo in a 2D or a 3D (such as TGS' Amapi 3D version 5) application, and then modify the original image to reflect the change.

To learn more about Amapi 3D, visit the ***www.tgs.com*** *Web site.*

Another Modification Example

You can also add prices or other information to the side of the building—or to the client's product packaging design, giving your client a true 3D representation of how it looks to people driving down the street or on the store shelves next to its competition.

Infinite Creativity, Part 1

This method opens an infinite number of possibilities for your creativity. You don't have to live with an unsuitable image.

Infinite Creativity, Part 2

Instead, you can manipulate it to create an interactive environment designed to your client's specifications—one that will etch your client's name into the public consciousness. Creating interactive images is discussed in more detail in Chapters 6 and 10.

RAM is the only limitation here. We have arranged with Crucial Technologies for a special offer on memor upgrades. For more information, see the Crucial folder in this book's FTP site.

Creating QuickTime And AVI Video

You can save Canoma files as still images for use in advertisements, as MetaStream files for use on the Web, or as QuickTime and AVI videos. The first two formats are straightforward; simply save your file in the desired format. To create QuickTime videos and AVIs, you need to know how to use the Animation controls.

The Video Control Panel

Using a simple keyframe system, you can create impressive *flythroughs* of your model within seconds—even if you've never created an animation before. Flythroughs are basically animations where you move the camera over, around, and through areas of your model so that viewers are able to see your work from all angles.

Select The Animation Controls

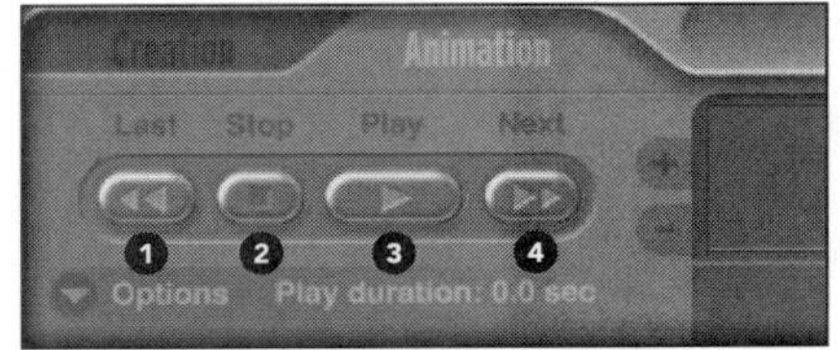

First, complete your model. Next, create a flythrough animation that will show off your work by selecting the Animation tab (next to the Create tab, at the bottom left side of the screen). You'll see a simple VCR-like control panel and a series of empty frames.

The main controls are set up like a VCR, allowing you to:

1. Move back one keyframe at a time
2. Stop the playback
3. Play the animation
4. Skip ahead one keyframe at a time

To Loop

In the Options pop-up menu, you can set whether the animation loops, or stops at the end. You also can call up the Animations Settings dialog box, where you set the overall length of the rendered animation in minutes, seconds, or frames.

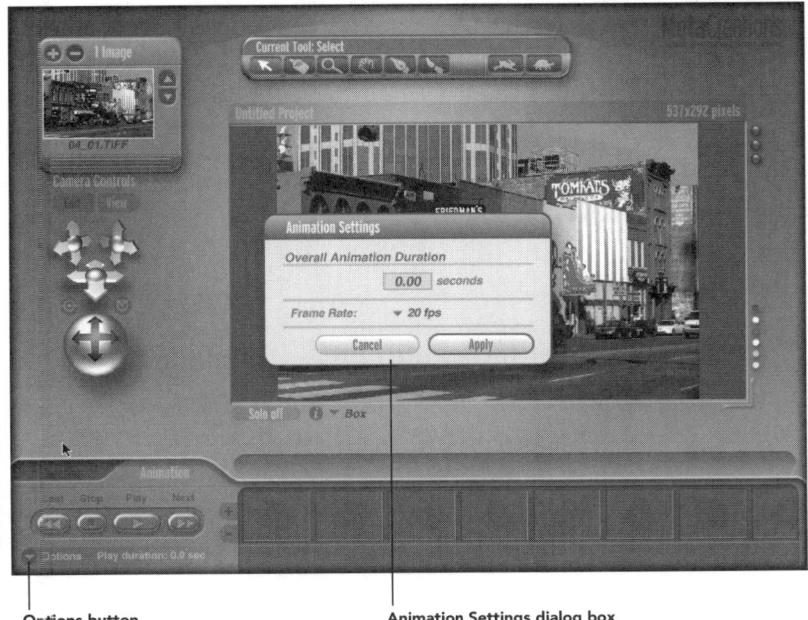

Options button

Animation Settings dialog box

Add/Delete Buttons

Immediately to the right of these controls are a plus (+) and a minus (–) button. Plus adds frames to your animation; minus deletes frames. You can delete intermediate frames as well as sequential frames; you have plenty of room to modify the animation before the final render.

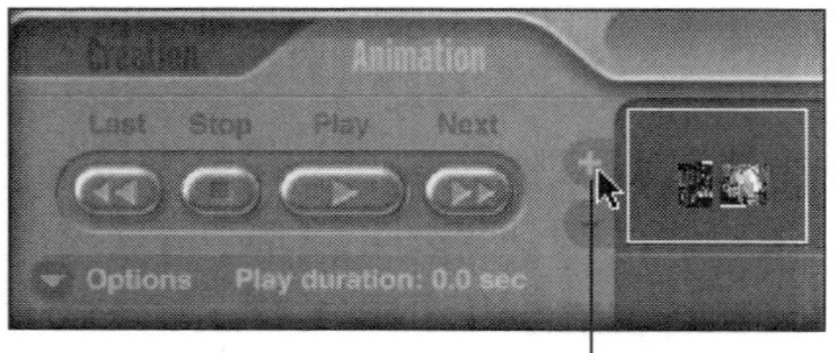

The plus (add) button

Deleting Frames

To delete a keyframe, select the one you want to remove by clicking on the appropriate frame and then click on minus or press the Del key. This causes your animation to change drastically, but don't worry.

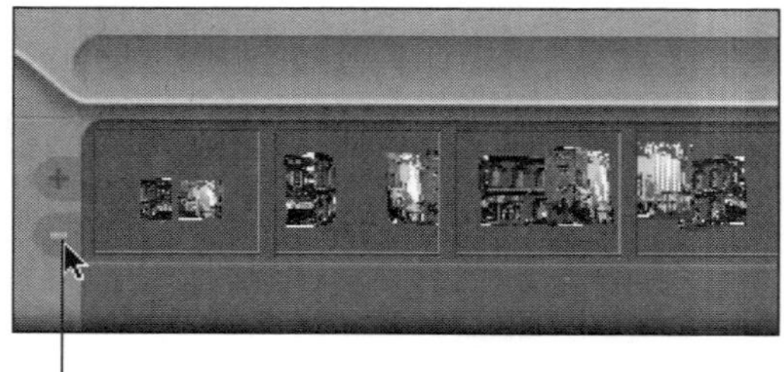
The minus (delete) button

Creating A Replacement Keyframe

To insert a new frame, click on the preceding frame. When you select plus, a new keyframe is placed between the existing keyframes. Canoma automatically calculates the new in-betweens.

Deleting An Unneeded Keyframe

To delete a frame, click on the frame. When you select minus, the unwanted keyframe is removed from the existing keyframe sequence and the now-empty space is closed up. Canoma automatically calculates the new in-betweens.

What Is A Keyframe?

In digital animation, a *keyframe* represents a specific point in an animation that tells the program you want to go from the prior saved frame to the current one. The program then creates all the "in between" images needed to represent fluid motion.

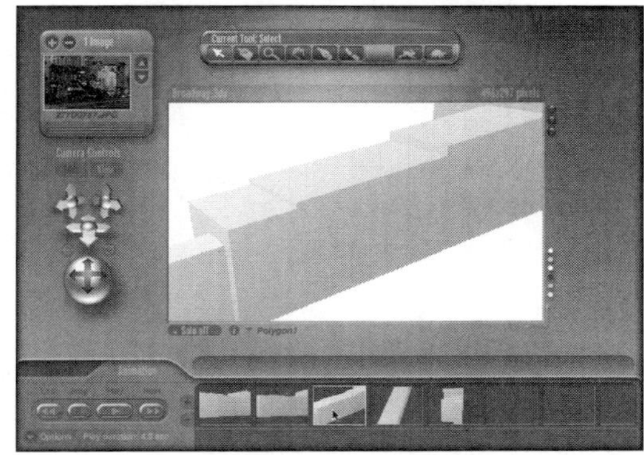

How Many In-Betweens Are Created?

It depends on how you set up an animation, and you really don't have to worry about it. Canoma does the math, based on the frames-per-second rate specified, creating enough in-betweens to make the animation fluid while staying within the time frame you've set.

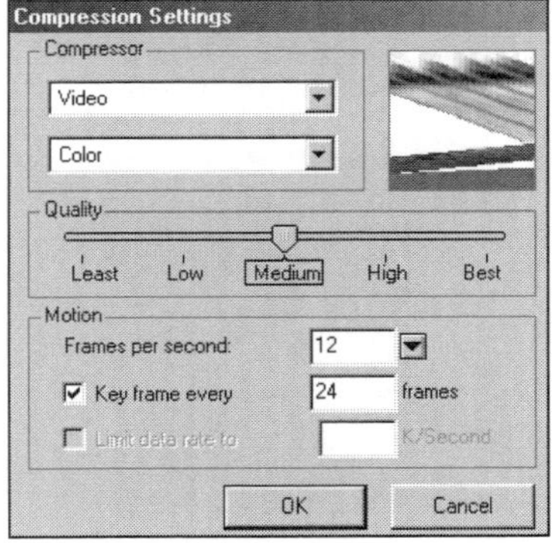

Keyframing is a powerful animation tool used in most 3D animation packages. To learn more about keyframing, read that section in the Canoma User Guide or in the documentation of your other 3D software packages.

Creating An AVI

When saving an animation in Canoma, you don't actually get an AVI option. When setting up your export parameters, you will see numerous file choices that give you the flexibility to import your finished work into your video playback software.

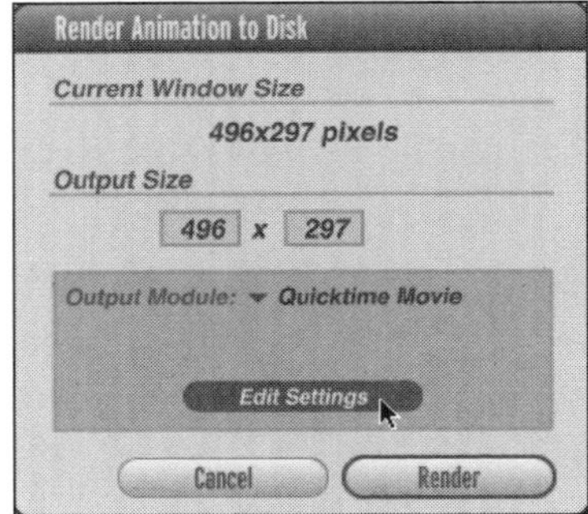

The Animation Choices

When you create the parameters for your animation(s), you'll find these in the pull-down menu on the setup screen. (When creating a file for AVI, I suggest using either Intel Indeo® Video R3.2, Sorenson Video, or the Video settings.)

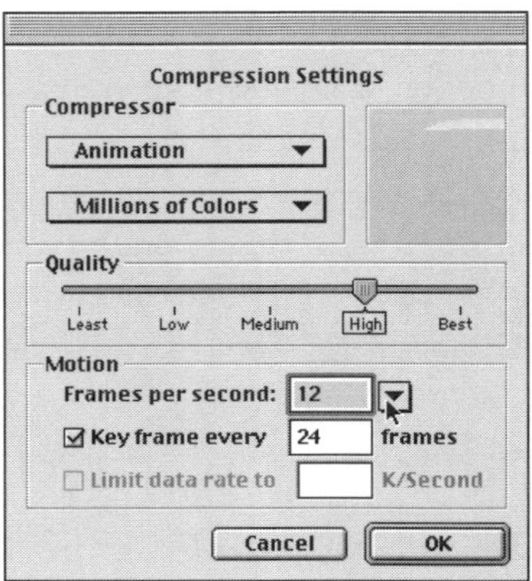

- Animation
- BMP
- Cinepak
- Component Video
- DV-NTSC (US Broadcast/Videotape format)
- DV-PAL (Non-US Broadcast/Videotape format)
- Graphics
- H.261
- H.263
- Intel Indeo® Video R3.2
- Intel Raw
- Motion JPEG A
- Motion JPEG B
- Photo JPEG
- Planar RGB
- PNG (quickly becoming a replacement format for GIF and JPEG on the Web)
- Sorenson Video
- TGA
- TIFF
- Video

You can learn more about these formats and what their differences are by experimentation or by reading Digital Compositing In Depth, *published by The Coriolis Group.*

Exporting Models For Use In Other Programs

As you learn more about creating in Canoma, you will want to see how complex you can make your images. Often, this involves saving your model so that you can import it into other 3D applications, such as Bryce 4 or Poser 4, or into an organic modeler such as Hash:Animation Master, Ray Dream Studio, or Pixels:3D.

Expanding Your Format Horizons

Canoma allows you to export in DXF, MTS, OBJ, and WRL, which are easily read by other 3D applications, such as Ray Dream 5.5, Carrara, trueSpace, and Pixels:3D. You can also save in PP2—the MetaCreations Poser 3/4 format—so that you can create animations using 3D characters.

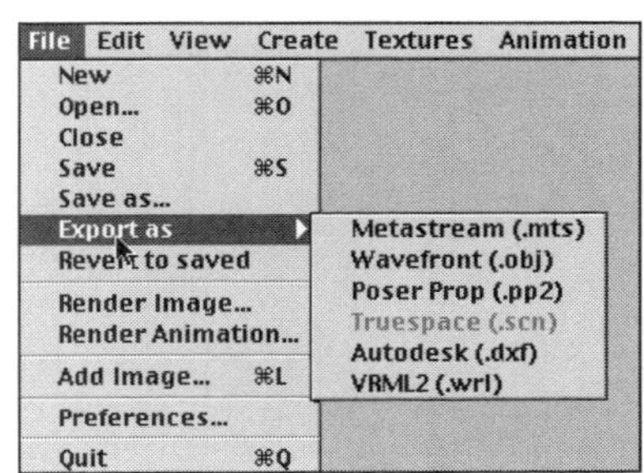

DXF And OBJ

DXF doesn't automatically map your photograph. When imported into a program, it's as an untextured wireframe. OBJ acts the same as DXF, only it includes mapped image information. If your 3D program accepts this format (nearly all do), your model is imported exactly as it was saved.

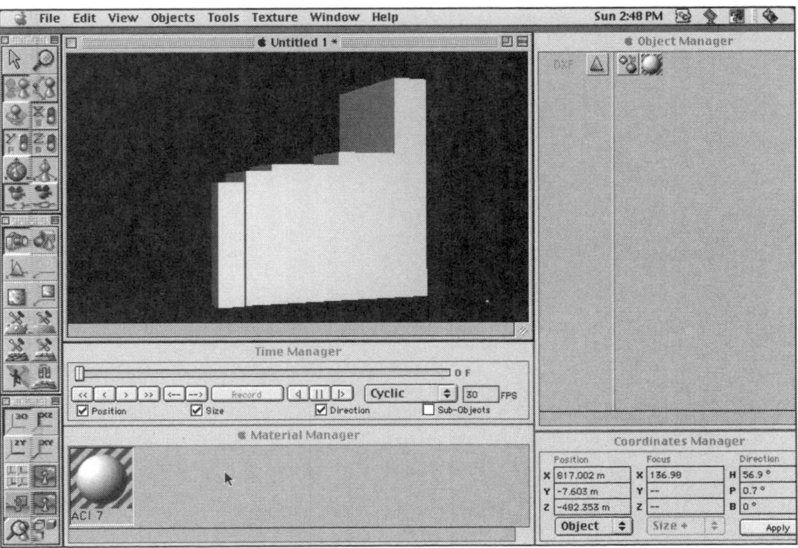

MetaStream And Experiment

MetaStream format (MTS) lets you place the model on the Web or, for presentations, to burn it onto CD-ROM or DVD. In this way, viewers can manipulate the image. Experiment with every format, but prepare to save files in MTS almost every time, whether or not the file is specifically designed to be used in another program.

Create An Interactive Flash Movie

You can import Canoma files into a Web-based application—Flash. The Flash format was created by Macromedia (**www.macromedia.com**), Flash and Shockwave players have become staples for Web animation and interactivity. The Flash and Shockwave players are so commonplace now that you probably you have the plug-in for viewing these files in your Web browser, whether you know it or not.

You can download the Flash file (SuitDisplay.swf) and the html file (SuitDisplay.html) to see the completed animation from the Chapter 9 folder on the book's FTP site (where you will use it as part of a project).

Macromedia Flash Or Fireworks

These applications, along with Director, are the granddads of streaming technology. You can obtain Demos of these programs at **www.macromedia.com**, and it's well worth purchasing one or both. The latest versions of these packages are Flash 4 and Fireworks 3.

Macromedia Director

This is Macromedia's high-end multimedia creator; it's truly among the best programs on the market. You've seen Director's work everywhere from the Web to CD-ROM to television and the movies. When you see a computer screen on the *Star Trek: The Next Generation* TV shows or movies, it's probably Director. The latest version is Director 8 Shockwave Studio. It comes with Fireworks 3.

LiveMotion

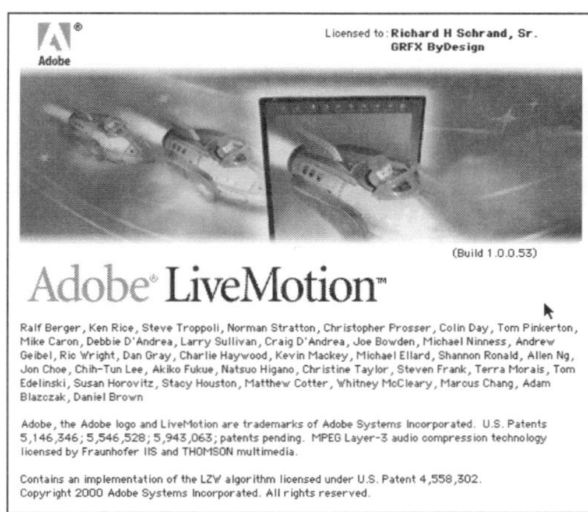

Adobe is now in the Flash creation business with LiveMotion, its latest software package. As of this writing, the program is still in public beta and is available for download at Adobe's Web site (**www.adobe.com/**). If you're used to Adobe products, you'll feel at home creating fully interactive animations with this program.

Chapter 5
Canoma For Sales Campaigns

- Build models for print
- Create a store walk-through and use Guide Lines to set perspective
- Blend different styles
- Generate a Web presentation

E-Commerce Applications With Canoma

If you have your own graphic design firm or work on freelance projects, Canoma-created images can give you the edge in acquiring new clients. If you already work with retail outlets, you can offer these clients new ways to sell their products—*e-commerce*. (The *e* stands for *electronic* and refers to the selling of products on the Web.)

The traditional method of retail advertising, especially print advertising, is to promote by showing a flat photographic image. These images are okay when transferred to the Web—but if you look closely at a potential buyer's incentive quotient, these images do little to bring him or her into an e-commerce store. Using Canoma, you can create interesting ads that stand apart from others, making a high-tech e-commerce site that blows away the competition.

*The files for this chapter's tutorials can be found in the Chapter 5 folder on the Coriolis FTP site (**ftp.coriolis.com**), in the **Canoma_Visual_Insight** folder.*

Using Canoma To Sell Yourself

The use of 3D imagery—whether static or the kind created with Canoma—is new to the general population and to retailers in particular. Your job is to prove how the potential increase in design cost will be more than offset by an increase in sales. This is difficult to do, but there are ways you can use images such as this one to show your clients how such images can make their products stand out from the competition and potentially increase sales.

Create A Product Model

In this section, you use Canoma in a way you might not have considered: creating interactive 3D line art. You might overlook this eye-catching use of Canoma's modeling capabilities because of the program's rich photographic-texturing engine. If you have an art tablet and electronic pen, it's easy to trace a photograph of the product in a program such as Painter 6. If you can draw by hand and have a scanner, you can scan and then use your line art.

With the release of Metastream 3, there are changes in the way you can create e-commerce sites. Refer to Chapter 1.

Draw A Product

Suppose that your client's sales materials contain hand-drawn art or the client wants to use line art rather than photographs for the Web site or ads. At first, you might think it won't work. Canoma, however, lets you work with line art as well as photographs.

1.

You have two options of primitive objects. You can use a basic Box primitive and then more boxes for the legs, or you can use the Table primitive. Here, the Table primitive is the best choice for the body.

If you consider the part of the model you're building as a single entity—and for the moment ignore other elements—you can begin to see other options for creating sophisticated models.

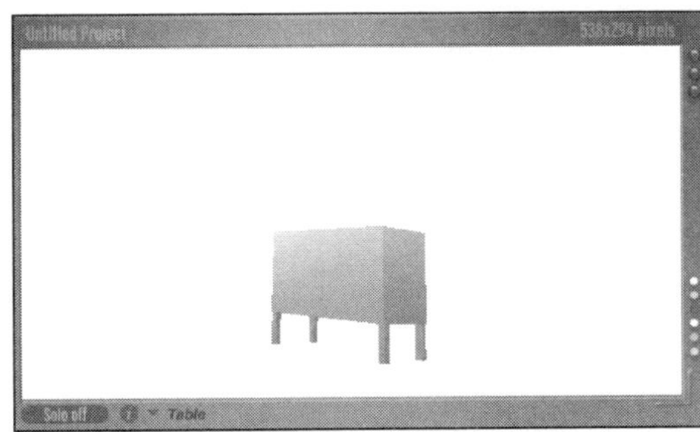

2.

Now create the body. Starting with the table top, pin the corners around the body of the dresser. Ignore the mirror for now; all you want to create is the base of the unit.

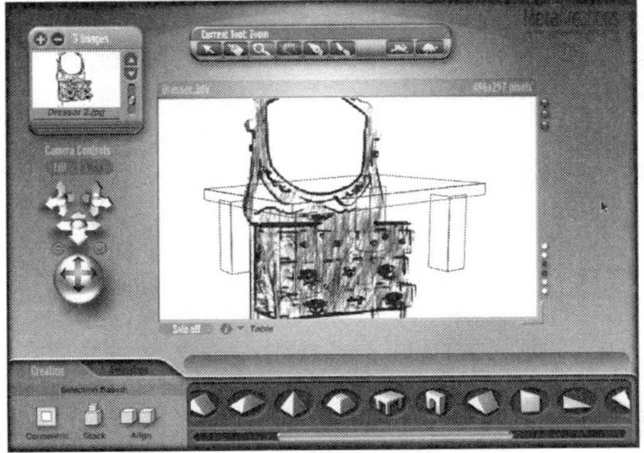

3.

Here's a Table primitive anomaly. When you work with the top portion of the Table primitive, the legs can go haywire (refer to Chapter 1). As you form the dresser body, don't worry if the legs look as if they've become detached.

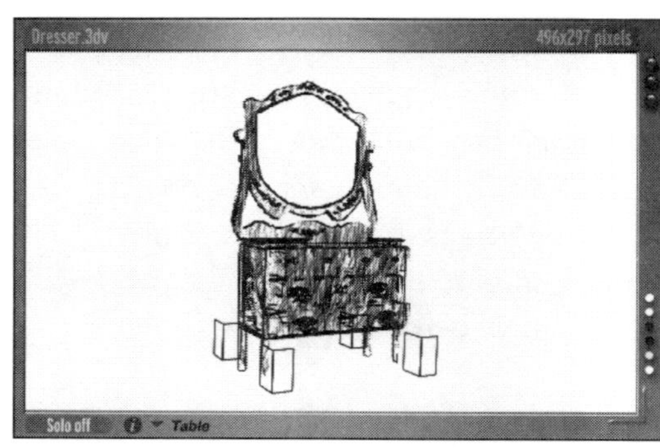

If you take a few moments after creating the chest of drawers body, watch the legs start to slowly work their way back into position. After this is done, and as you modify the legs to fit the image, you'll also notice that what you do to one leg affects all the others.

4.

The image shown here has been manipulated so that you can better see the drawer primitive.

5.

Now, you'll create the drawer and learn a new trick at the same time. With the dresser body primitive active, select Create|Align|Box Primitive and hold down Shift. You now have a primitive resting on the ground plane in front of the dresser body.

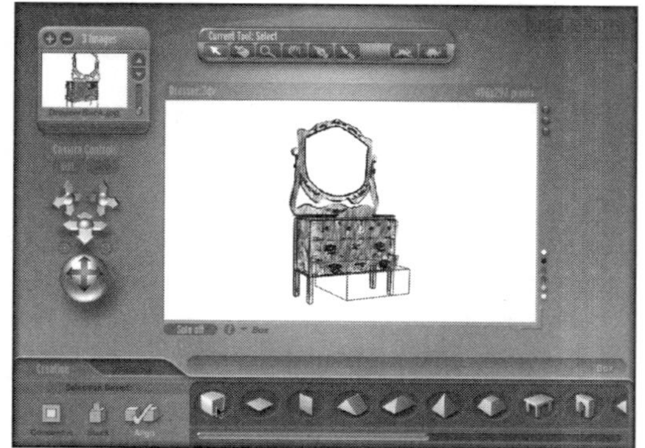

6.

A trick that can help you align objects correctly: Select Menu|Unfix Y (Height) Parameter. Select a top rear edge of the Box primitive and then hold down Command (Mac) or Ctrl (Windows) as you move the corner into place.

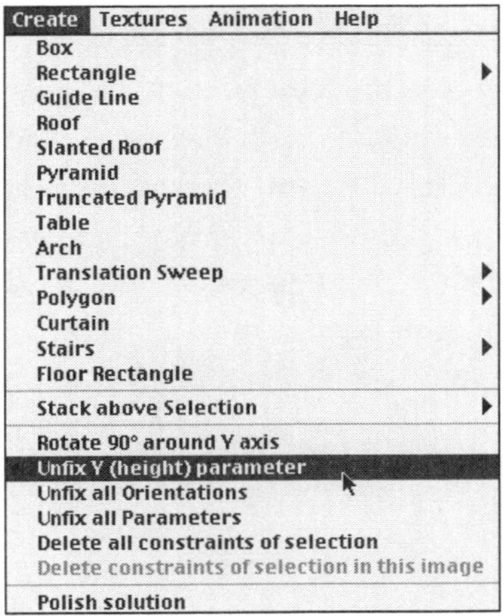

7.

The cursor changes into the glue bottle, and you can pin and glue at the same time. You really should remember this shortcut. Using the Glue option is a major part of modeling in Canoma; if you use this shortcut, you'll soon tire of selecting the Glue tool manually.

8.

Pin the other corners of the drawer and do a Quick Render. The drawer (bottom) should be perfectly aligned with the body of the dresser.

The Sliding Trick

You can use this technique to place model elements into nonaligned areas. Press and hold Command or Ctrl when you click on the rear edge of the new primitive, then glue it to the vertical edge of the main primitive to force the new primitive flush against the center face of the main primitive. Select Menu|Unfix Y (Height) Parameter. You can move the primitive without having to position it against a vertical edge by dragging the dot on the glued intersection.

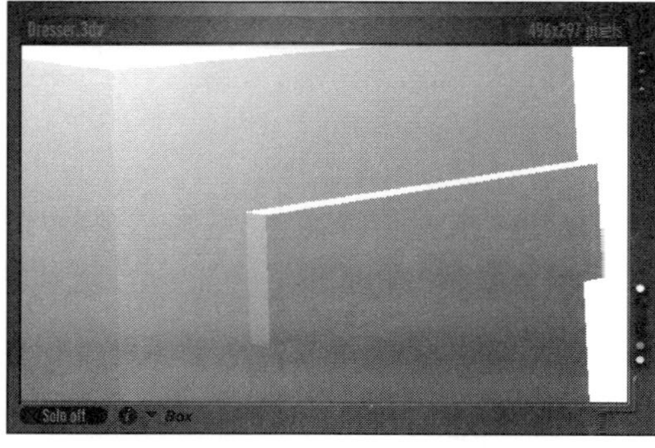

1.

To prepare the final image for print, select File|Render Image To Disk to create a JPEG, TIFF, PICT, Photoshop (PSD), or other image file and select the parameters (settings) for the file size. *Do not* specify a size larger than the size of your image.

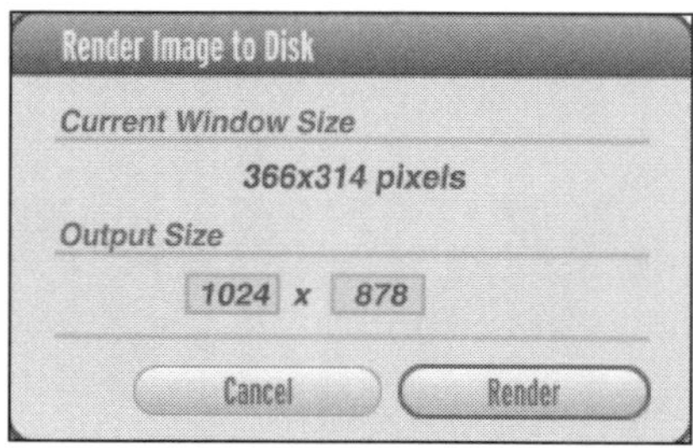

2.

If you use a 1,200x1,200 pixel image, for example, don't save it larger than this, or the file will become pixelated (see "Finishing The Walk-Through" later in this chapter for more on pixelated images.

When you change the first size parameter (either vertical or horizontal) and then press the Tab key to move to the next size adjustment box, the dimension will be automatically adjusted, based on your workspace dimensions.

3.

To prepare the file for other 3D applications, choose OBJ, .pp2 (Poser Prop), .scn, or .dxf. For Web site use, save your file in the MetaStream format. Later in this chapter, I go into more detail on MetaStream file format.

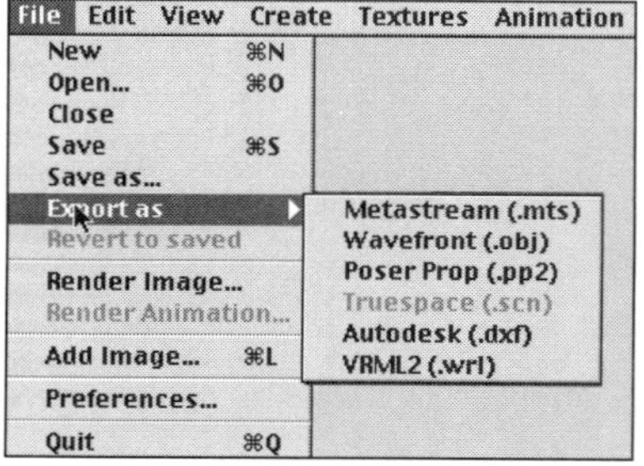

Incorporating Files Into Print

By saving your image in one of the photo formats (refer to the preceding step 1), you can import it into a page layout or design program and build your ad. Then you can re-create the ad as a Web page, using the MetaStream file you created to give the site visitors full interactivity with the product. It gives online customers extra value while retaining the store's overall theme and advertising look.

Create A Retail Walk-Through

Get permission to shoot some photographs inside your client's store, making sure to keep customers out of the shot. It's always best to take elevated shots so that you can get the correct perspective. If this is impossible (because ceilings are too low, there is no ladder, or the manager won't let you climb onto tables or counters), photograph as many sides of the object as you can. In this way, you can stitch together the photos later. Bring the images into Canoma and begin building your scene.

The Campaign Begins

This image shows a number of display stands, some clothes racks, and background. Unfortunately, this kind of image gives you only a single angle so make sure that the Mirror Texture feature is turned on (Command|Ctrl+N or Textures|Mirror Textures).

Extra Work For Canoma

Also, because you don't have textures to fill in areas that are blocked from sight, Canoma must do some calculations. Therefore, the textures look strange in some areas.

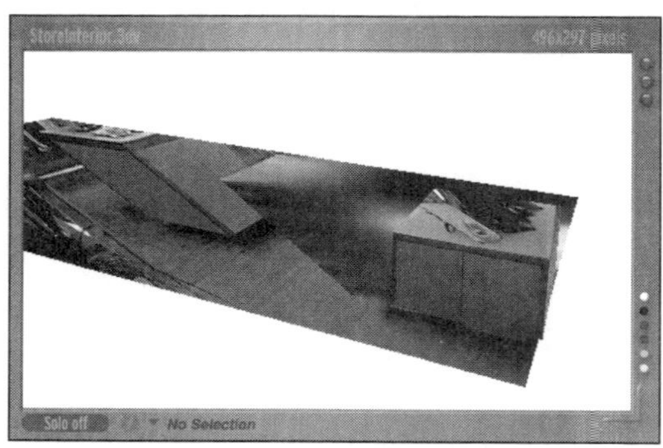

Challenges For The Program

Another challenge: The display stands have a base, hidden from view, that raises the main body of the stand off the floor. You can cheat by creating the model as a single piece, or you can create the stand and stack a second Box primitive on top. This is the approach we'll take.

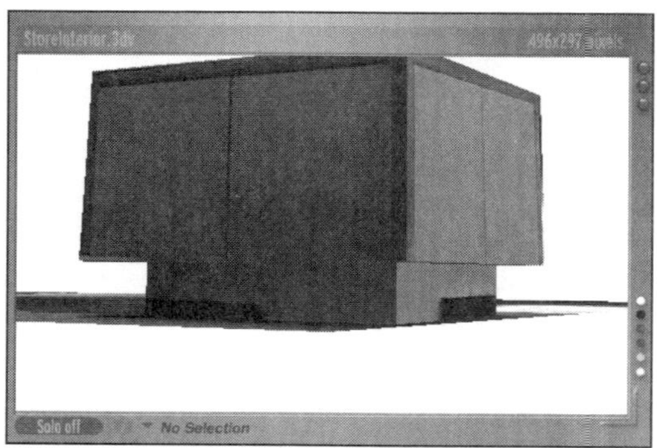

Estimate Positions On Hidden Areas

When you create the bottom portion of the display stand, you need to estimate its position in relation to the upper body. Luckily, this is fairly simple: Create a box and make sure that it isn't stressed. Stack a second box on top of the first one. This example shows what the unmapped display stand should look like.

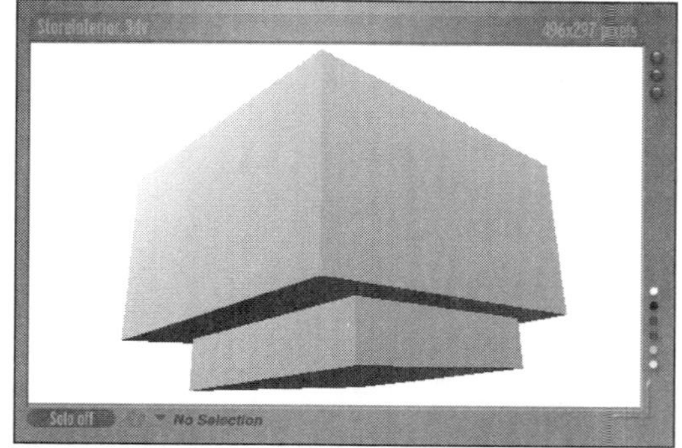

You must build the stand without actually seeing the backside of the object: You have to guess the final placement of that portion. With practice, your ability to visualize size and dimension will benefit your modeling efforts.

Create The Floor

Until now, you've been looking at how to create a single product. Everything is floating in space, defying gravity. Now it's time to give the model a base to rest on. Select the Horizontal Rectangle primitive; then resize it to fit your image. Use the trackball (rather than rendering) to rotate around the model to make sure that everything lines up. Finally, do a Quality Render.

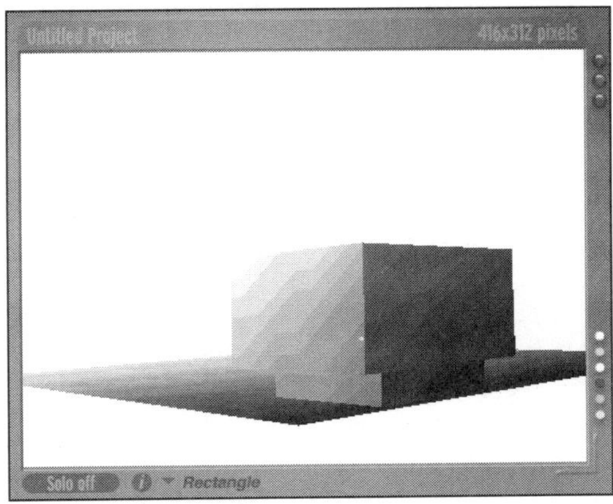

Why Did This Happen?

The floor and top of the display cube look strange; Canoma rendered the image onto the primitives you've built. So, the perspective looks strange—like a slide being projected on an off-kilter screen. As you place subsequent primitives into the scene, this no longer is an issue because the different elements cover up those specific misaligned spots.

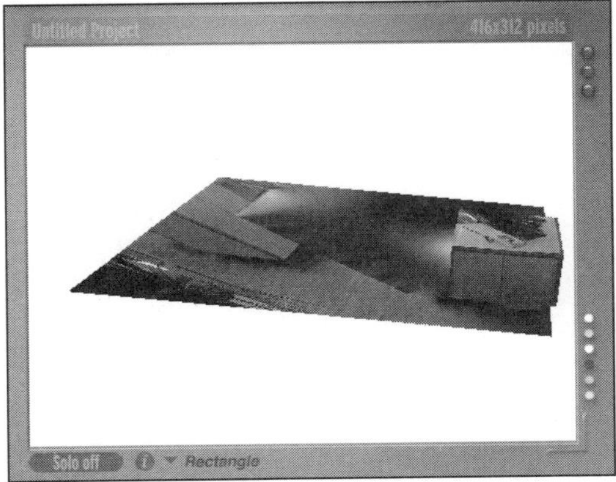

The Curtain Tool

You also want to create the back wall. For this, use a new primitive: the Curtain (shown here as the fourth tool from the left). Beyond being a great tool for creating walls and backgrounds, curtains have the added bonus of becoming invisible when viewed from the opposite side.

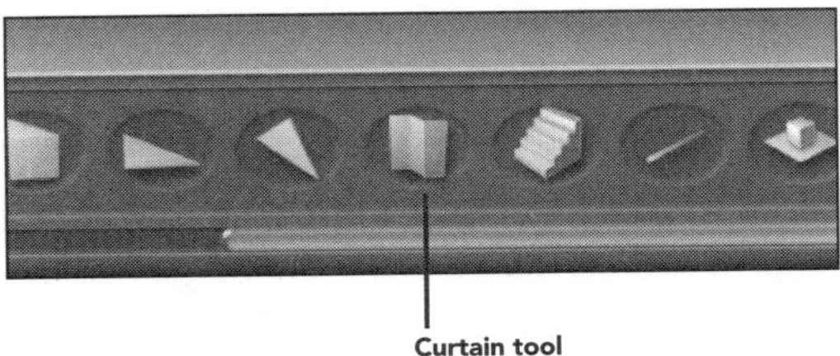

The Incredible Disappearing Primitive

What does this mean? From the front—or textured—side, the Curtain primitive acts as a wall or background.

A Two-Way Curtain

As viewers move outside the model and into an area "behind" a Curtain primitive, the primitive disappears, allowing them to see the room from that angle.

Add The Background

Make sure that the Horizontal Plane is selected (click anywhere inside it). Then select Stack and then the Curtain primitive. Note that it's segmented, giving you greater control over placements around numerous corners. You learn more uses for Horizontal and Vertical Planes in Chapter 8. For now, pin the bottom edge of the Curtain to the left rear, center, and right corners of the Horizontal Plane. It's also a good idea to glue the corners.

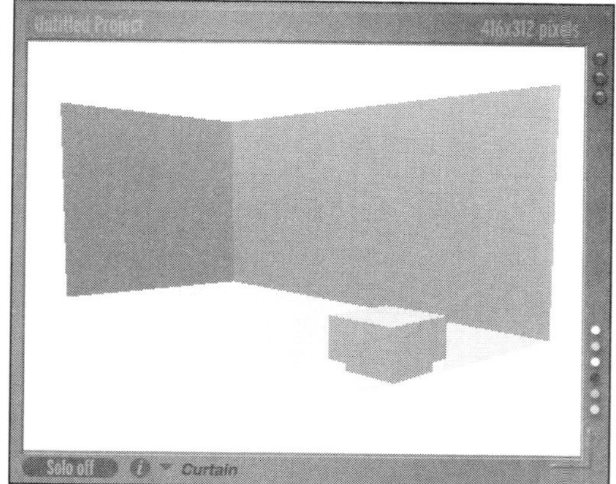

Duplicate The Displays

Place a second display cube into the image. Here, assume that the cubes are the same size, and simply duplicate the original display cubes. Select Command|Ctrl+D or Edit|Duplicate and move the duplicates into place. You'd have to do a lot of manipulating to get them to fit together correctly. In this case, create a new Box primitive. Activate the Horizontal Plane (or floor) and stack a new box on it. To create a second stand, make the base and then stack a second Box primitive on top of it.

But Is It On The Floor?

Now make the block sit on the floor (not float in space). The right topmost button on the display area turns Shadows on or off. When highlighted, it's on; when gray, it's off. You also can turn Shadows on by selecting Display|Shadows On. Using Shadows helps in the overall alignment of objects by giving you a graphical representation of the relationships between objects.

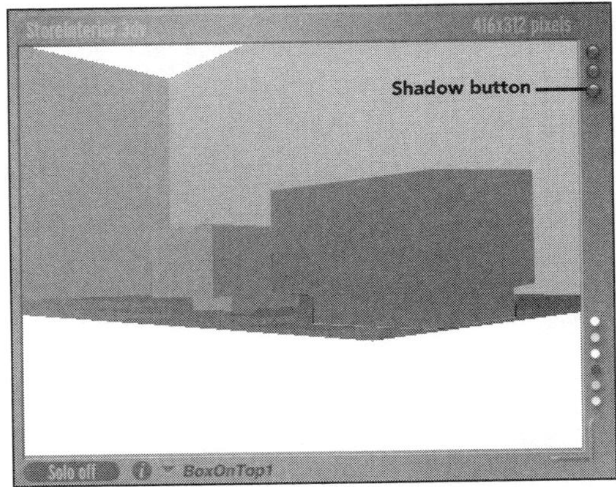

Introducing Guide Lines

Guide Lines are another tool to help you control the relationships between objects and to aid in measurement and perspective. (A Guide Line is created with the Line tool, so it isn't a true primitive.) Guide Lines don't render in your image or your preview, so you don't have to worry about having unwanted information in your scene.

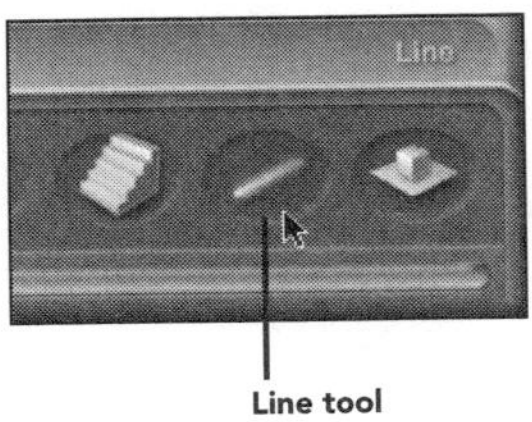

Setting Measurements

When you place a Guide Line, extra options become available. Selecting Object Information opens a dialog box in which you can enter a numerical value to set the size of a primitive. By duplicating the line, rotating it, and gluing the ends, you can force a primitive to take on dimensions that you set.

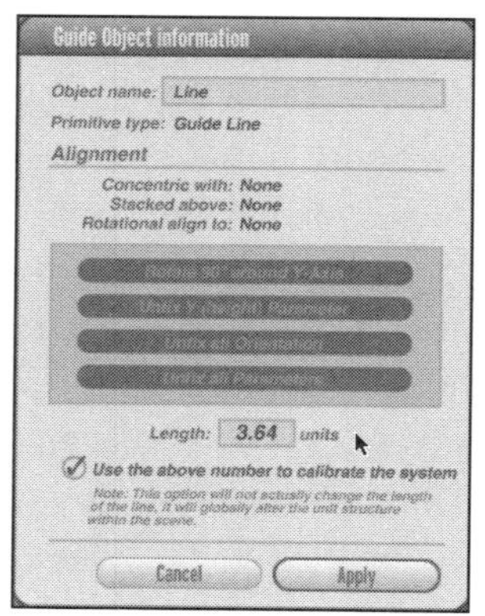

Using Guide Lines—Locking In The Perspective

Save the file so you can come back to it later, but don't close the image. Delete the ground plane and the back wall so that the scene has only the two cubes. Create a Guide Line, and move the left end to the lower-right corner of the foremost cube by clicking on and dragging the Guide Line's end point. Following the perspective of this cube, stretch the Guide Line and pin it as close as you can to the far side of the second cube.

Using Guide Lines—Aligning To The Guide

If the Guide Line and cubes don't touch, it isn't an unsolvable problem. Move each cube to the Guide Line, and then glue it to the Guide Line. Now the two objects will be perfectly aligned. If you did a Fast Render now, you'd see only the cubes; the Guide Line doesn't become part of the image.

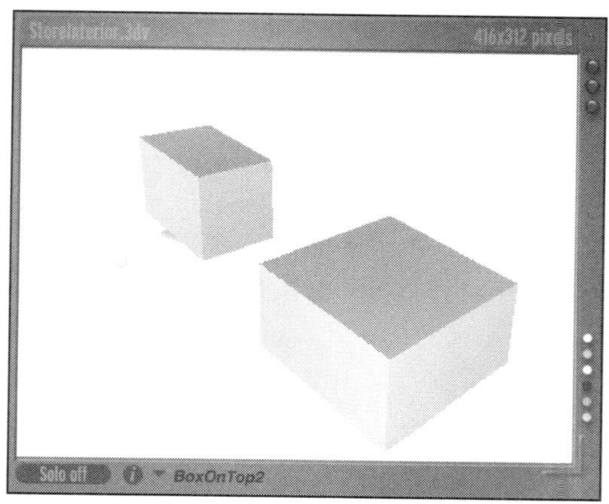

Sizing With Guide Lines

To lock in the sizes of the objects, first make sure that you unfix all parameters by selecting Menu|Unfix. Create a Guide Line object (visible only in Edit mode, it doesn't show in this View image), and glue it to the bottom edge of one of the cubes.

Duplicate The Guide Line

Duplicate the line (Command/Ctrl+D or Edit|Duplicate) and rotate it into a vertical position along the edge of the cube. Make sure that the bottom end of this line and the end of the other line are touching, and then glue the points.

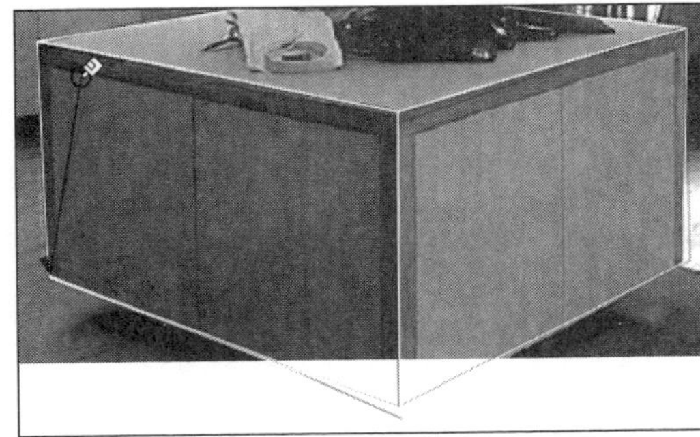

Make Another Copy

Rotate the Guide Line again to create a top edge and glue the lines together. Your cube is now resized to the Guide Line lengths.

Finishing The Walk-Through

Now, return to the image you were creating. To open the saved scene, select either File|Open or Command/Ctrl+O or select File|Revert To Saved. You have set a floor, two cubes, and a background. Now let's finish the model by creating the products.

1.

To create the display items, select the frontmost cube, click on Create|Stack, and click on the Box primitive. Reshape the box around the shirt. (For some fun, shape this primitive to match the shirt and then use the Stack and Box primitives on that one to create the collar.)

2.

Repeat the procedure for each item on the display cubes. You need to do a lot of zooming in to make sure that the elements are pinned correctly. Doing so *pixelates* your image, which makes it difficult to see edges clearly. Images are made up of pixels, so smooth edges aren't actually smooth. The antialiasing process blurs pixel edges, giving the appearance of smoothness. As you zoom in, the pixel edges become pronounced, which is referred to as pixelation.

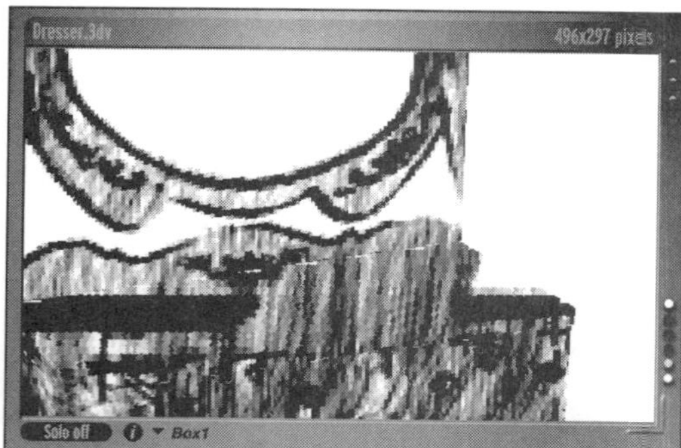

You can also try experimenting with various primitives to see which ones work best to complete your model.

3.

To create the display case shown in the back, select the Curtain primitive and then select Create|Align, and the Box primitive. Resize the primitive to fit the display case and glue the edges to the edge of the Curtain primitive.

4.

To create the clothes rack, repeat the preceding steps; but this time, align to the Display Case primitive and not the Curtain primitive. If you do the latter, you'll lose the correct proportion of the objects and the proper positioning between the elements. When you build the models, you should always be aware of this point; if something isn't aligning correctly, it's probably because the wrong object was picked as the aligning one.

View The Walk-Through

Now do a Quick or a Quality Render. Test your walk-through by moving in and out of the model and between the display cubes. Fly around the image to look at it from all sides. You might also want to do a quick animated fly-through and save it. If you don't, you'll probably need it at the least opportune moment—when you're somewhere and with someone who needs to see it, and you can't build the animation.

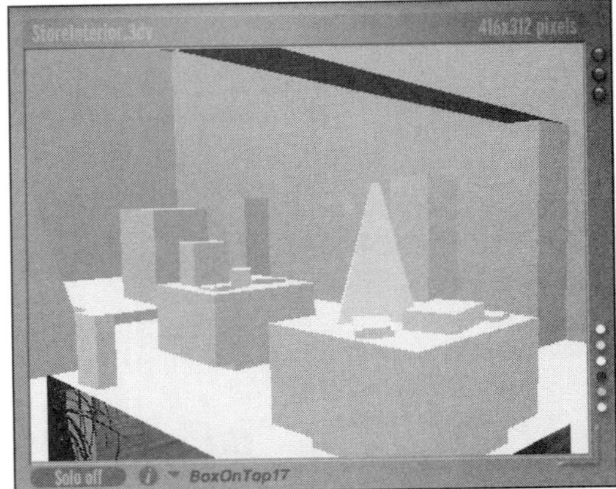

Blending Styles

Now let's create the same scene, but this time, as a combination of hand-drawn and photographic images. This mix of styles can produce an eye-catching model.

Why Combine Genres?

In advertising, the name of the game is to produce a strong impression so that the public associates your client's product with the brand name as well as with characteristics such as quality and economy. By finding new, exciting ways to highlight a product, you have a better chance to create a strong impression.

The Idea Is To Stand Out

If you, as a client, saw this image in a catalog—with the line art as the main element contrasted with the sale item in photographic form—you more than likely would read the attached copy or would want to get more information about the product. Add to this your ability—thanks to Canoma—to provide this type of image in fully interactive 3D on the Web, and it's easy for your client to see the potential for increased traffic and sales.

Draw The Background

Suppose that you want to focus on the front display stand in the image you just created. Draw the sales area: the display stands, the background, the display shelf, and the clothes rack. If you're using Adobe Photoshop, Painter 6, or a similar program, build a second layer and place on it the photographic image of the shoes. Now repeat the steps in the preceding section to create the combined image and save it as a MetaStream file.

You can see a color version of this image in the Color Studio section of the book.

Linking To The Web

A Canoma strong suit is its capability to export image files in MetaStream format. MetaStream allows for complete user interactivity—from pushing in and pulling out of the model to user-controlled fly-arounds. The easiest way to visualize a fly-around is to picture yourself in a small airplane and flying over an area. You can create a link on each page for viewers who don't have the MetaStream plug-in; otherwise, they won't be able to see the image. Using MetaStream technology, you can embed MTS files in your page to build an online catalog for your company or client. After you create the page, you can show it to your client on the Web, or you can open the file in your Web-site creation program. Your client or superiors will never again want to show their product in a static, two-dimensional way.

The Slow Connection

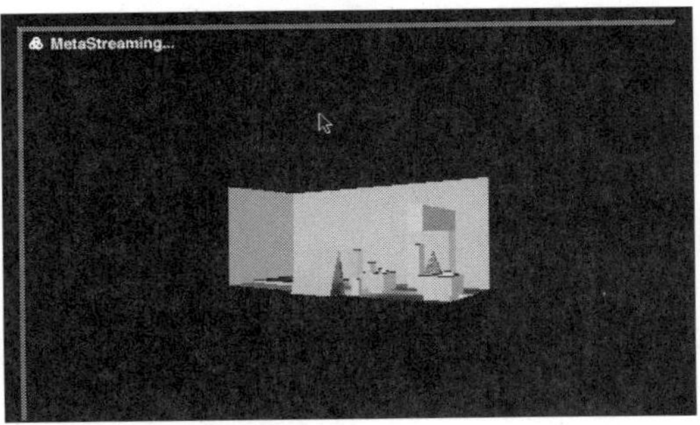

The MetaStream format has one drawback: For those with slower Internet connections, it takes time for highly intricate images to map onto the model. While waiting for the image to load, the visitor sees the model as a two-toned image (the same as an unmapped primitive).

Use Low Resolution Pictures For The Web

Don't go overboard when adding images or using high-resolution textures. The slow load time diminishes the mystery of the Canoma creation process. To shorten load time, use single images or smaller files. Also remember that the ability to interact with an object—viewing a product from all sides as if you were actually holding it—is new. Make it a manageable size so that visitors know what they're buying.

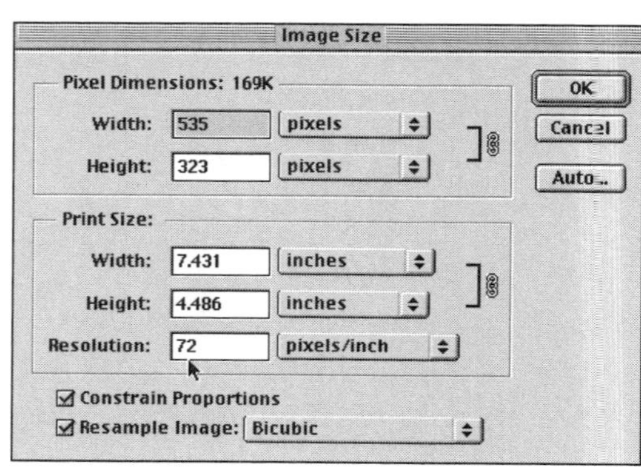

---

*A link on the official Canoma site (**www.canoma.com**) shows another workaround for this problem. It involves placing a completely different, unrelated element well away from the main model to act as a curtain to hide the model while the image maps load.*

HTML Or MTS Files; Which To Use?

When you save in MTS format, you get two files: an HTML and an MTS file. The HTML file is built over a black background and contains directions on how to manipulate the image. It also contains code that others can copy to put the file onto their Web sites.

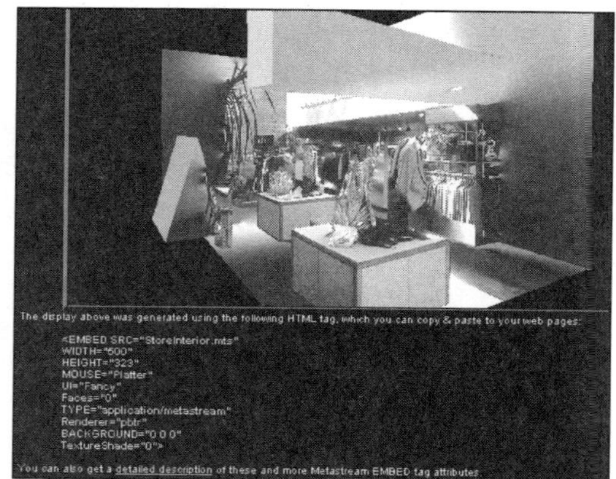

I'm Not A Fan Of HTML

By including any type of HTML code on your pages, it opens the possibility of others taking your work and posting it on their sites. You can link this page to your Web site, or you can design your own page and import the MTS file to the page.

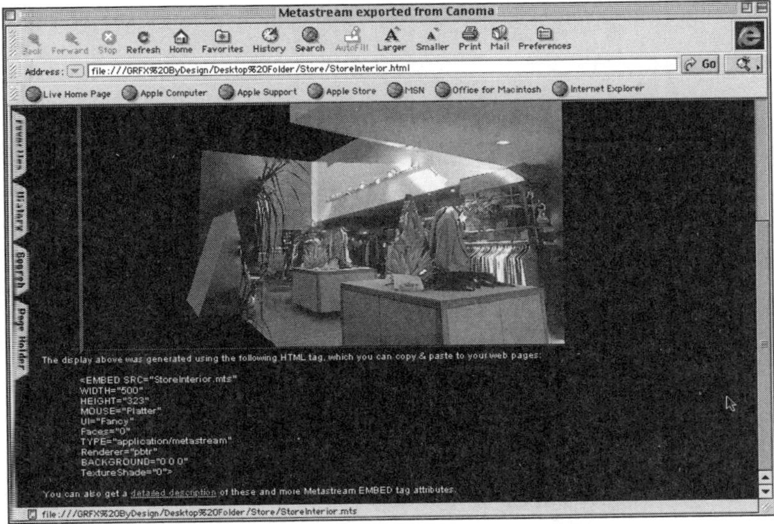

My Web Recommendation

For professional work that requires trademark or copyright security, I recommend using the MTS file only. To learn more about recent changes to the usage rights of MetaStream technology, visit **www.metastream.com**.

Chapter 6
E-Commerce Solutions

- Construct photorealistic items
- Build 3D clip art from existing clipart files
- Create a banner ad using your Canoma models
- Use the images on an e-commerce site

Use Canoma To Build Revenue On The Web

Now you will explore e-commerce. Canoma is the perfect tool for creating unique presentations on the Web, especially to sell merchandise. E-commerce is tricky and setting up Web sites is afield of this book's subject. However, this chapter explores options for creating unique elements to place on e-commerce sites that will set your work apart from others.

3D MetaStreaming

You can now build 3D photomodels and let Web surfers manipulate products in size from screws to football stadiums. Although detractors agree that the ability to rotate and zoom images can dazzle visitors, they argue that it gets boring. Potential buyers, however, don't visit sites for the dazzle; they just want to walk around and pick up a product—just as they do in any showroom.

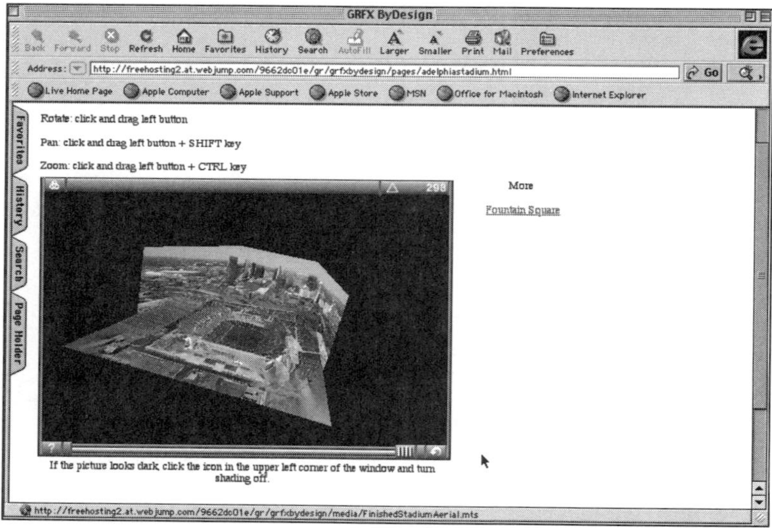

Product Design, Laptop

In the first exercise, you build a G3 iMac laptop, working from only one image. Previously, you used multiple images to map both the front and back of objects and modified images within Canoma with a Helper application. When *you* shoot the products, it'll be easier because you'll use what you learned in this book to set up and show your subjects in their best light.

Build A Round-Edged Product

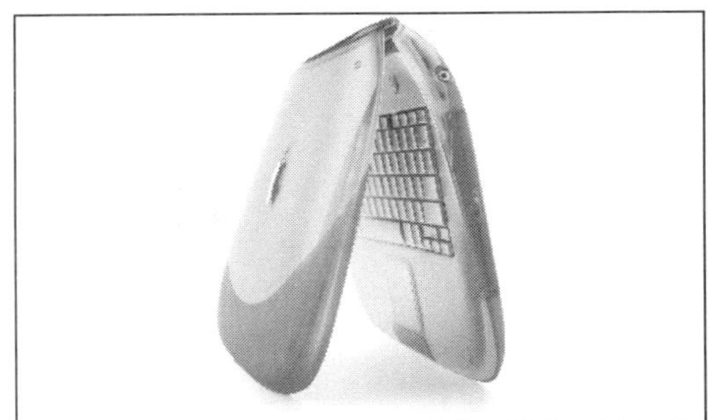

Open the Laptop.jpg file found in the Chapter 6 folder on this book's FTP site (**ftp.coriolis.com**, in the **Canoma_Visual_Insight** folder). Study the image and decide how you're going to create this file. With rounded edges, a Box primitive would look bad when rotated, so you need to use a Horizontal Translation Sweep.

1.

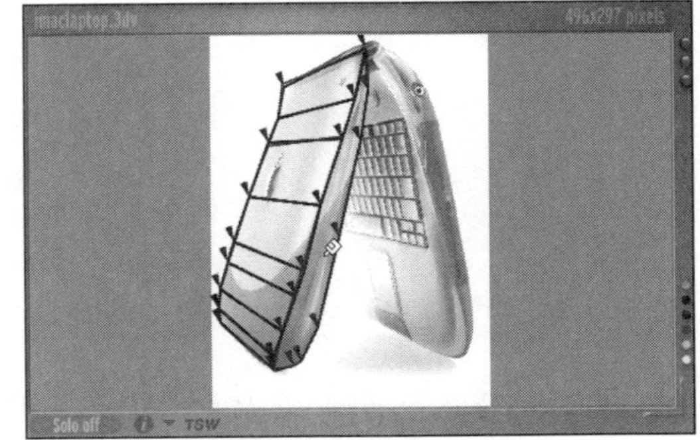

Create the base. As with all your images, you build from the ground up. Start by creating the base. Here, start with the left side (or top) of the laptop.

2.

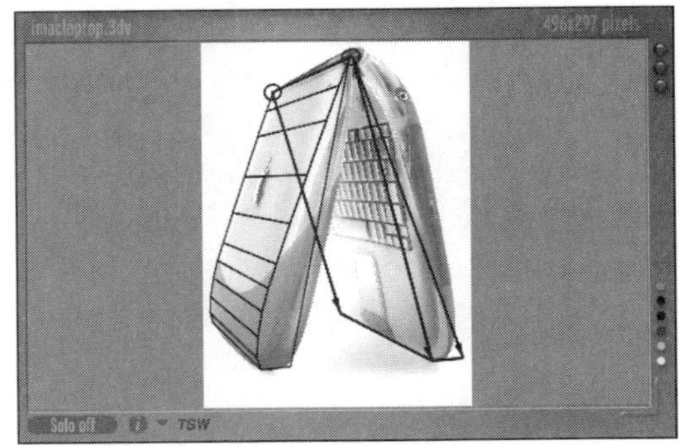

Create the rough outline. With the Horizontal Translation Sweep selected, create a rough outline of the case. Start with the lower-left corner of the image, and then outline the lower-right, upper-right, and upper-left corners.

3.

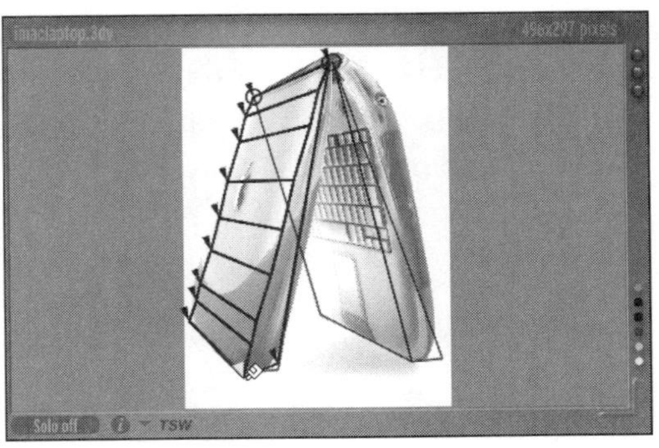

Now, rough out the other side. Click on the upper-right corner of the primitive you just created. Then select Align, and place another Horizontal Translation Sweep primitive in the scene.

4.

Make the two sweeps meet. Starting with the frontmost top corner of this new HTS, bring it up into position against the first HTS, and glue the corner either by selecting the Glue icon or using the Command/Ctrl+drag technique.

5.

Glue the primitives together. Then glue the upper-left corners at the rear of the primitive. After they are in place, move the other corners into place so that you end up with a pyramid-like shape.

Add Points

It's now time to modify the HTSes, using their reshaping power to round out the laptop. Select the Add Point tool (right of the Hand icon). Beginning with the first primitive you built, create additional points along the rear vertical edge of the cover. Start with a small number of points, and add others if needed.

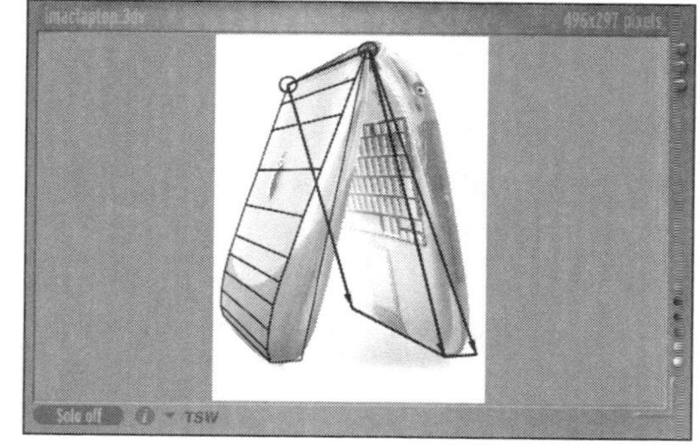

Why Add More Points

As you work with the HTS and the Point Tool, you'll see how the number of points you add to the HTS increases your ability to create rounded shapes. With this laptop, you'll want to add more points so you can more accurately re-create the curved shape.

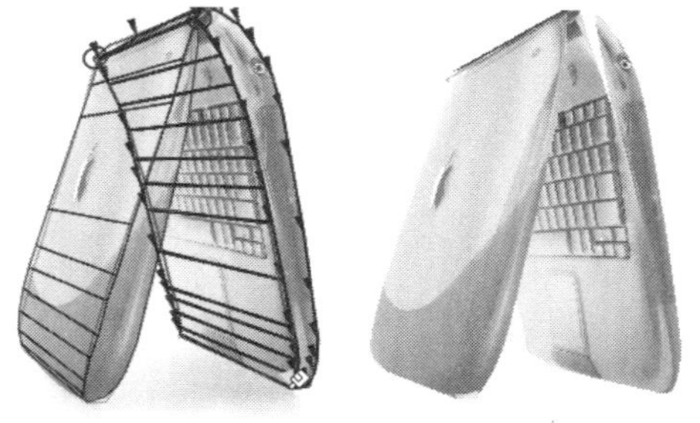

1.

Use Select to begin moving points into position around the outer edge of the laptop. Add more points to smooth the curves. After you position the points along the rear edge, move to the front edge and modify the corresponding points to match the far side. Watch the Stress indicator to make sure you're not moving points too far out of position, which avoids mapping problems.

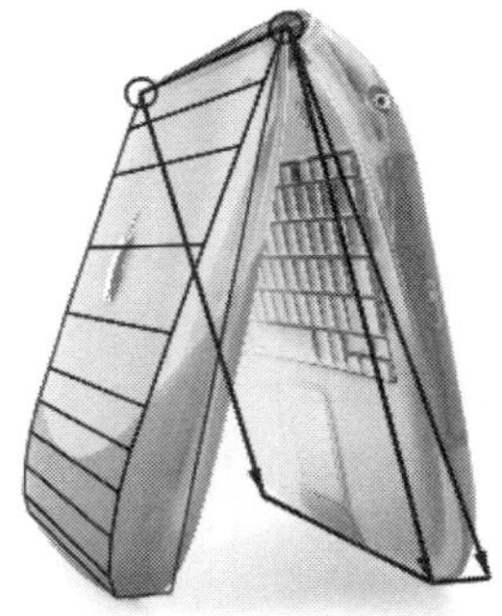

2.

Notice that you haven't added points to the back side. Now work on that part; repeat the previous process—add points to the interior top portion, and then manipulate the points to meet the outline of the upper part of the case as best you can. Try to put the same number of points on each side of the primitive. This symmetry isn't strictly necessary, but it's good design procedure.

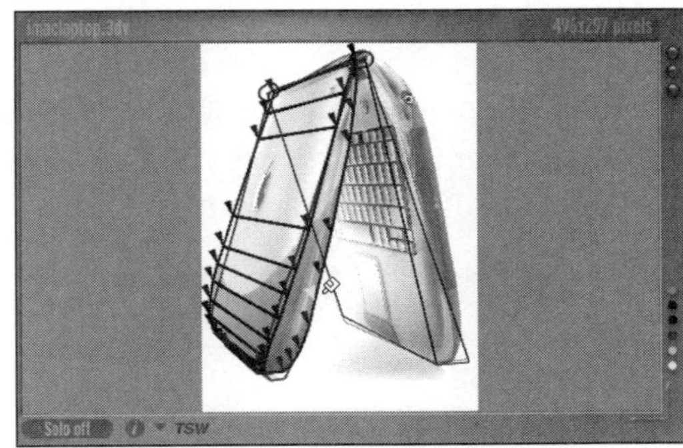

3.

Now model the rest of the laptop, the keyboard and the bottom, by repeating the steps you just took. You may have noticed that this HTS got a bit out of whack with the other one when you modified the first one. This tendency for the primitive to warp is normal and will correct itself as you outline the image. As long as the wireframe doesn't go crazy—something that occasionally happens when you do something the program doesn't like—you're fine.

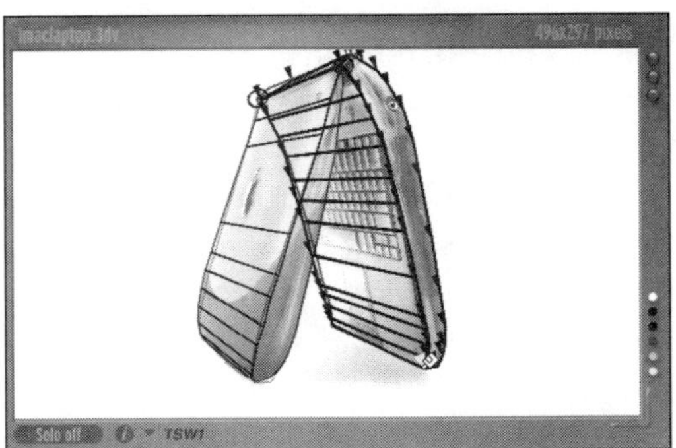

If your modifications suddenly cause your work to stick out in all directions, you need to use File|Revert To Saved. Save often!

Optional Modeling

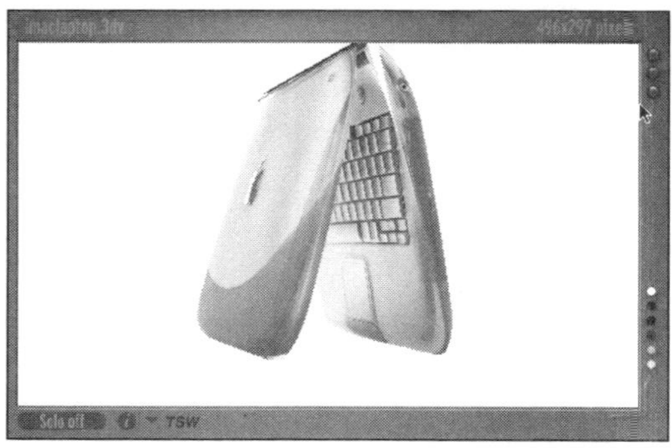

Occasionally, building the front side first ruins the quality of the finished image. Depending on how carefully you add points and mold the HTS, creating the front half of the laptop can result in some nearly uncorrectable stress points on the primitive. If this happens, start over and model from the back (keyboard) side.

Modeling With Nonphotographic Images

You modeled from photographs and added these models in nonphotographic scenes created in other modeling programs. You learned how to create interactive images in Canoma using images from other kinds of media. Often, clients supply only line (or clip) art. They expect you to scan and use these images as static representations.

Building and mapping this first model should take about three minutes, but it's an integral part of the overall concept of using clip art for Web marketing and e-commerce. Download the needed files from the Chapter 6 folder on the Coriolis FTP site.

Getting Boxed In

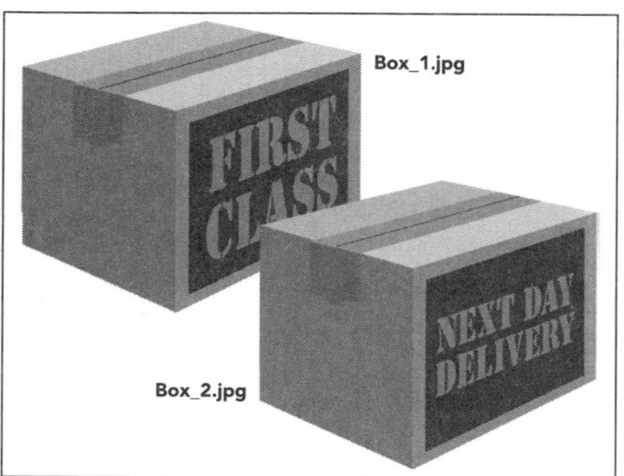

Using Box_1.jpg and Box_2.jpg, you'll create a simple model that you can use on an online order screen. The first box has a sticker reading "First Class", and the second has "Next Day". Using techniques you mastered in the previous chapters, import both images into Canoma and use the Box primitive to create the First Class side.

The Second Image

Now do a Quick Render with Mirror Texture turned off. The back side will be plain. Select the second picture, rotate the Box primitive, resize it, and do another Quick Render. Don't be afraid to zoom in close if the box doesn't seem to fit together well. Tweak the primitive until you're satisfied, and then perform a Quality Render.

Export

As with all the models, you will export this file in numerous formats. You'll save it as a Wavefront OBJ and render the image from both sides—but because it's destined for the Web, you don't need to size the image to anything other than that assigned.

Create A QuickTime Animation

You'll also create a QuickTime animation. For this, set up two frames—one for each side—at 12 frames per second, and specify a five-second animation.

Set The File Size

On the Render Animation screen (File|Render Animation), set the height field file size to 50 pixels, approximately the same height as a standard Web banner. Save the animation in two ways: as a QuickTime movie proper and as a series of JPEG stills.

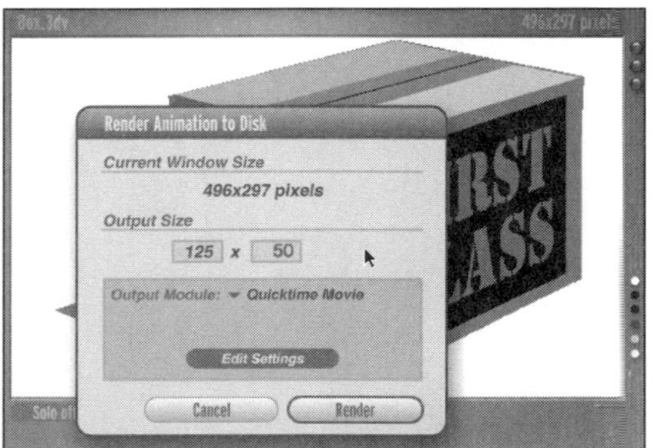

A Different Type Of Clip Art

Now the site features a box showing that you feature next-day delivery—but if no product is in the box, you probably won't see paying customers. Your client, Gloomy Day Outfitters wants to feature backpacks this month on its Web site. The only available image of the backpack is a bland clip art file. Import it into Canoma.

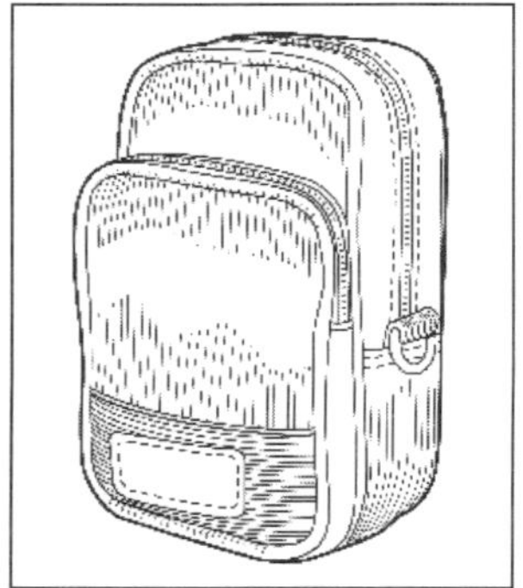

Model The Backpack

Again, you see rounded corners, but this time both backgrounds—of the image and of GDO's Web site—are white. You won't have problems creating the image with standard Box primitives; matching backgrounds means that you don't need to round the corners. Create your 3D backpack, and remember to turn Mirror Texturing back on.

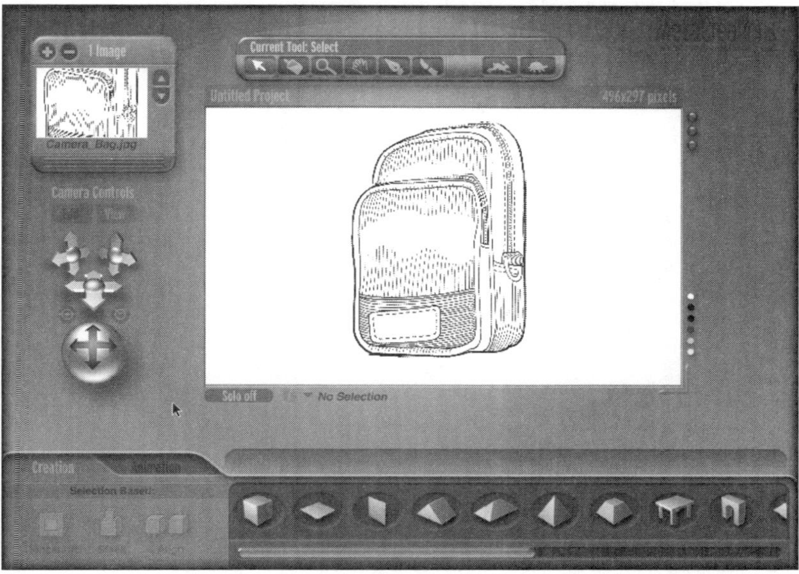

In the Helper application, remove the front pocket to create a flat back image, flip the completed image horizontally so that it models correctly in Canoma, and flip the untouched image on the horizontal plane so you can model the other side of the front pocket.

Create A Web Banner

You can direct traffic to Web sites with banner ads (they usually appear at the top of a page, with hyperlinks to sponsoring sites). With Canoma, you can wrangle space on other sites to sell client wares, generate leads, and build revenue. Use a GIF animation program (such as GIF Builder or Headline Studio), some ideas, and Canoma images.

*A Headline Studio demo is available from the Chapter 6 folder on this book's FTP site or from the MetaCreations site at **www.metacreations.com**. You use this program in the following section, so familiarize yourself with its basic controls before continuing.*

The Types Of Files To Use

Headline Studio has many controls that help you create broadcast-quality Web banners. Unlike some of the other GIF animation software, Headline Studio allows you to import image formats such as JPEG, PICT, and GIF. You have two options for this banner: Match the timing to the QuickTime file you just created or import separate JPEG image files for the animation.

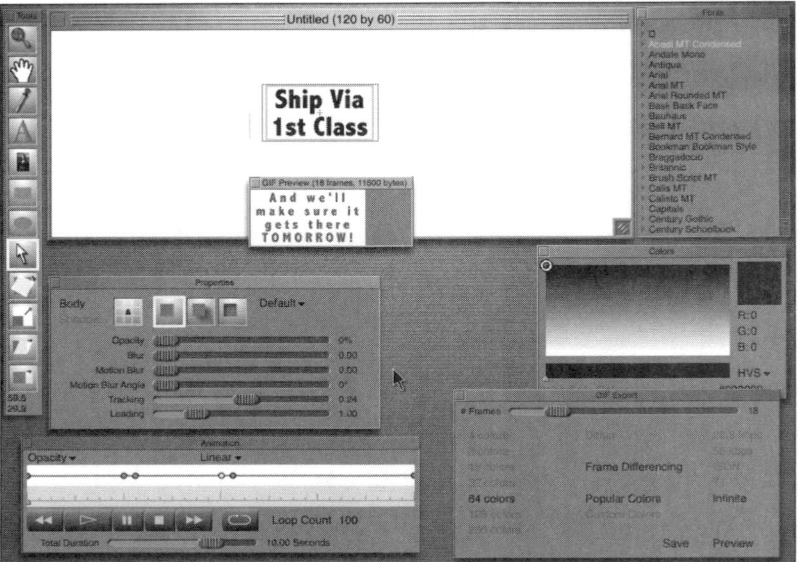

The Cons And Pros Of Using JPEG Files

Unfortunately, when you work with multiple files within a GIF animation program, it takes time to build your file. To create the illusion of animation, you must time the appearance and disappearance of each shot. On the positive side, as you bring in the text, you have instant feedback about the timing and can correct errors immediately.

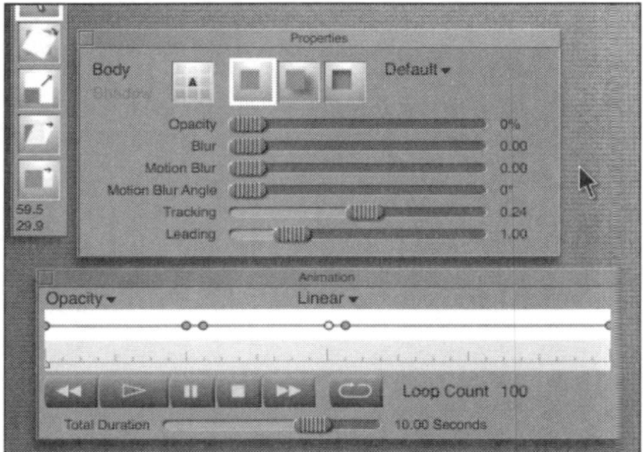

The Pros And Cons Of Using MOV Files

The MOV file is completed, and you can build a banner without video or stills manipulation. A finished animation containing JPEG still frames saves you hours of work.

The Final MOV File Settings

You must estimate the timing of text to coincide with major movement in the animation. Knowing the animation's length and frame rate helps, but you may not always get it right the first time.

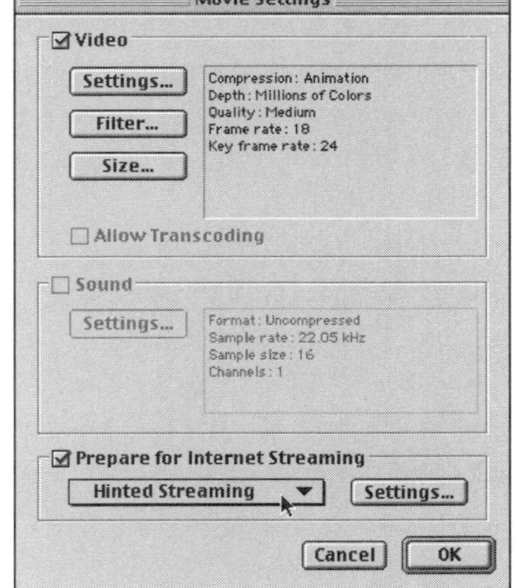

Use The MOV File

Here, use the MOV file to save time. If you have the QuickTime player installed, open the file and move it forward until you reach the middle frame (the one with the seam of the top flaps filling the screen). When you know the length of time between the start and this point, most of your work is completed.

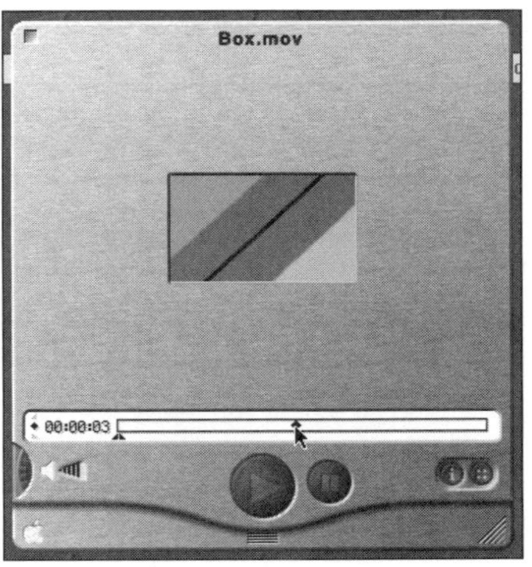

Create Text In Headline Studio

Create a banner about the same height as the animation file, and then type some text that matches the label on the beginning side of the box. Just before the midpoint of the animation, fade out the text and bring in new text. To do this, use any of the effect styles by working with the dial parameters below the main screen.

The Final Step

Save your final Headline Studio text animation as a GIF file, and prepare to import it into your Web design software. The following section uses Adobe GoLive! 4 you can download a demo version at **www.adobe.com**. If you use FrontPage, PageMill, or any other Web development program, you'll need to put this together using your particular program's settings.

Finish Your E-Commerce Page

For this exercise, you'll build a page to generate sales for your client, Gloomy Day Outfitters. You'll use the QuickTime file, the text animation you just created, and the MetaStream file.

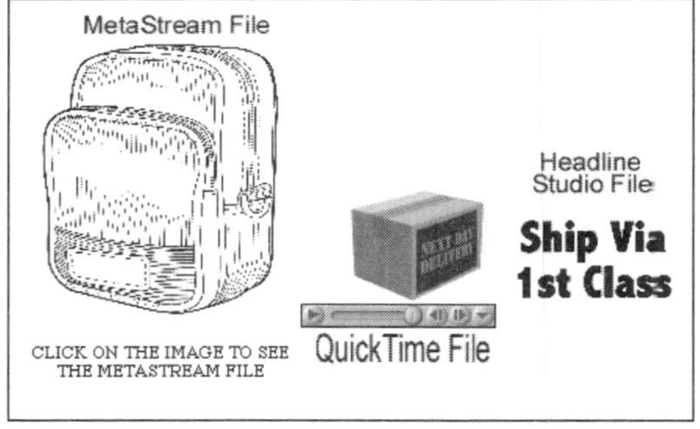

Get A Feel For The Design

This quick-and-dirty page gives you a feel for how all the elements can come together. It also shows you a way to create links to the MetaStream file. The company offers free animated GIF files for your use in linking to the MetaStream download site.

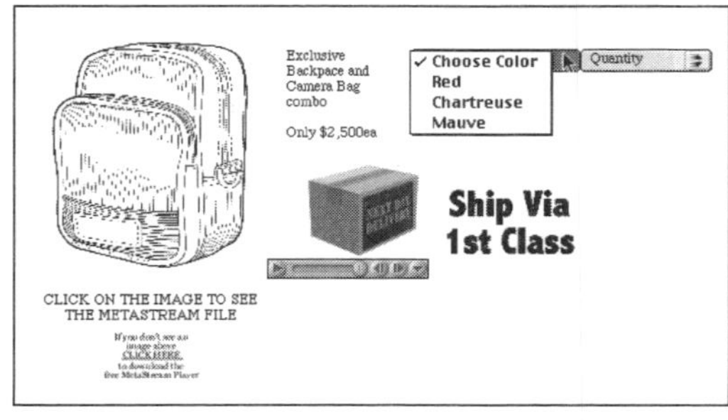

Where To Get The MetaStream Plug-In

You can download the plug-in in both PC and Mac formats. If you create a link to a MetaStream file, you should also include the downloading link there. People often ignore the first plug-in warning and try to view the page anyway.

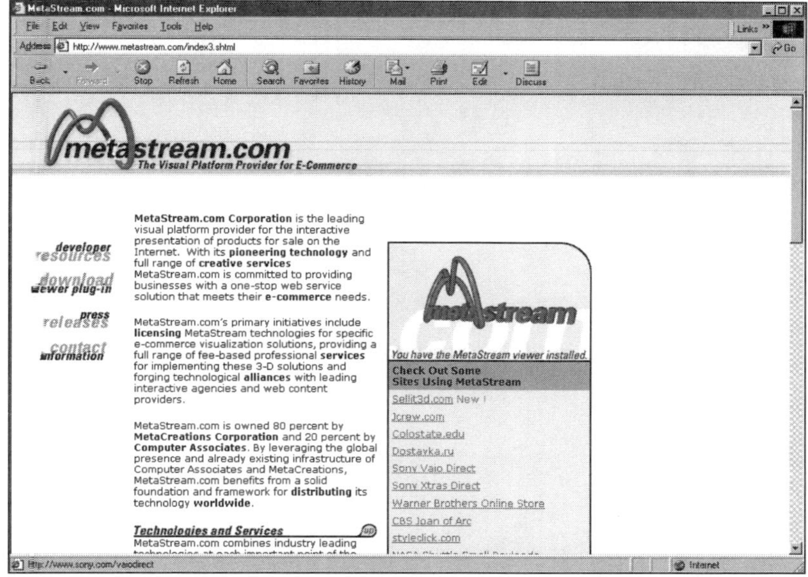

At this writing, the MetaStream 2.0 plug-in is available. MetaStream 3.0 will soon be available. Check at ***www.metastream.com*** *for the update.*

What Visitors Will See Without The Plug-In

When surfers get to the page and an icon like this appears, they'll use the link to get the software. Remember that the basic design and marketing idea is to make it easy for people to see the product. If this means including a link on every page, so be it.

Create The Design

Use your creative expertise to create an overall design for the product. This approach combines two pages: the product page, showing the backpack/camera bag and the initial order page. A link takes visitors to the product's MetaStream file. The easier the site is to navigate, the more comfortable people are, and the more willing they are to spend money.

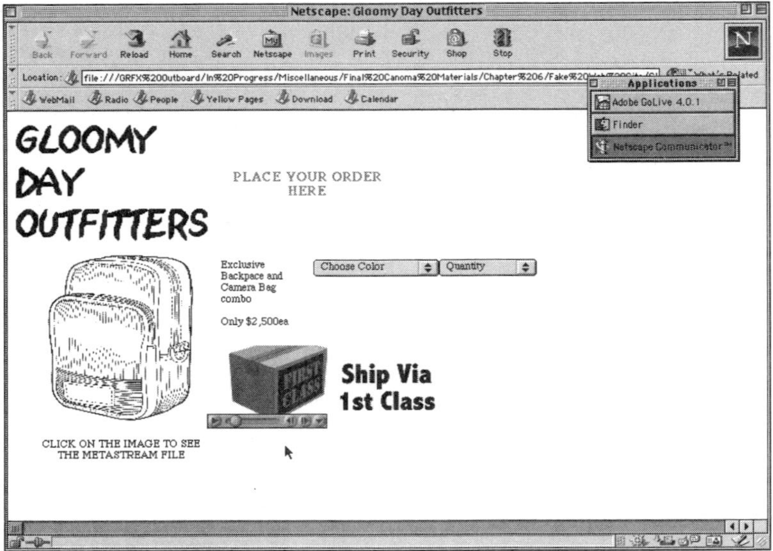

E-Commerce And Technology

E-commerce architecture changes so fast, it's difficult to stay abreast of it. New and exciting venues are continually being developed. If you're one of those who are on the cutting edge of this technology—either through providing improved scripts or through design and layout—using programs such as Canoma will help you create a stronger image for yourself and your client.

Canoma Studio

The following pages contain color examples of the topics and techniques presented in this book.

Canoma And Other Applications

Objects built in Canoma can be saved and imported into other programs, such as MetaCreations' Bryce 4, to create intriguing scenes.

The lighthouse (right) and the house (below) were modeled in Canoma.

Using Filters

Filters applied in a 2D image application can add new and interesting looks to your finished models.

This splash screen was created for a Web site. This image was created using Photoshop 5 and KPT filters, importing the images into Canoma, and then building the final scene in Bryce 4.

The filters used here are from the KPT6 collection (left) for Photoshop 4 or later and MetaCreations' Painter 6 (above).

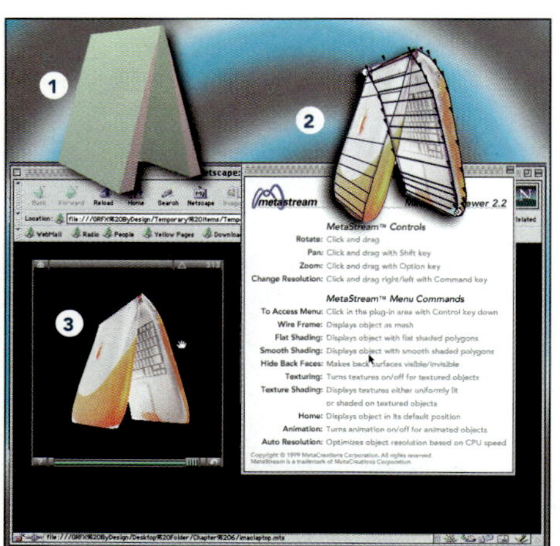

Modeling An Odd-Shaped Object

A look at three versions of the same model as it goes through the Canoma 3D process.

1. The primitives before applying the image.
2. Modification of the Horizontal Translation Sweep.
3. A MetaStream model on the Web.

YOU WON'T WANT TO MISS...

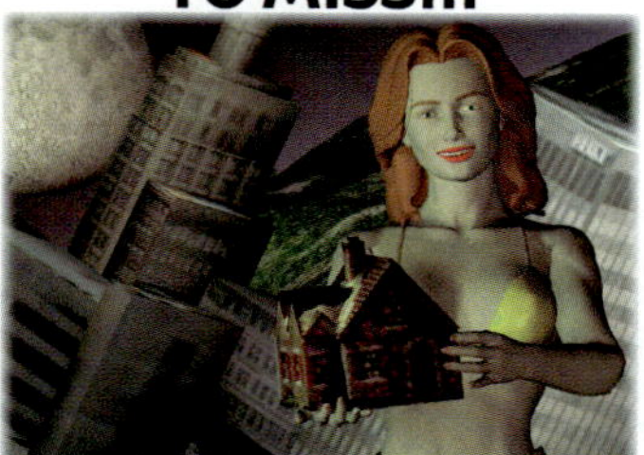

THE CERAMICS EXTRAVAGANZA!

Every Nite NOW Thru Y3K

One-Of-A Kind:

Figurines Houses

Scenic Wonders

Network

CyberActive Cable Ch. 5,975

Print And Web Variations

By importing a finished Canoma model into various media applications, you can create one-of-a-kind looks that go well beyond standard photography-based ad campaigns.

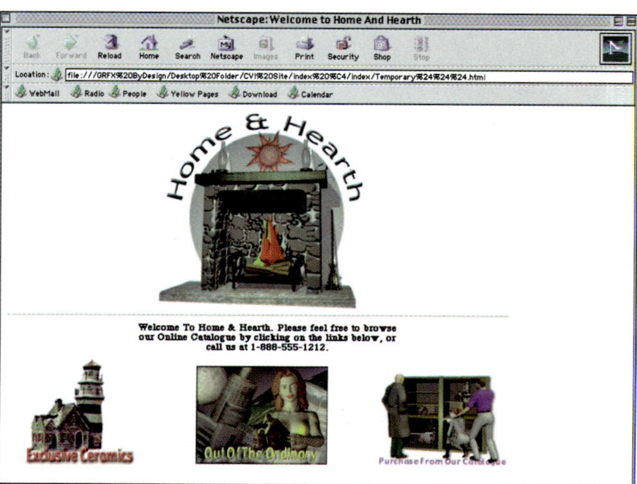

Combining Canoma Models With Other Artistic Styles

Combine two dissimilar rendering styles, hand drawing and Canoma, to create an eye-catching look.

By combining Pixels:3D and Poser 4 with a Canoma model saved as an OBJ file, this model shows off the latest in home decoration. Note the floating car (below the second storefront from the left) held in place by invisible wires.

Complex Projects

These two views of Asheville, N.C., are good representations of a complicated modeling assignment that uses more than 150 primitives. They also show modifications of the photograph, which was accomplished without leaving Canoma. Chapter 10 walks you through creating this image.

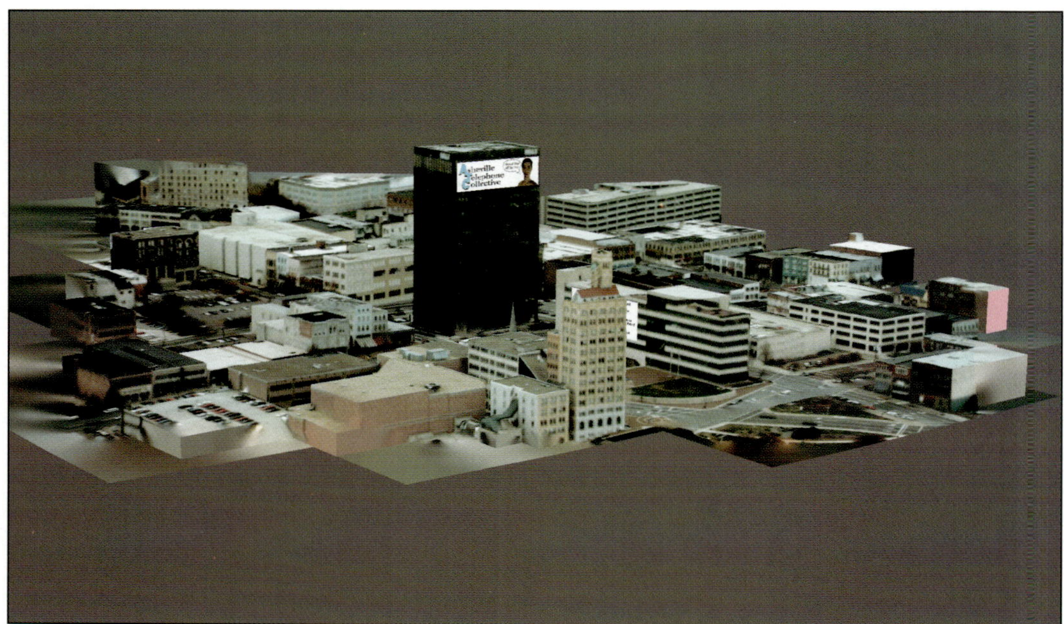

Print Or Web Projects

Using Canoma models in conjunction with other 3D programs can offer many alternatives to your designs.

The top image uses a bookshelf created in Amapi 3D. The image was then imported into Poser 4, where the two shoppers were added. These kinds of images could be used in print ads or as Web graphics. All of the 3D buildings in both images were created with Canoma.

Creating A Fantasy

Taking an original image and creating a totally different look is an intriguing function of Canoma.

The image in Canoma is shown with a Horizontal Sweep modified around the subjects. You learn about Sweep Tools in Chapter 4.

The image was rendered using the Quality Render feature and exported at 1,400×860 pixels.

The original photo used to create this image was a bit blurry. In Chapter 3, you learn the effective ways to shoot photographs for use in Canoma.

The image was reopened in Photoshop and, using the KPT 6 Sky Effects and KPT 5 Noize filters, the background was created. Using the Cloning tool expanded the leaves to fill the bottom of the image.

Finally, Fairies from the Zygote collection were posed in Poser 4, imported into Photoshop, and placed in the image. Gaussian blur effects were used to give them a glowing appearance.

Working With Canoma And Bryce

You can create science fiction–based scenes with Canoma models.

Here, a building put together in Canoma and imported into Bryce 4 becomes the centerpiece for an Armageddon-like image.

Another "distant future" image was created by importing a Canoma model into Bryce 4. You create this Canoma city-street model (prior to its futuristic destruction) in Chapter 4.

Working With Art Images

You can use Canoma for more than creating 3D versions of photographs. It's also a useful tool for creating 3D clip art.

Image courtesy of Dynamic Graphics, Inc., www.dgusa.com.

Here, you see the process of building a model from a painting of a front porch. You create this image in Chapter 6.

Animation Projects

By animating from within Canoma or by exporting the scene as an OBJ file (which retains the photographic texture-mapping information), you can achieve effects results in minutes that would have originally taken hours. You can find the completed animation on the Coriolis FTP site.

A Trip Through A Painting

Scenes from the San Marcos animation (included on the FTP site).

More Complex Projects

Chapter 10 guides you through creating these kinds of complex models.

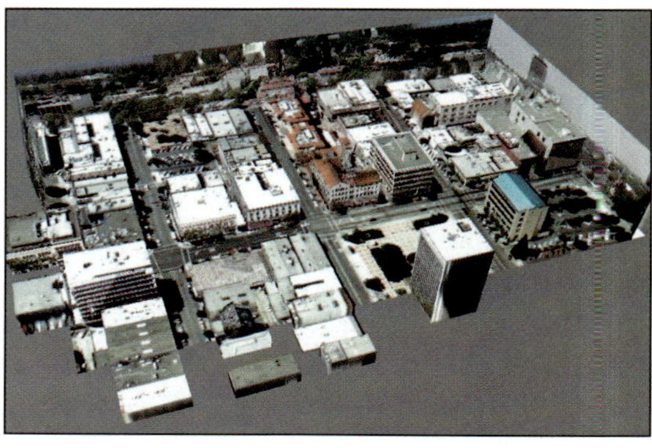

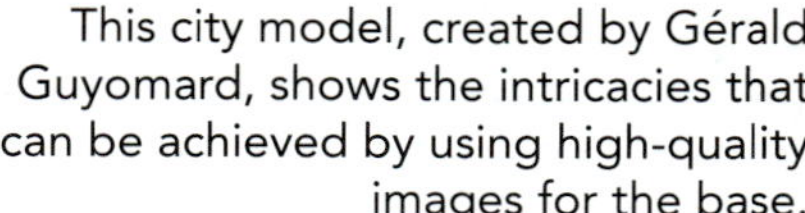

This city model, created by Gérald Guyomard, shows the intricacies that can be achieved by using high-quality images for the base.

A look at the original sketch (left) made on a napkin, by Robert Seidl, and the Canoma model created from it (right).

The original photo of Fountain Square in Cincinnati, Ohio was a 72-dpi screen capture. After creating the model in Canoma, it was brought into Photoshop. Extensis PhotoFrame and PhotoGraphics effects were used to add interest.

"Canaletto"

This Canoma model was built by Gérald Guyomard, a highly-regarded Canoma artist. The original JPEG image and the completed Canoma model are included on the FTP site.

Painting by 17th century artist, Canaletto.

The original digital artwork.

A look at the various elements used to create the model.

The rendered image.

Palace

The Palace painting was an interesting challenge due to the stairs and the elements hanging from the side of the building at right. Using various techniques discussed in the book, you'll be able to re-create this model. The original digital artwork, in JPEG format, is included on this book's FTP site.

Painting by 17th Century artist, Canaletto.

The original digital artwork.

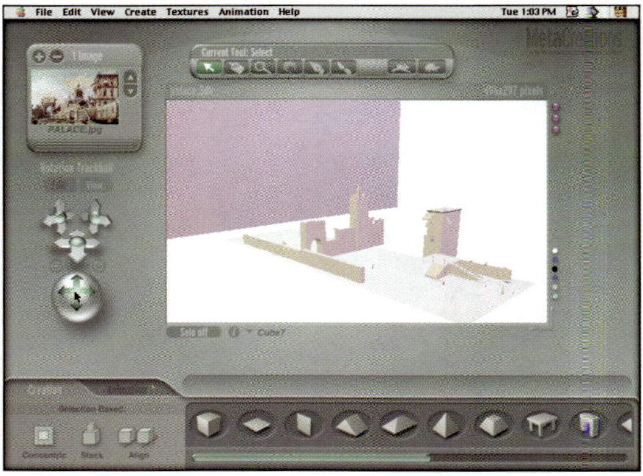

A look at how the various elements fit into the overall scheme of the model.

The rendered image.

Using Canoma For Creating A 3D Comic Book

The uses for Canoma run well beyond what you might expect. Canoma and Poser 4 were used on the images on this page to create scenes for a possible 3D comic book. Chapter 7 discusses how to use Canoma to design comic books in detail.

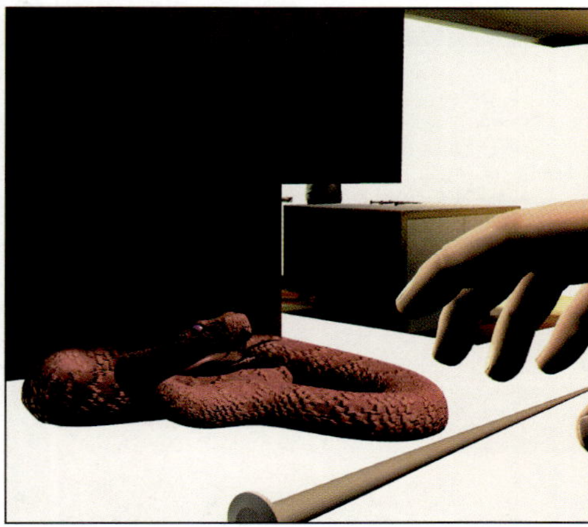

Using Canoma For Creating A 3D Comic Book *(continued)*

The full-page rendering of a comic book prototype used Canoma models and other 3D packages. Extra Poser models were supplied by Zygote and the Renderosity Web site.

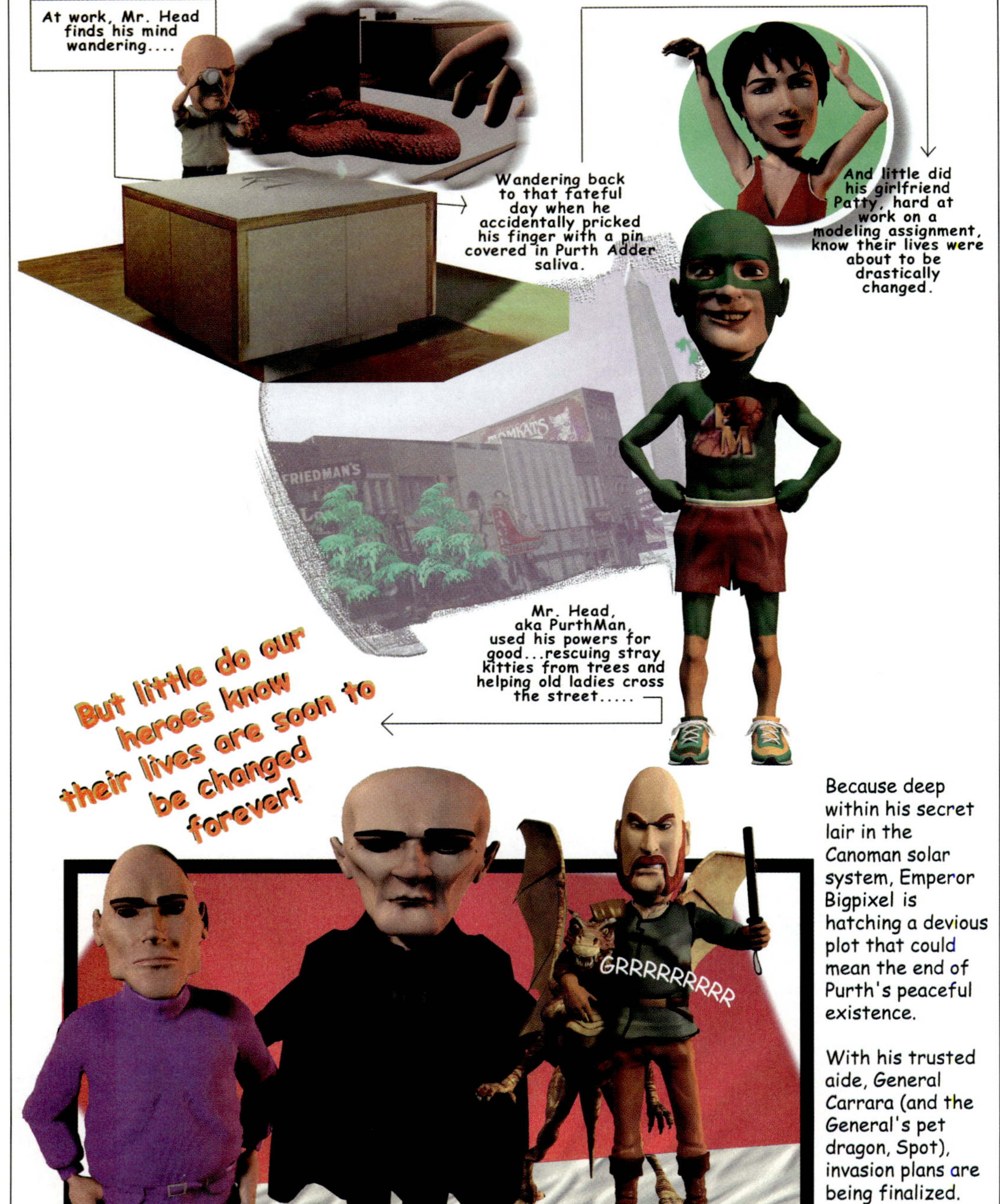

Chapter 7 Canoma For Fun

- Create a fantasy world for fun
- Create characters to populate your world
- Build set pieces in Canoma
- Build your scenes
- Render your scenes in other programs
- Create your comic layout

"Second Star On The Right"

It's now time to lighten up and use Canoma to create comic books. Artists have long sought to create new realities in their stories and art. Comic book publishers produce books featuring characters with extraordinary powers and fantastic cities. By including models created in other programs (such as Poser 4 and Bryce), you can easily create a 3D comic book or strip. This chapter presents a totally off-the-wall story; do not use it if you plan on a career as a graphic novelist.

Setting The Scene

You need a bible (a guidebook that reveals the overall storyline for at least one year, and up to five), a comprehensive idea of the settings, and full history for the main characters—unique heroes and villains. You'll use the Canoma models you previously built to create the frames. You'll build, pose, and save the models. Then you'll mix and match all the elements to design the frames.

If you use Poser 4, you can find free, alterable character models at ***www.renderosity.com*** *(I used models and props from here) and links to other sites that offer free or inexpensive models. Also,* ***www.zygote.com****, has high-quality Poser props and characters (free models change each Wednesday evening), or you can purchase high-end models to give totally new looks to your scenes.*

Our Hero, Mr. Head

Mr. Head is a superhero wannabe. By day, he's a pin processor at the Pin City Pin Plant on the planet Purth. He makes sure that all pins the plant produces have proper points.

Such Are The Dreams

Privately, Mr. Head wants to help when trouble arises. Purth, though, is peaceful. Then a freak accident at the plant gives him super powers. A Point man responsible for creating the points on the pins drops a pin on the floor. A Pin supervisor stationed at each processing point counts the pins made and tested. If the number varies by even one, all pin processors are fired.

The Fateful Pin

A Purthadder—a dangerous snake with saliva that causes fatal indigestion—licks the tip of the pin. The point pricked its tongue, causing it to retreat (luckily for the Point man). Wanting to keep his job, the pin producer searches for and finally locates the pin. Mr. Head was the (un)lucky pin processor to get the pin and the poisoned point pokes him.

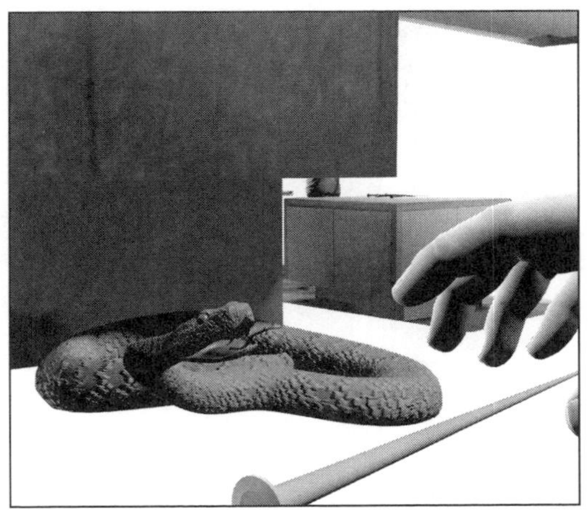

Mr. Head's Powers Develop

Soon, Mr. Head develops strange powers. His sense of smell heightens, and his strength increases. Not concerned with how it happened, as the new powers are revealed, he begins to understand that he can now realize his dream. He purchases a superhero suit from Mr. Hands at the neighborhood PurthMart. And so is born PurthMan, the Provider Of Peace.

Mr. Head's Girlfriend

Patty, Mr. Head's sweet natured girlfriend, is a model with the Purth Modeling Society. There, she is a Posette (because she's currently unemployed). Only she and Mr. Hands know that Mr. Head is PurthMan.

The Bad Guys

Neighboring Purth (in a cosmic sense) is the Canoman system, which contains two populated worlds, both controlled by the evil Emperor Bigpixel V. Bigpixel has an overlord of Militaristic Mayhem, the fear-inducing (because of his pet dragon, Spot) General Carrara.

The Story

Bigpixel's scientists couldn't develop a telescope powerful enough to study Purth, so BP V orders Carrara to go to Purth to learn if it is inhabited. Meanwhile, on Purth, Mr. Head (using his new powers) patrols the streets at night, looking for would-be hoodlums. He doesn't know that danger is on the way and he, PurthMan, is the only one who can save the planet.

Creating Characters

Here, we'll give you an inside look at how the characters are developed—how you can use Poser 3 or 4 and Canoma to do your initial design work. Remember, when working with any 3D project, you'll use as many different programs as you can afford (and that fill the gaps left by other programs). No 3D program is perfect or fills every need.

The Mr. Head Character

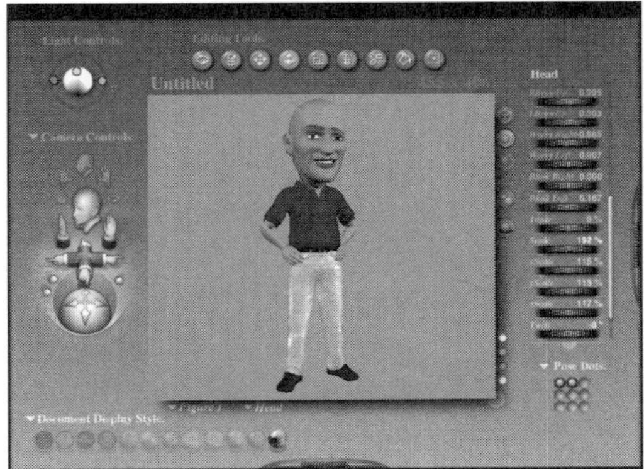

Mr. Head is the standard Nude Casual Male character that comes with Poser 4. He has been modified substantially in the following ways:

- The Body Type was changed to Adolescent.
- His head was resized 193%.
- His hands were resized on the X and Z axes by 115%.
- Genitalia was turned off.

These changes produce a cartoonish character while retaining the human facial structure. I wanted to create a comical, yet realistic, look, often called a Living Toon look, a term coined by author and 3D artist Bill Fleming. All other characters were modified by using the same parameters.

Write down the parameter settings that you changed so you can use them to create other Purth people later. Do this whenever you modify characters in this kind of 3D program—Bryce included—so you don't have to remember dozens of parameter changes.

Creating A Uniform

The superhero suit was created using the P4 Nude Man texture template. I imported it into Photoshop 5 and, with heavy use of Layers, built the various elements of the suit. I used KPT 5 Fractal effects for the logo, as well as Photoshop 5 native filters. When I was happy with the template, I saved it, then changed it to a black and white image, adding more filters to the uniform. Again, when I finished that, I saved it as the bump map.

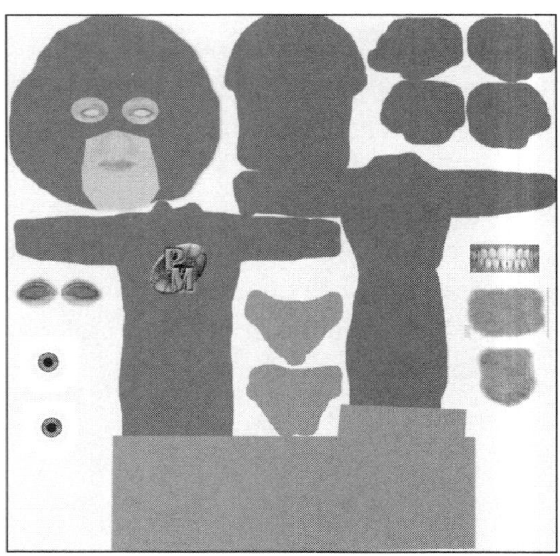

Saving Files By Exporting

Save your files in two formats: as an OBJ file and as a rendered image. First, save the model in an OBJ format so you can import it into other programs. Remember that the OBJ format saves mapped texture information with the model so you don't have to reassign the textures when you import the model into another program. The Export submenu shows the different formats in which you can save a file, including Hash Animation:Master.

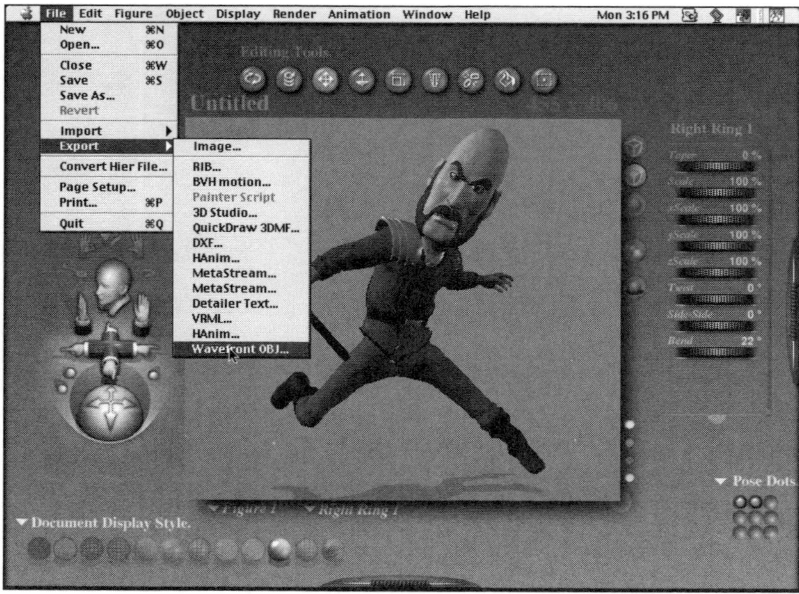

Rendering Files

Second, and most important, render the image at a high ppi (pixels per inch) ratio (Refer to Chapter 3.), which you can downsample to a higher resolution in your 2D editing software. Use a background color that does not match any color on your model so you can easily mask the characters for different uses.

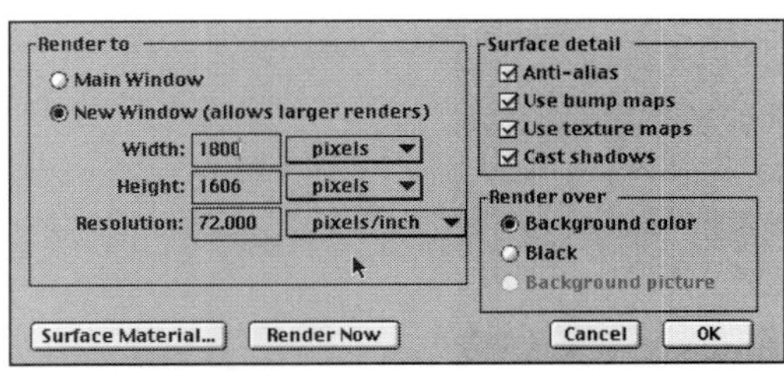

Creating The Scenery

Now use Canoma. In this section, you re-create some of the previous models, as well as build some new pieces and save them for inclusion in Bryce and Poser to create the scenery.

Build Purth—Part 1

In the center of Purthville, Capital City of Purth and Mr. Head's home, is a monolithic structure called the Purthington Monument, which looks strangely familiar. If you didn't save the Washington Monument model, go back and do so now; save it as an OBJ file.

If You Saved The Monument

If you saved the model as a Canoma file, remap the image, save it as an OBJ, then bring it into Bryce 4 for placement. You're going to use the Washington Monument as the centerpiece of the town square, and Bryce is the perfect program in which to use Canoma models to help build that area.

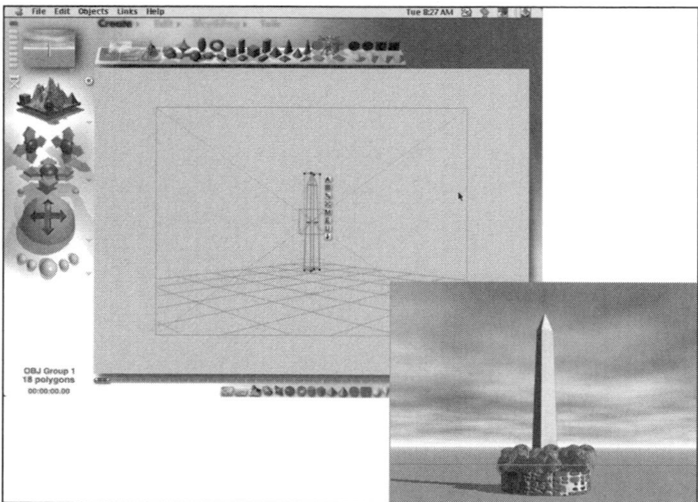

Build Purth—Part 2

For this comic, you need only the Broadway Street portion of the town model you created in Chapter 4. It shouldn't take too much time lining up the Box primitives. Again, make sure that Mirror Image is turned on. Save this as an OBJ file, but *don't quit the program!*

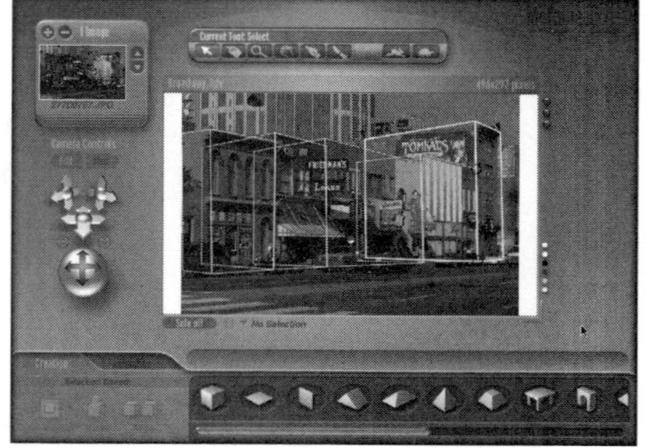

Modify The Image

Use the photo-editing feature to access your 2D manipulation program to modify the storefronts. Change the business names and remove the more recognizable earthbound signage so you can use this for either the other side of the street or businesses on a cross street.

Save For Bryce

Save the file as a second OBJ and import it into Bryce 4 for final layout, as seen here. You can keep the file in a separate area of your computer or you can save it within the Bryce program for use at a later date. Refer to the Bryce 4 manual to learn how to do this.

The easiest method for renaming the file is putting a number after the name. If the initial OBJ file was saved as Broadway_Street.obj, save this one as "Broadway_Street1.obj".

Build Purth—Part 3

You also need to prepare some other Canoma models—some interior pieces, if you want to do indoor scenes for this comic book. You'll use the store interior from an earlier chapter.

More Rebuilding

If needed, rebuild the display cube in the foreground, a simple task that should only take a few moments. Again, use the Helper application to remove the clothing images from the top of the cube. Once mapped, save it as an OBJ file. Import it into Poser 4 so you can add our hero into the scene to show him diligently inspecting the pin points.

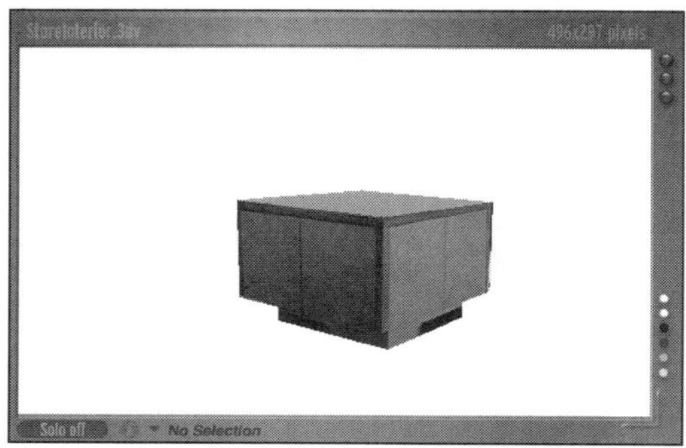

An OBJ and Macintosh Poser (.pp2) models of the pin and loop are available on the Coriolis FTP site in the Chapter 7 folder.

Don't Limit Your Options

Use more than a few models for set pieces. If you can't take photographs for your project, numerous sites on the Internet have inexpensive, royalty-free photo collections. You can also find CD-ROM collections, such as ClickArt's (**www.broderbund.com**) box sets of photographic images, at local software shops. You can use the photo collections in these sets and import clipart files into Canoma to build 3D line-art files for a unique look.

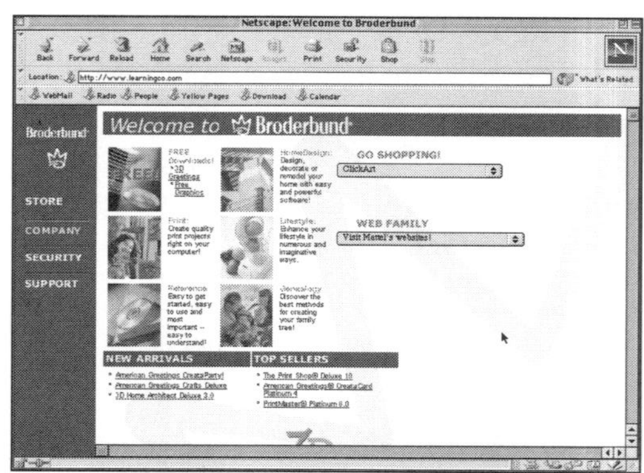

Scene Building

Now that you have all the elements built, and have (hopefully) created extra models, it's time to place them into their "natural" environment. In this section, you'll focus on using our Broadway models and Bryce 4 to create your Main Street set. As you move through this section, you learn how to save files so you can render them at a quality high enough for print use.

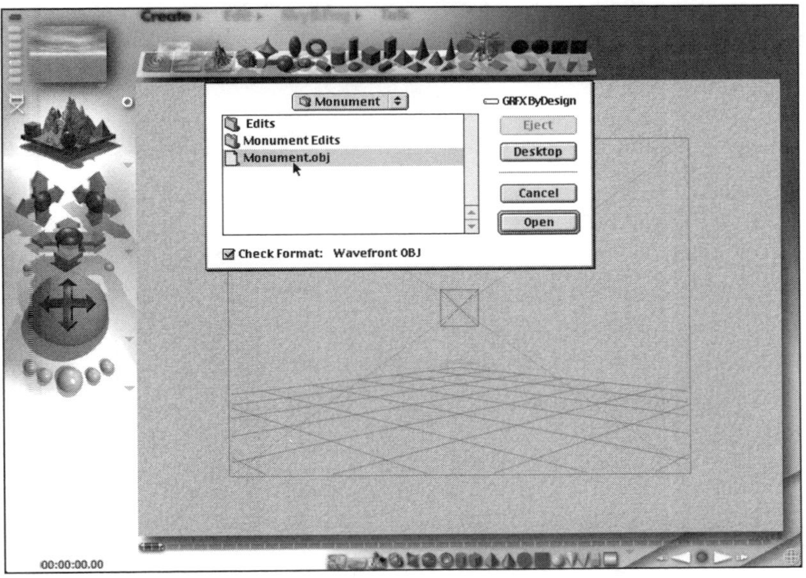

The Plains Of Purth

It's time to go into Bryce 4 to get our overall scene built. There are books on Bryce 3D and 4 written by R. Shamms Mortier that give you excellent ideas on building landscapes.

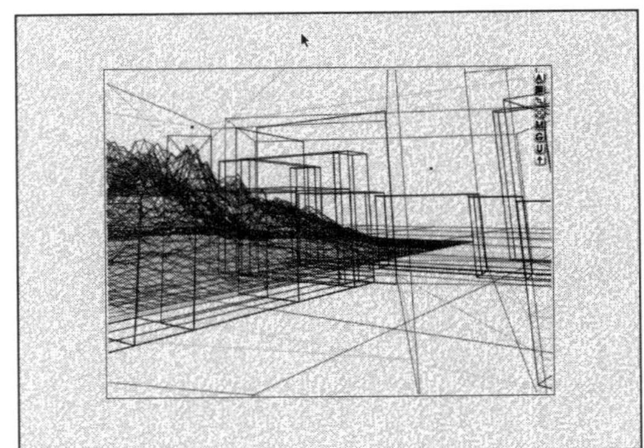

1.

Create a landscape. You can make it as strange and otherworldly as you like, but leave some flatlands on which to place your new OBJs. After this is finished and you're happy with the results, save the Bryce file and prepare to create the lonely streets of Purth.

2.

You can access the U.S. Geological Survey site **www.usgs.gov/** or **www.monumental.com/rshorne/downloads.html** to download inexpensive or free Digital Elevation Maps (DEM) files. These files include elevation information on the real world and planets that Bryce 4 can read. Using this type of file, you can create the landmass area of Cincinnati, Ohio or Paris, France.

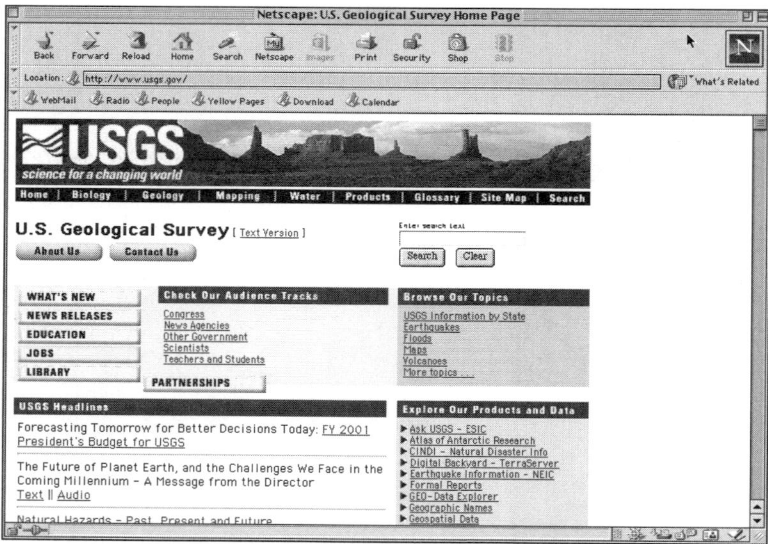

3.

Import the Canoma OBJ files you saved and begin arranging them. This is where your talent for city design comes in handy. If you lack this talent, you have two options: You can buy expensive books on city planning (which will drain your funds), or you can just learn as you go. I suggest the latter.

Decisions, Decisions

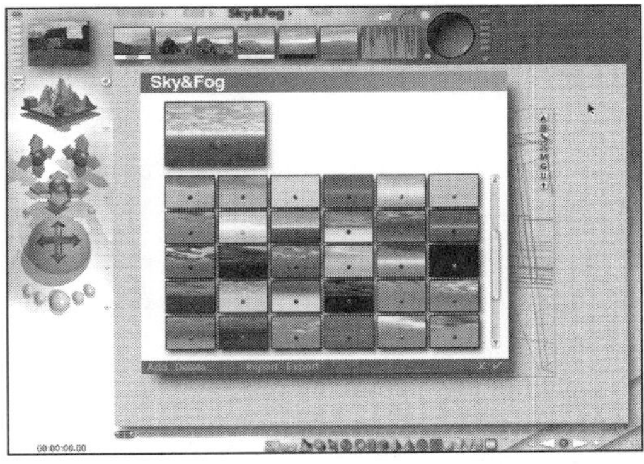

What is the atmosphere like on Purth? Is it earthlike, or does it have a strange, otherworldly look—purple clouds floating through green skies, with pink stars stippling the highlights? It's up to you. By selecting the Sky & Fog area of Bryce, you can choose from a library of atmospheres, or you can create your own.

Atmospheric Conditions

Here, Purth is earthlike with blue sky and hazy clouds—the perfect setting for PurthMan to rescue stray kittens.

Populate And Propagate

If you haven't done so, create extra Purth people to populate the streets. Use the animal models supplied with Poser 4, either real (such as cats, dogs, horses, and frogs) or fantastic (such as Zygote's wonderful Dragon Model, seen with General Carrara earlier in this chapter) to use as pets.

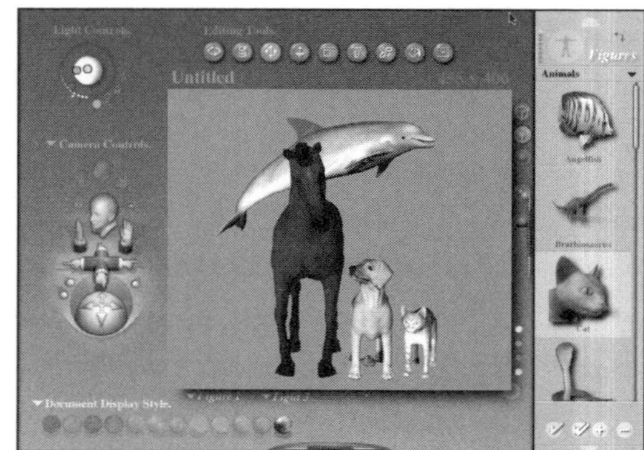

1.

Modify them so they appear to be walking, running, jogging, or looking at the Purthington Monument. For example, you can have a Purth person holding a pet by saving them as a file within Poser 4 (see the Poser documentation to learn how to save models within the program).

2.

If you created a crowd pose (two plus characters), export the models separately (delete one, reload the saved model, and delete the other). In this way, the texture maps read onto the correct model when you import the models into other programs. An OBJ file is viewed as a singular object, unless you ungroup it in Bryce or another program, which then leaves you with the task of regrouping dozens of parts.

Realistic animal posing is difficult. Many artists have created pose sets free for downloading from ***www.renderosity.com, http://PoserWorld.com****, and other sites, and Credo Interactive (****www.charactermotion.com****) has extremely high quality animal-animation sets for sale.*

Rendering Your Scenes

In Chapter 3, you learned the best ways to scan photographs so they can be resized to a higher resolution without losing quality. It's the same principle when rendering a scene for inclusion as high-resolution files in programs such as Photoshop, PaintShop Pro, Illustrator, Canvas, or other 2D image programs.

The Render Process

When doing your final render in Bryce, here is what you want to do (and the same goes for Poser):

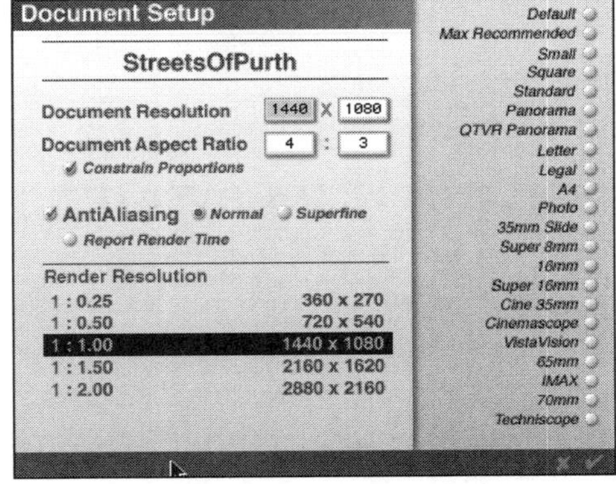

1.

Choose File|Document Set Up. If you plan on using the image as a full-page background, choose the Letter option to the right of the menu screen, or choose the format that fits best for how you'll use the image.

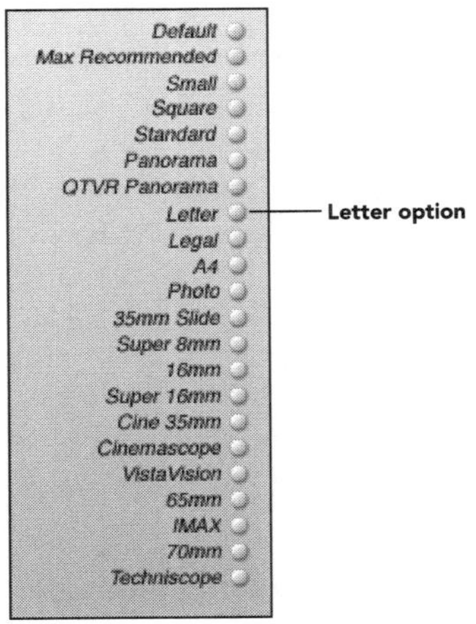

2.

Using the Pixels Per Inch guide in the lower-left quadrant, type the size into the fields in the upper-left part of the menu screen. In this situation size matters, so select the largest file size your system allows.

Render Resolution	
1 : 0.25	153 x 198
1 : 0.50	306 x 396
1 : 1.00	612 x 792
1 : 1.50	918 x 1188
1 : 2.00	1224 x 1584
1 : 3.00	1836 x 2376
1 : 4.00	2448 x 3168

3.

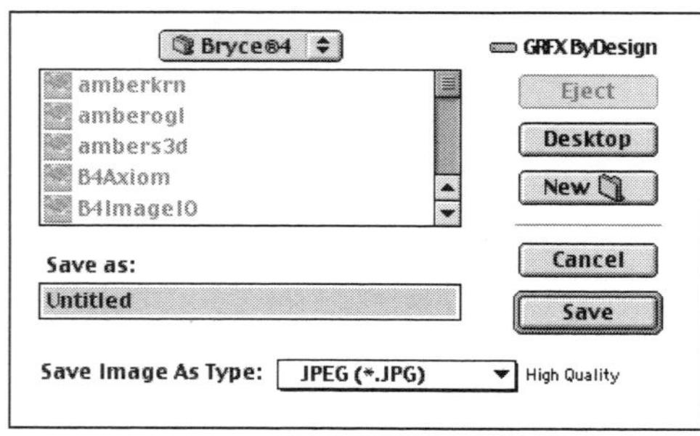

Save the file and use Command/Ctrl+R to render the scene. Then, choose File|Save Image As to save the rendered scene. The number of primitives in your scene, and the processor speed and amount of RAM you have determines the time needed to render a scene. Depending on scene complexity and size, a file could take days to render. So be prepared.

Creating The Layout

Using boxed frames to represent each picture in a comic book was once the standard. Free-flowing layouts, with pictures or elements violating (breaking out of and laying over) framed areas, are popular today. The former design style is still viable, but specific formats aren't needed—just so it tells a story. Here, you'll add text to a comic book page, using the images you've created, modifying them in your Helper application, and then finish with a layout program such as Illustrator.

---

*Here, you use Photoshop with the following Extensis plug-ins: PhotoGraphics 1.0 (to manipulate text along paths and other effects) and PhotoFrame (to create framed borders for your images). You can get a fully working demo of these plug-ins at this book's FTP site. For more information on Extensis products, go to **www.creativepro.com**.*

Design Your Layout

Form the habit of sketching your ideas—not only for these layouts but also for all modeling you do outside of Canoma. Having an idea of how you want a story told and how it will flow makes the work quicker and more organized. Don't make it high art (this is for your eyes only), just put your designs on paper!

Create A New Document

Usually, comic books are printed on 8.5×11-inch paper with a 1/4- or 1/2-inch margin, for a content space of about 7.5×10 inches. The paper varies from a stock slightly heavier than newspaper weight to a 50- to 80-lb. glossy stock. Knowing the type of paper used for printing is very important. Because you're creating this project for your portfolio (not for publication), create the image for printing on a 720dpi printer or higher, using a good photo stock paper with a file size of 300dpi. This gives you bright, clean images that show your work to its best advantage.

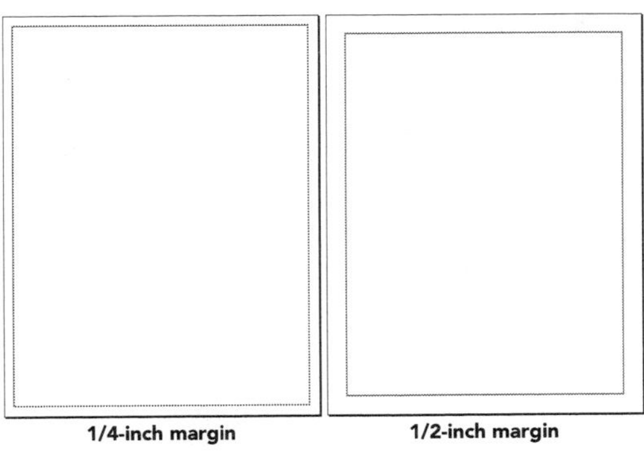

1/4-inch margin   1/2-inch margin

The paper weight refers to thickness and strength. Differences exist between paper weight and card stock, although both are graded in the same way (pounds). Build a relationship with your professional printer; learn about paper. They'll respond to you better if you understand a bit of their world.

Import Your First Image

Now import the StreetsOfPurth.tif image, the one that uses the model of Broadway Street you built earlier in the book. If you saved this file at a large enough ratio, 2000×2000 *pixels per inch* (*ppi*), it will be huge. That's fine because you'll downsample the image (change from 72dpi to 300dpi).

What This Does

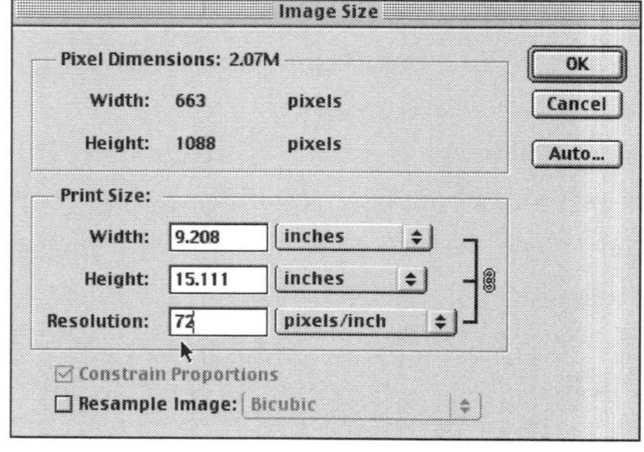

Choose Image|Image Size to open the Image information screen. Make sure Resample Image is deselected, and change the Resolution setting from 72 to 300. This produces a high-resolution image with no loss of clarity to the image.

Using The Image As An Anchor

In this design, StreetsOfPurth.tif will be your anchor image—your background. Using the PhotoFrame plug-in, create an interesting look for the picture (I used Canvas_02.frm, which comes with the demo program) and apply it. Photoshop allows drag and drop between screens, so transfer this new layer onto your layout page and place it as you like.

Bring In Our Characters

Import the main characters you created or downloaded from the FTP site and place them in the general positions you designed earlier. Don't get too locked into staying with your original drawing because you'll tweak positioning to best fit the overall flow of the page and the differences in image sizes. Create additional generic backgrounds for some of the characters (as I did with the bad guys) to add more interest and some borders to give the feel of comic book frames.

Add Text

If you're using Photoshop and you installed the PhotoGraphics plug-in, you'll see a new Extensis pull-down menu at the top of the screen. Choose PhotoText and design your text. When finished, save it to a new layer and continue to build your comic page blurbs. To spread copy to various areas around the page, add some lines with the Line tool to help the reader figure out which part to read next.

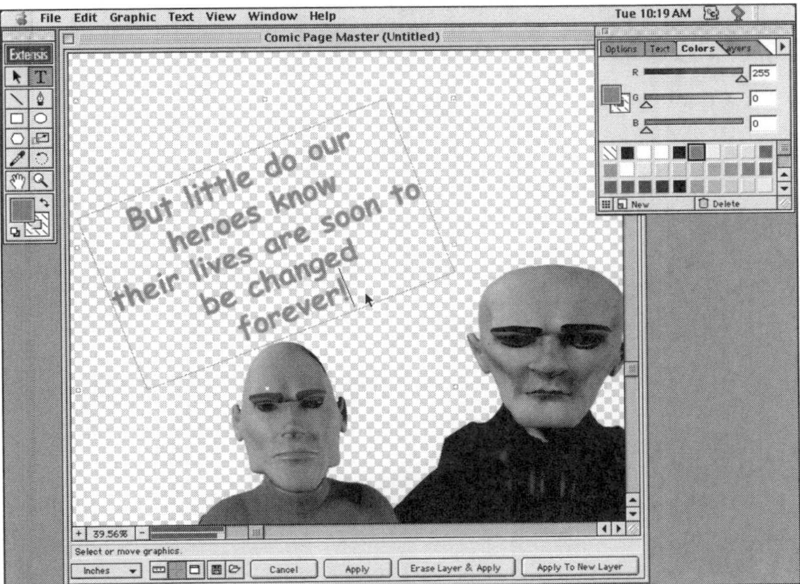

Completed Page

Here is the all-important comic page that begins building tension for the reader. You can see a full-color rendition in the Canoma Studio section. As you can see, the possibilities for using Canoma and other 3D and image editing programs is vast. It gives a whole new appearance to your work.

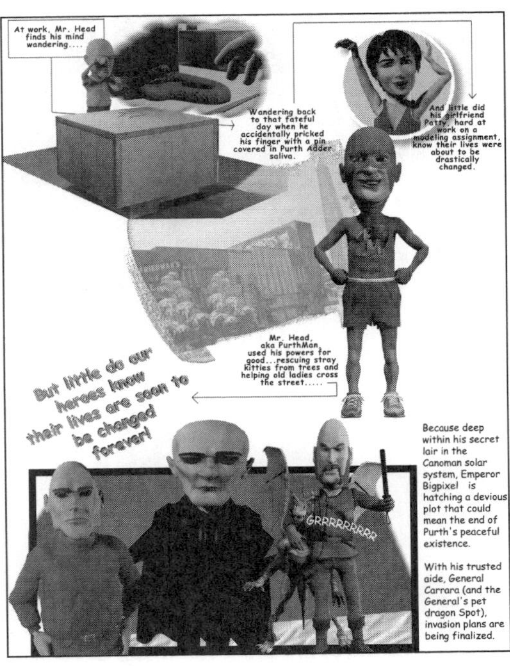

Part II

Projects

Chapter 8
The Canoma Architect

Project 1: Build a complex facade

Project 2: Create a building to place in a scene

Project 3: Place buildings in a construction site by using two different images

Project 4: Produce a multimedia presentation

Visualize Growth

The previous chapters showed you how to use Canoma in various situations, including sales presentations. In this chapter, you learn another important use of Canoma that can help you gain a foothold in a highly competitive market: producing print and multimedia presentations to help officials manage community growth. Traditionally, city officials made building and siting decisions by viewing artists' concepts and architectural plans. These tools will never be replaced, but Canoma introduces a new element of interactivity to this process.

Project 1: Practice Creating A Complex Model

Using Canoma, you can build a complex model that can be viewed from all angles. This kind of creation can give decision makers a true feel for how a proposed building will fit into the overall environment. This practice will help you when you get to the main theme of this chapter—building and combining both model and scene.

1.

Let's begin building a complex model, as shown here, by using numerous primitives and glue. This model is complex due to its many angles and curves. First, you start with a front view of the stadium.

*The files for these tutorials can be found in the Chapter 8 folder on the FTP site (**ftp.coriolis.com**, in the **Canoma_Visual_Insight** folder).*

2.

Let's re-create a portion of Adelphia Stadium in Nashville first. For non-American football fans, Adelphia Stadium is the new home of the Tennessee Titans football team.

Adelphia Stadium photographs ©1999, Donn Jones, Team Photographer, Tennessee Titans. Photos courtesy of the Tennessee Titans.

3.

Adelphia Stadium is an oval building, and as you know, handling rounded objects isn't a Canoma strong suit. That's why you must consider what's important in the image and include extra information to help present the structure properly.

4.

If you look closely, you'll see a number of recessed areas that should show in the finished model. Therefore, use Stack to create the various levels of the stadium.

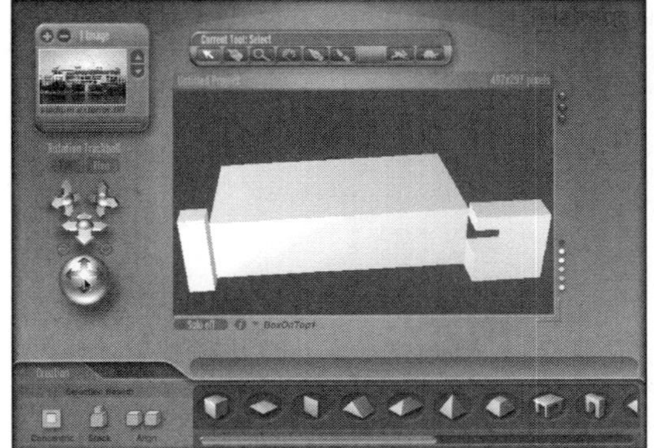

5.

Using this side view, select the Box primitive and outline the stadium. As you get into more complicated modeling, you'll use stacked primitives to make a more detailed model. Sometimes, a single primitive will suffice—and in this case, it can be argued that it would—but this is too appealing a model to create with a single primitive.

6.

Until now, you glued corners to corners, (called Point-To-Point Glue) in "Canomanclature." Here, you'll use Point-To-Edge Glue. Starting with the lower-left corner, glue this corner of the top object to the top-left edge of the bottom primitive.

Adelphia Stadium, Step-By-Step

Using Point-To-Edge gluing, Stack, Duplicate, and Align, complete the model of the stadium. Here's the way to do it.

1.

Create the right upright column of the stadium. Be exacting in how you manipulate this first primitive because it will be used for the placement of the next primitive. So zoom in close, as you see here, to make sure the back right corner is in the correct position.

2.

With the initial box element selected, choose Align and the Box primitive. Move in very close on this so you can place the left bottom corner against the back left corner of the first primitive. Then extend this box across the front of the building, as you see here.

3.

Choose Align again while keeping this second Box primitive active and create the next upright. Make sure you position the back corner of this new primitive against the front lower corner of the other. After you outline the area, glue the lower corners of the two primitives.

4.

Use this third primitive as the active one, and Align one more Box primitive to it. Place this box to the lower-left area of the third primitive to create that extension. Glue the bottom right-front corner to the bottom left-front corner of the right column primitive.

5.

Now select the second primitive (the one in the middle of the two uprights) and extend the top of it until it aligns with the top of the stadium bleachers. Click the view button to make sure everything is still aligned. Now select the Glue icon and glue the upper corners of the uprights to the vertical columns of this center primitive. This is the part called Point-To-Edge gluing.

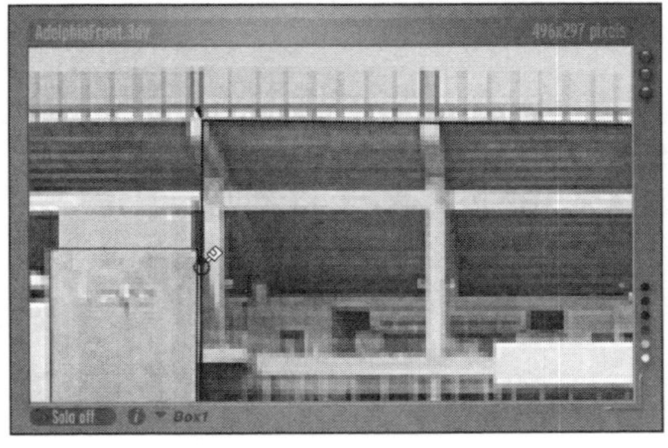

6.

Take your time. Do as many Quick Renders as you need to get a feel for how the stadium is coming along. When you're finished, save the file. Using these various techniques and primitives, finish building your model.

7.

Now, prepare to render your model. Select File|Render Image. Select the desired image size (no larger than the actual size of the master image) and then click on Render.

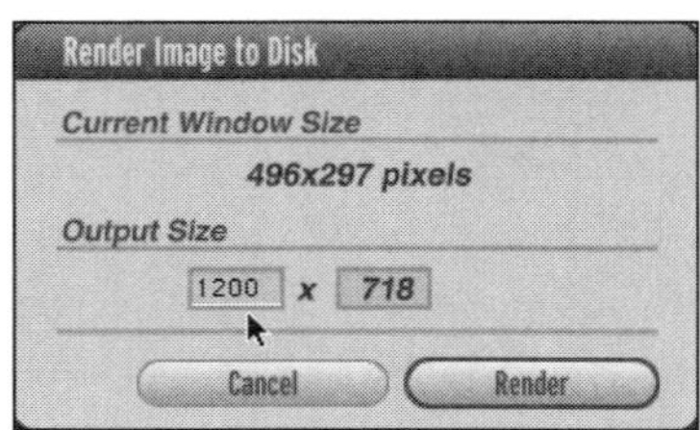

8.

Next, select the format you will use. In the pull-down menu that appears, you can save the file in any of the following formats: BMP, JPEG, PICT, PSD (Photoshop), PNG (a new image format competing with JPEG for use on the Web), or TIF.

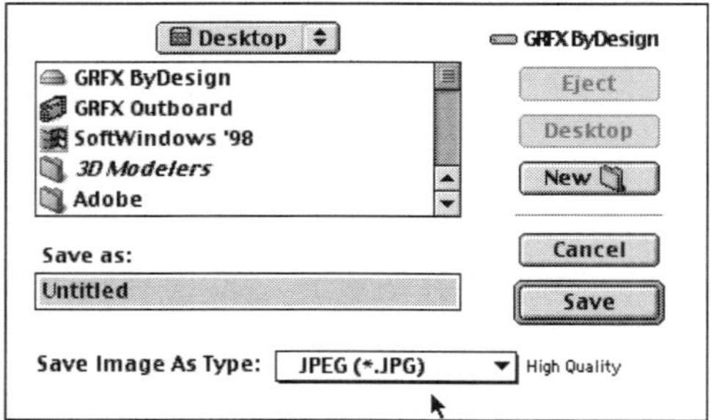

Create An Animation

Now you can create an animation to use in the presentation. Because this is a practice session, consider it a "rough cut."

1.

Click on View to return to the editing mode and do a Quick Render. Then click on the Animation tab and the + button to add your first frame.

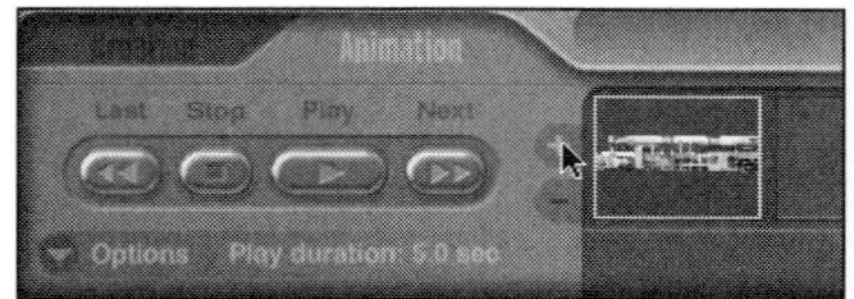

2.

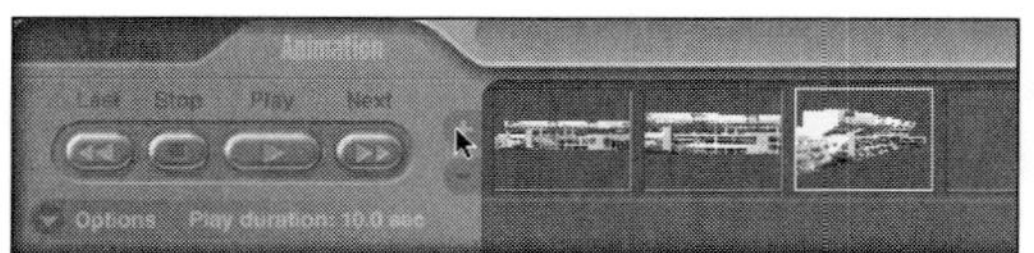

Now you are ready to create keyframes. Using the Trackball control, the Move X/Y control, and the Move X/Z control, move around the model, clicking on the + button at different intervals to create a number of keyframes. Using these controls is also known as moving the "camera" around the model. Canoma will fill in the blanks by creating all the in-between frames.

3.

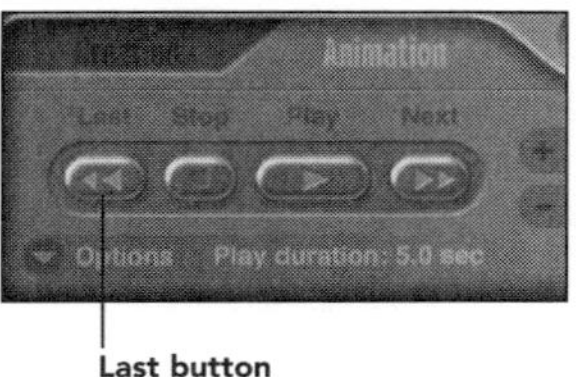

Preview your animation to make sure that it comes out the way you expect. To return to the first frame, click on the Last button on the Animation control panel.

4.

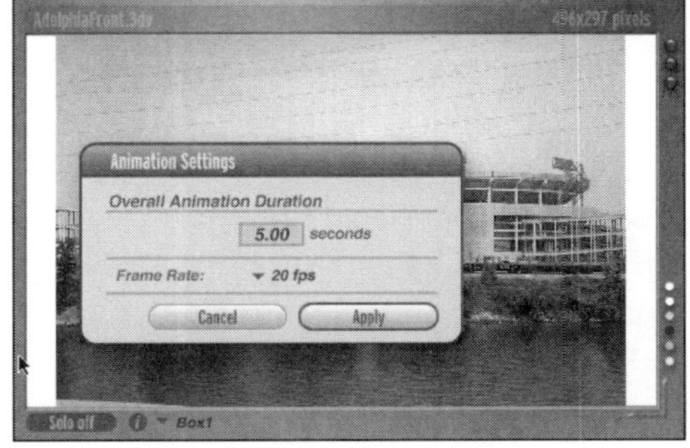

If the animation isn't as you envisioned, you need to re-time your effort. Start the animation. If you want to change the time of the video or set it up to *loop* (play over and over), click on the Options button at the bottom of the control panel.

5.

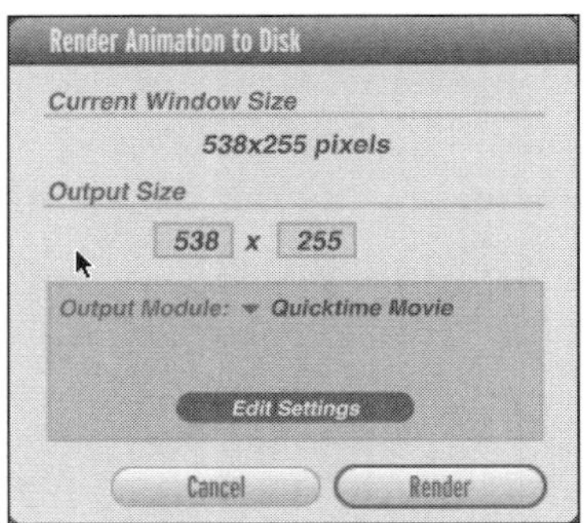

Now, save the animation for later use. Select File Render Animation. In the panel that comes up, set the size of the screen, whether to save as a QuickTime file or as individual frames, and, by clicking on the Edit Settings button, everything else you need to create your file. Also, save the master file as Stadium.3dv or something similar. You may want to come back to this file, clean it up, and use it for a Web presentation.

Project 2: Create The Entire Stadium

You now have three files to use in a formal presentation: one image to use in a page layout program for print and two files for a multimedia presentation. Let's create an image that incorporates the physical location of the stadium along with the facility. This is one way to build a model. See Chapter 11 for a way to build this stadium with even more detail.

Stadium Construction

With Nashville as the backdrop, you can do one of two things. You can create a static file in which you place the stadium image you just created. Optionally, you can use two images (supplied in the Chapter 8 folder on the FTP site) to build an animation and MetaStream file.

1.

Open the stadium_aerial.tif and stadium_construction.jpg files. You will start with stadium_aerial.tif, building the stadium and then placing it in stadium_construction.jpg to create the final scene. This model will be complex by the time you're finished, so leave plenty of room on your hard drive and have plenty of patience. Begin by creating a Block that will become the field. Then create a Horizontal Plane for the ground.

2.

Begin working on the exterior of the stadium. Select the Block primitive, select Align, and create another Block to serve as the entrance to the stadium.

3.

To make everything fit, use Stack|Build to create the other layers of the entrance. Some pictures can be deceiving, so experiment here to see how best to make everything fit.

You'll need to check your model continuously to make sure everything stacks up as it should.

4.

Now start on the far side construction. Repeat the preceding process for the screen and the structures at the back of the stadium, beginning by stacking your first primitive. Don't worry if these structures are too tall. They'll be covered up soon by other primitives.

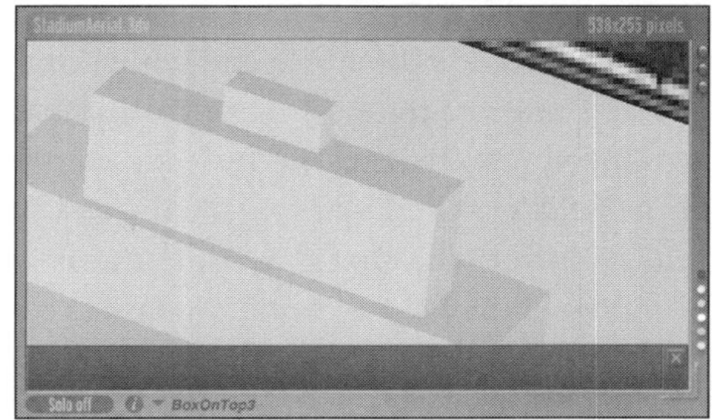

5.

Building the stands (the area where the fans sit) is probably the most complicated part of creating the model. As you see, the stadium angles out as it gets taller. You can't use a Box primitive because it would stretch so much that it would look horrible. Select the Horizontal Translation Sweep primitive and reshape it to fit the angle.

6.

Now pin the edge. In this case, you want to use the Stack option while the Ground Plane is active and pin it to the Horizontal Translation Sweep's lowest edge to the center of the football field (the area where the players collide).

7.

Test your work. At this point, don't worry about rendering. Instead, use the Trackball control to make sure this new primitive is lining up correctly. If you glued the lowest edge of the Sweep to the bottom of the field box, things should work fine.

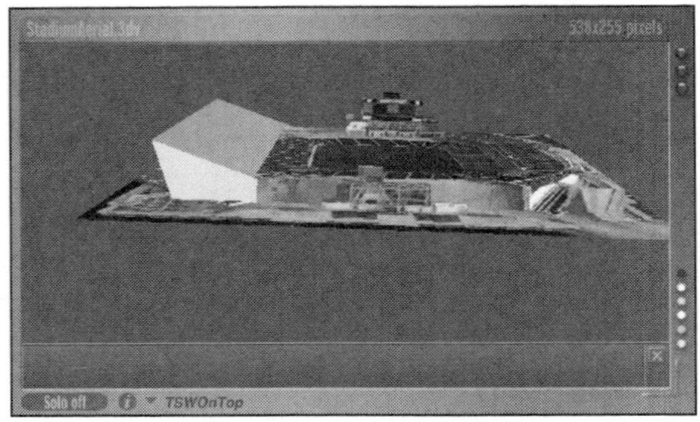

8.

Next, you need to duplicate and adjust your efforts. Duplicate the Horizontal Translation Sweep you just created. Then select a corner of the field level and rotate it 180 degrees so that it mirrors the first one. Glue the new primitive to the field box and prepare to repeat this process.

9.

You need to make two more copies. Duplicate either of the stands primitives, rotate it 90 degrees, place the two primitives at the two ends of the stadium, and carefully resize them. Be extra careful on the back side (the corner at the top of the screen) of this new primitive; otherwise, the primitives won't line up correctly and will leave a noticeable gap in your finished model. Keep using the Trackball control to rotate the model to make sure everything fits correctly.

10.

The stairwells on either side of the front of the stadium appear to be triangles, and it might seem best to use a Horizontal or Vertical Translation Sweep or one of the Triangle primitives to model them. In reality, though, it's best to use a Block primitive and create a square that violates the premodeled portion of the structure. You can then minimize the amount of stretching and manipulating you must do. If you doubt this, use a triangular shape and try to get it to fit properly—especially when adding Point-to-Point or Point-to-Edge Glue!

11.

Now it's time to do a Quality Render to set the images to the primitives. Click on the Turtle icon, sit back, and watch your stadium come to life. Notice that, even with Mirror Textures turned on, many areas remain unmapped. Unfortunately, you don't have images of these missing sides. This is one reason why you need as many photos as possible—so you can fill in the gaps.

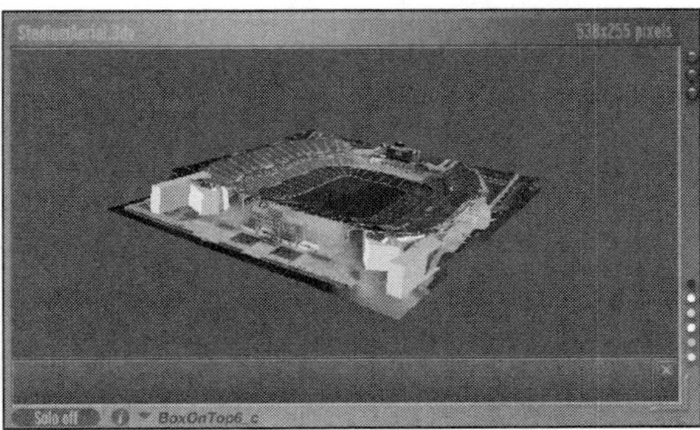

Project 3: Put The Stadium Into The City Scene

Now it's time to make Canoma shine. You have a fully rendered football stadium; next, you want to place it on its planned location. This is where your second shot comes in, and it makes a wonderful example of how Canoma works when you're using numerous images.

1.

When you select the second picture, you'll see the stadium's wireframe superimposed over it. Because the two photos are shot from different angles, use the Camera controls, the Banking control, and the Trackball to position the stadium onto the scene. Don't worry; you've already rendered the stadium, so when you move it around in this scene, the textures stay mapped. Additionally, as you position the model, you'll see a ghost image to help you align it.

2.

After you're happy with the stadium's placement, model the buildings in the background. Don't get overly precise here because the foreground buildings are low, but they're so close together it's easy to use a single Block primitive to model them. For the Batman Building (refer to Chapter 3), you didn't model the spires separately. Here, I modeled the rear buildings on the right using one primitive. It didn't work, so I reset them.

3.

As an alternative and better way of handling step 2's approach to the background buildings, try this. Taking a quick look, you can see that by modeling each building as a separate primitive, you add depth to it. It's starting to look like a city back there. I suggest that you use the Trackball to view your progress after you place each new primitive. In this way, you can make sure the city is growing as you planned.

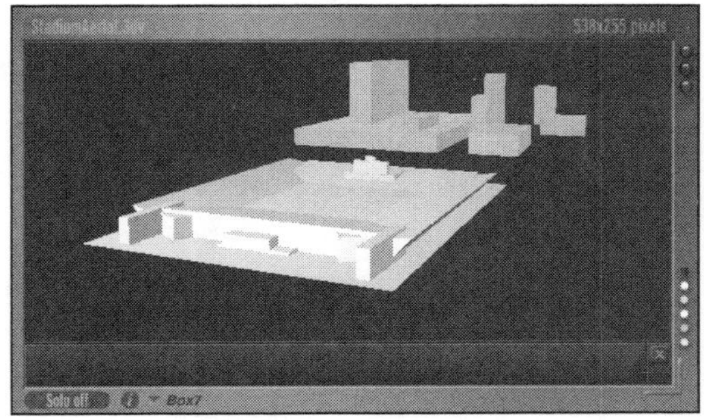

4.

Because you need to see the construction area as well as the river, you need to add a second Horizontal Plane. To get the right perspective, the front corners of the plane must extend outside the photograph but in this case, you can live with it. A good way to tell whether your perspective will be right—without using the Guide Line tool—is to match the sides of the plane with the farthest outside Box primitive corner.

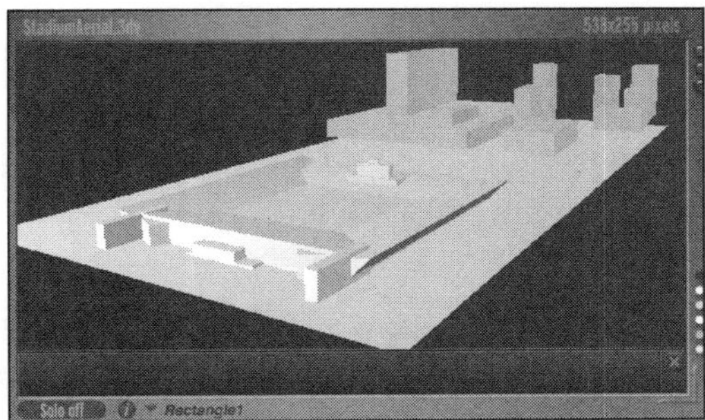

5.

To finish this model, create a background screen. First, select the Screen tool. Notice that it's segmented, and, as luck would have it, the segments match up with the left, rear, and right sides of the model.

6.

Resize the Screen primitive to extend from one edge of the photograph to the other. Do some Point-to-Edge gluing and then check to make sure everything is lined up correctly, especially the buildings in the background. You don't want them to be jutting out from the backdrop.

7.

After you're satisfied, do a Quality Render and admire your work. Also, create a fly-around animation (you can see the one I created by downloading it from the FTP site). As you move around the model, you'll see that the screen disappears in the foreground so that it doesn't block anything.

Project 4: Use The Images To Create A Full Presentation

To recap, you have a still image of the front of the stadium and have placed the stadium in the construction zone. You also have either a MOV or an AVI animation of the front of the stadium. You'll also want to create a special animation for the completed model. Then you'll be ready to model any building anywhere in the world. Redesign New York, Sydney, Australia, or Butte, Montana. You can create and put these cities on the moon or on Mars. To do so, however, you need funds. To generate those funds, you need to put together all the elements into a presentation for your client.

1.

For stills, you can generate high-resolution images to place into a print presentation by exporting the mapped image at an appropriate ratio (at least 1200 x 750 pixels per inch). By bringing these images into a page layout program or graphic design program such as Painter 6, you can create eye-catching visuals that correspond 100 percent to your video presentation.

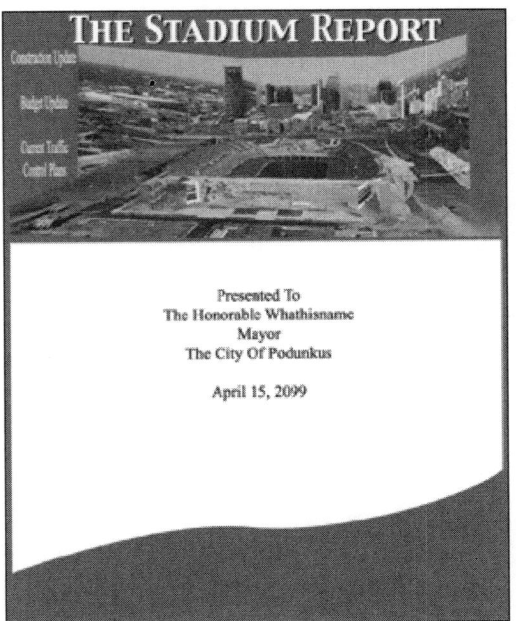

2.

For animations, you can buy or rent projection attachments for your laptop fairly economically. Then you can create animations within Canoma or put animated characters into scenes—you'll see how in Chapter 9—to create full-fledged multimedia presentations that, again, work in conjunction with your printed pieces.

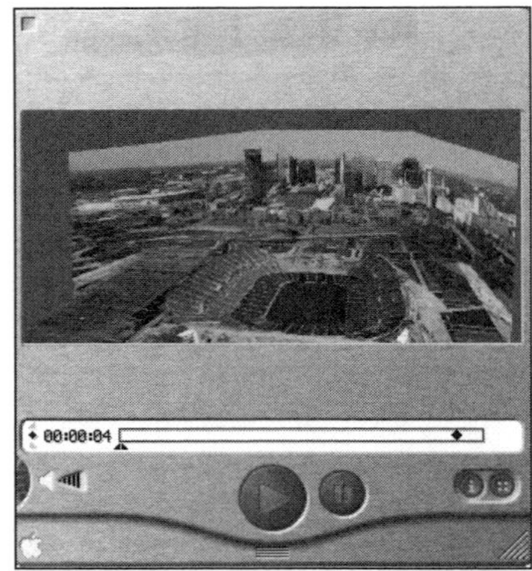

3.

Finally, there's the Web. Using Canoma, you can create interactive pieces that go beyond the current norm. If you've stitched together photographs, you can create full QuickTime VR scenes like those you've seen all over the Web, or you can create an interactive image that will immerse viewers in the world you've created.

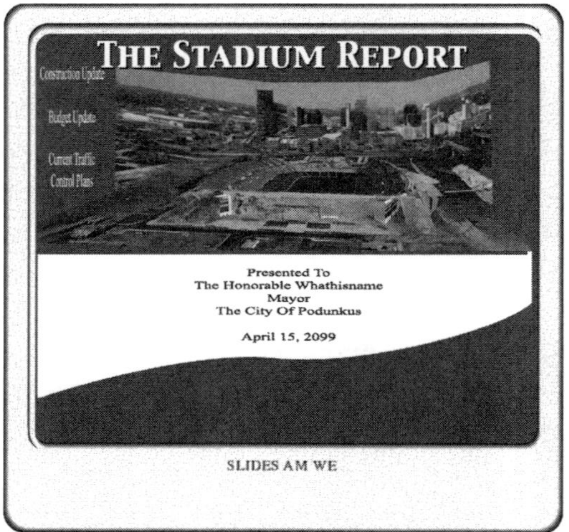

Chapter 9
Using Canoma With Other Applications

Project 1: Create a Web splash screen

Project 2: Use advanced techniques with Bryce 4 and Poser 4

Project 3: Create a presentation with Poser, Bryce, a 2D image program, and Canoma

Project 4: Create a print ad with Poser, a 2D image program, and Canoma

Project 5: Create a video using Poser, Bryce, and Canoma

Interacting With Other Software

Your computer toolbox is probably filled with programs that can enhance your Canoma presentations. Importing your creations into programs such as MetaCreations' Bryce 4 and Poser 4 can help you produce exciting images and videos. You've already learned how to assign your favorite 2D image-editing program, such as Adobe Photoshop, as the default editor from within Canoma. In this chapter, you create work outside Canoma and combine it within Canoma and other programs to create basic and advanced e-commerce sites.

---

*Project 1 deals heavily with creating images in other programs for importation into Canoma. Demo filters discussed in this project can be downloaded from the Canoma Visual Impact FTP site or from Extensis (**www.extensis.com**) and MetaCreations (**www.metacreations.com**).*

Project 1: Create A Logo For Your Splash Screen

You can use 3D to enhance a splash screen logo's look, giving it "substance." A 3D logo is immediately identified as a substantial concept, and the entity it represents also seems more solid. Usually, to add 3D depth, you use a 3D text block or symbol. Suppose that you're designing a logo that represents Eyeful Tower Communications, a business of author R. Shamms Mortier. Because Mortier deals with clients who want some form of 3D output, he wants to craft a logo that has more 3D variety than a simple text block or symbol but will incorporate those elements.

1.

The piece is planned as the splash screen of a Web site.

For this project, you'll need MetaCreations' Canoma, Bryce, and Adobe Photoshop with the mentioned plug-ins.

2.

Start in Photoshop. For a 2D image application, I prefer Photoshop for most bitmap editing work because using it is familiar and intuitive. Using Photoshop 5, I can craft three images that can be mapped to a cube, each with some content that relates to the business name and logo concept. If you do this, substitute your own images. The concept is important, not the content of the image.

3.

Size matters. In Photoshop, create a 300 ppi, 6 × 6-inch image. You can use 72 ppi, but here your content includes intricate images, so you want high resolution. Canoma maps images so well that 300 ppi is worth the extra render time. The first image, a direct take on the logo (a pyramid with a sphere on top), is easy to create in Photoshop, where I could apply color gradients to both pyramid and sphere.

4.

To add the text blocks to the logo, use the Extensis PhotoGraphics plug-in filter, which has all the needed text modification tools that Photoshop lacks. This includes the capability to create text so sharp-edged you'll swear that it was imported vector text.

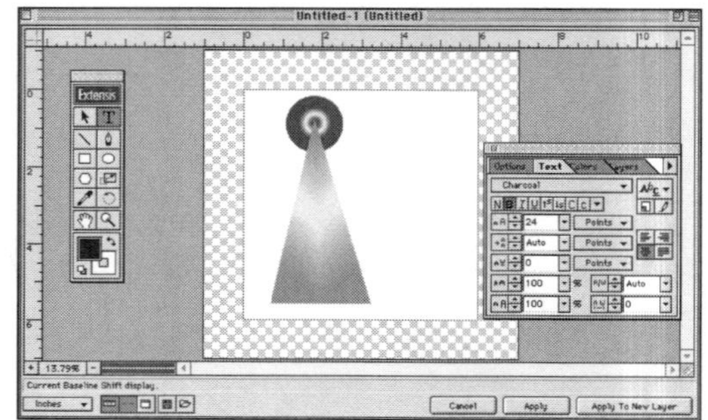

5.

Now, check the result. After you compose the text, use PhotoGraphics' interface to configure and place it as desired. PhotoGraphics has all the modification options—font selection, resizing, and rotation—built in. When you're finished, close PhotoGraphics. You'll see your text layer added to the image in Photoshop.

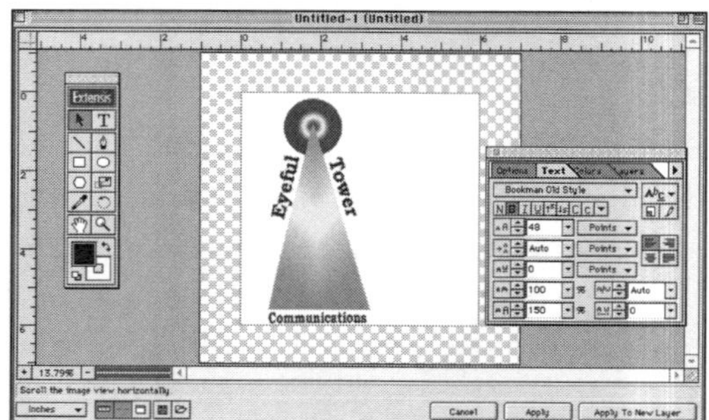

Building A Background

Next, you need to add a backdrop behind the logo image.

6.

First, duplicate the background layer and move it down behind the logo layer. Erase everything on this new layer. On the original logo layer, clear the background outside the graphics. Then, turn off visibility of all layers except the new background layer and open KPT5 Fraxplorer. Explore this great fractal-image tool until you find a background you like, and then add it to the background layer.

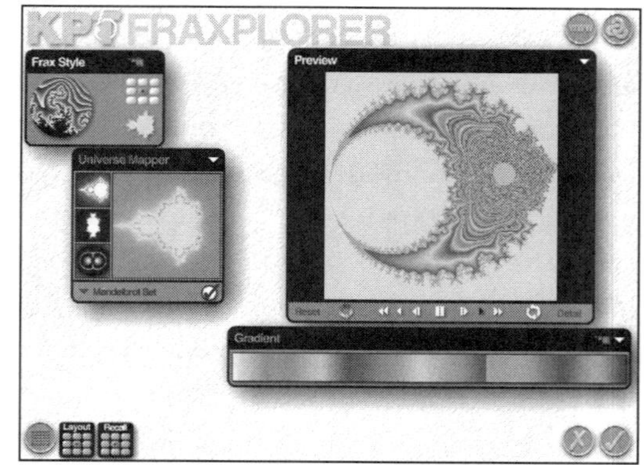

7.

Next, you will blend the elements. Make all the layers visible again. If everything looks layer-separated instead of cohesive, select the logo image layer and make it 50 percent transparent. It ties the whole concept together nicely.

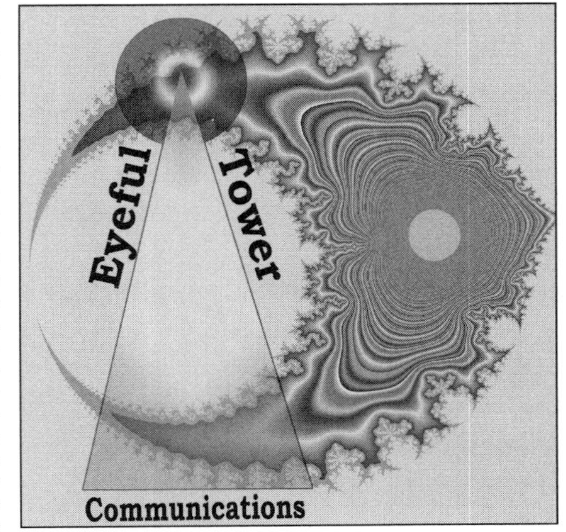

8.

Now develop two images for the sides of the cube. On one side, you can use an image layered with transparent and resized duplicates; this logo uses a self-portrait. On the other, create a 3D button. You can create the button with Photobevel and PhotoGraphics plug-ins. Create the background for the button using Xenofex Little Fluffy Clouds plug-in. The effect in the center is done with the Photoshop Stained Glass filter.

You can download free demos of Extensis' PhotoGraphics and other Extensis software from this book's FTP site. A demo version of AlienSkin Software's Xenofex can be downloaded from their site, ***www.xenofex.com****.*

Making It Fit With Canoma

Now that you've created the components of your logo, it's a good idea to work with your image a bit more. You'll tweak the various elements so that they'll work smoothly with Canoma.

9.

The next critical step is done to accommodate Canoma. In Photoshop, use the Perspective and Distort tools to create a false cube, to be used eventually in Canoma as a template. This image shows a single side of the cube, after distortion and perspective is applied.

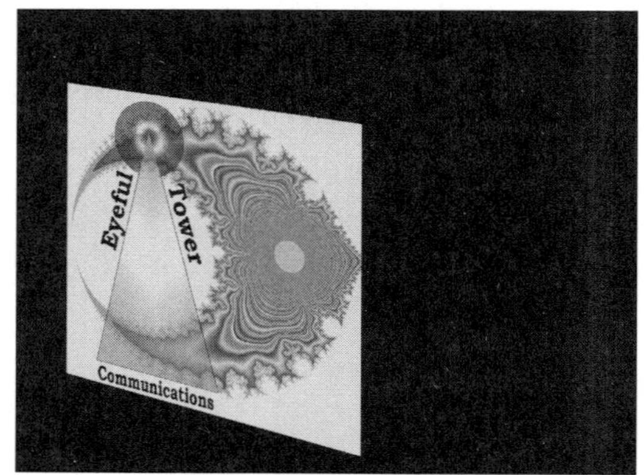

10.

Keep the cube to 72 ppi because you will replace the three images on its facets with the 300-ppi graphics. This image shows two sides completed.

11.

Then save the false cube along with all three of the 300-ppi images. This image shows the sides of the cube that you completed.

This cube doesn't need the correct perspective, only an approximation. You can make any necessary adjustments in Canoma.

12.

Open Canoma and import the false cube as a template. Create a Box primitive to build the shape around the image. Import each 300-ppi image to replace the lower-resolution images on the facets of the cube. Leave Image Stealing on so that these three images are automatically duplicated on the opposite facets. Zoom out so that you can see the relationship of all three images while they are being placed. Save the finished, mapped cube as a WaveFront OBJ file.

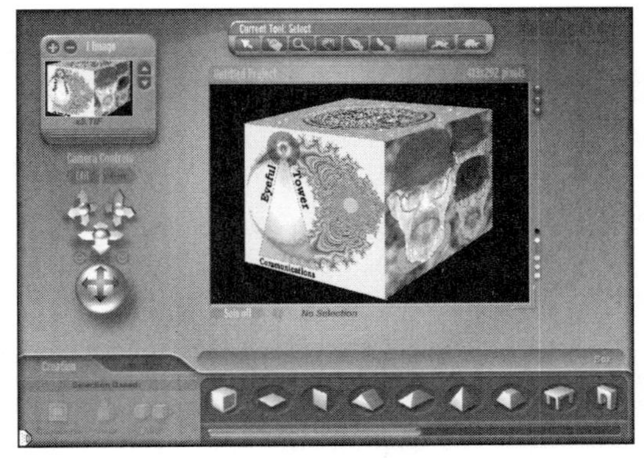

And Finally, Bryce

To complete the project, you need to import the cube into Bryce. You can think of a Web splash screen as a full screen or central image with various link elements. In Bryce 4, you can build this kind of model and assign buttons onto specific sides of the boxes. Each button links to a page within your site or to outside URLs. This step prepares the project for its final placement on the Web.

13.

Import the cube into Bryce. Canoma-mapped objects flow easily into Bryce, mapped and ready to place. It's always best to do a few test renders before your final one. The final image uses a number of rotated cubes, each of which can be used as a URL target for use as a Web splash screen.

Project 2: Advanced Canoma E-Commerce Combinations

Now that you've learned how to work with numerous programs, let's plunge into the ways you can build intricate images with other 3D programs. You'll begin with other MetaCreations' programs—Poser and Bryce—with an eye toward creating e-commerce images that are far different from the ones you'll find on other Web sites. Project 1 gave you an idea of what can be accomplished, but now let's take it a step further. Set up a master folder where you can save all the files you'll create, and read on.

The Background Information

You've been hired to create an e-commerce site for a new cable channel named Home & Hearth. This company sells limited-edition decorative products at high prices.

1.

The clients want a site that has the feel of the television network but also has its own look—one that exudes wealth and class.

2.

A new H&H featured product is a series of ceramic lighthouses. This lighthouse is the network's premiere piece and centerpiece of the home page you'll create. Import the photographs you've taken of the lighthouse (or download images—LighthouseBackHR.jpg, LighthouseBackLR.jpg, LighthouseFrontHR.jpg, and LighthouseFrontLR.jpg—from this book's FTP site).

Here, HR stands for high resolution; LR stands for low resolution.

3.

The lighthouse portion is rounded, so take your time. Use the Horizontal Sweep tool to create the base and then stack flat-topped Pyramids to create the top sections. These primitives contain extraneous background information (you'll fix that later in Photoshop or Photopaint). After you create the lighthouse, map the different angles to produce a high-quality model and save it as four files: WaveFront OBJ, MetaStream, a high-resolution PICT, and as a Canoma file (you'll use it again later).

Remember, the OBJ format retains the mapped information.

Create The Home Page Image

Now that the model is created, you'll render different images for various uses. This task incorporates both Bryce 4 and Poser 4, so make sure you have downloaded the demos of the programs if you don't have the full versions. Notice that all three programs have the same interface design, making it easy to move from one to the next with a minimum of effort.

4.

Open Bryce and create a scene for your lighthouse. You can create an original model or access to the U.S. Geological Survey site (**www.usgs.org**) and download DEMs (digital elevation maps) of actual areas. Your scene uses a DEM of Bar Harbor, Maine, expanded by 900 percent. It also has an added water plane.

5.

Import the Lighthouse OBJ into Bryce and position it where you think it fits best. You might want to position some lights to act as the beacons. Depending on your concept, you can have beams of light radiating from the tower in a dusk or nighttime setting. Because snow is on the roof, you'll want to assign a snowy texture to the landmass. Don't worry about extraneous image mapping from Canoma; you can remove it later in your 2D image program.

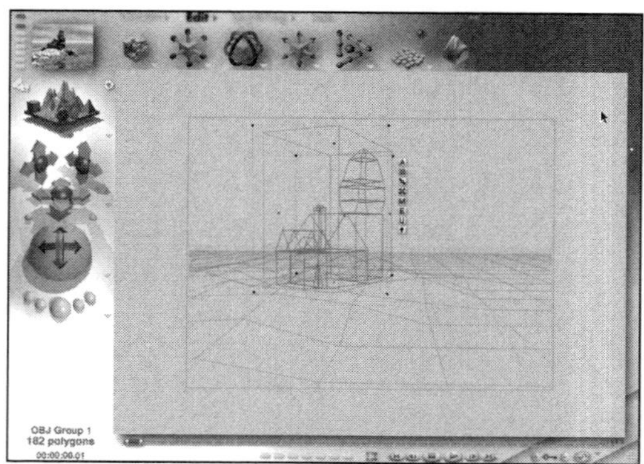

You can get detailed information on using Bryce in R. Shamms Mortier's book, Bryce 4 f/x and Design, *published by The Coriolis Group.*

6.

Now, you import a Poser model. To add interest to the scene, open Poser 4, create and pose a character or two (or three or four), and then export the images as OBJ files. These characters will be added to the Canoma/Bryce scene to lend reality to the image. After you import the characters into Bryce, you only need to resize them to fit and place them where you want.

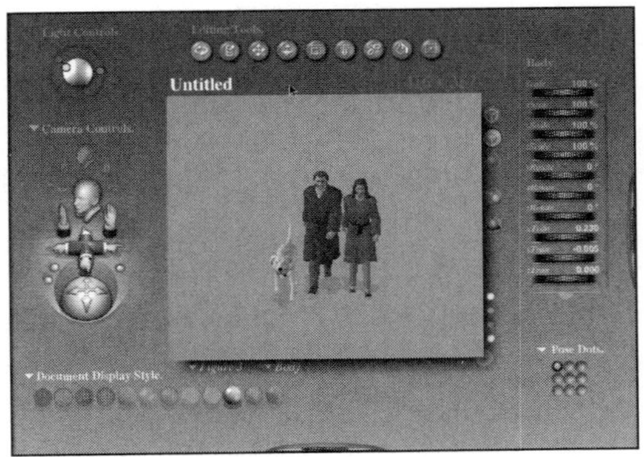

7.

Depending on how you are setting up the site, you can have the lighthouse contain one or multiple links. The single link would, of course, take visitors to the ceramic lighthouse portion of the site; other links could be set up to send visitors to the ceramics area, a home décor area, and so on. It all depends on how you, as the designer, want to incorporate your work. At this point, save your file in HTML format. Now everything is ready for the Web.

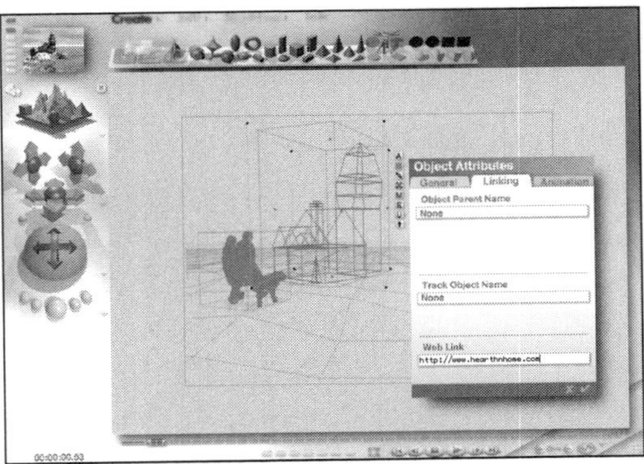

8.

Repeat the multiple save process. Again, you'll save this file in three different formats: as a large-scale PICT image, as an OBJ file (link all the elements together before you save), and as a series of PICT images viewed from different angles. Do the latter by moving the camera and re-rendering each new scene. Make sure you also render one image looking down on the entire scene. Then delete the Poser character(s), re-render, and save again.

9.

Here is how a Web home page could look that employs your Canoma models. Each image along the bottom would be a link to a specific area.

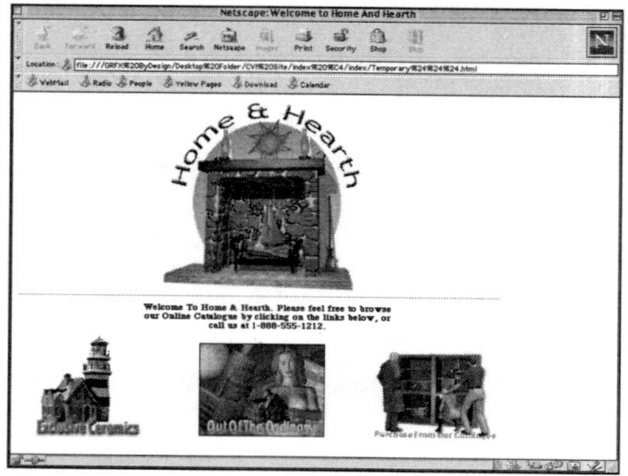

Project 3: Create An Interactive Flash Movie

Another Web-based application Canoma files can be incorporated into is Flash. Macromedia (**www.macromedia.com**) created the Flash format. The Flash and Shockwave players are so commonplace now, you probably have the plug-in for viewing these files in your Web browser, whether you know it or not.

You can download the Flash file (SuitDisplay.swf) and the html file (SuitDisplay.html) to see the completed animation from the Chapter 9 folder on the book's FTP site.

The Flash And Shockwave Software

To create Flash animations (also called Movies), you'll need one of the following: Macromedia Flash or Fireworks, Macromedia Director, or Adobe LiveMotion (as of this writing, in public beta form, downloadable from **www.adobe.com**). For more information about these applications, refer to the end of Chapter 4.

1.

You'll be creating two animations: a zoom in on a store and another zoom into a product. When you import them into the Flash creation program, you'll create a dissolve between the two, finishing up with an animated link to an order page.

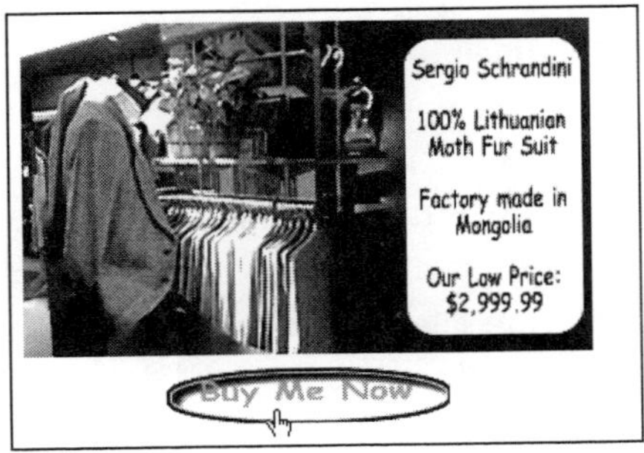

2.

The first animation consists of the Broadway Street model you have already created. Bring it into Canoma, and do a Quality Render on the model. Then select the Animation tab in the lower-left corner of the screen.

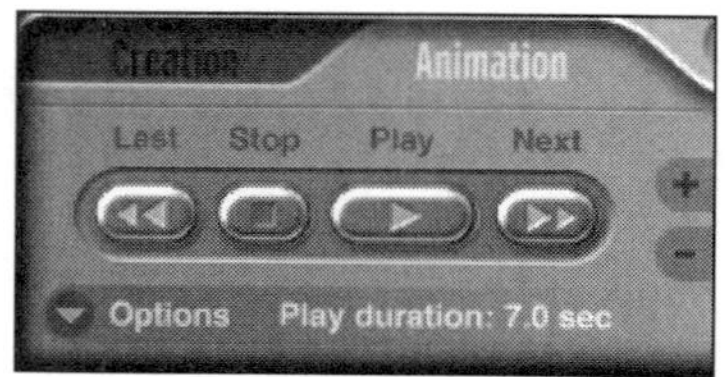

3.

For this you want a five-second animation. Select Options in the Animations panel. For the Duration, enter 5 and change the fps (frames per second) to 15. For slower connection speeds, this is a good speed. You can go up to 24fps, but you risk creating a jerky animation for those who have a slower online connection.

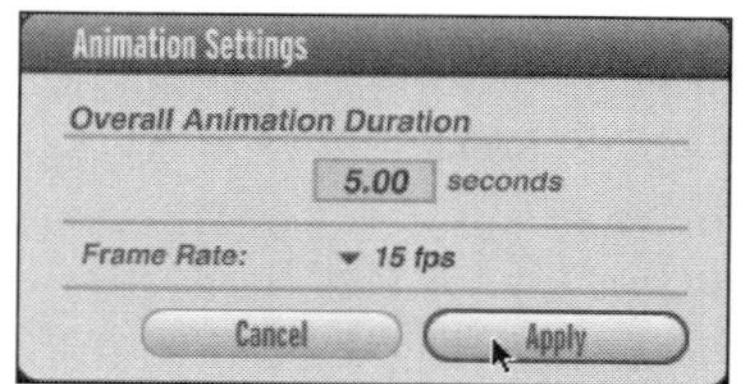

4.

With a five-second animation and 15 frames, three keyframes is enough to make a smooth zoom in. Start with a wide shot, click the + button, zoom in with the crosshair control until you're in front of the store with the book on the sign; click the + button again. Now zoom into the store window until your screen is filled with black. Click the + button again. Your Animation "timeline" should look like this.

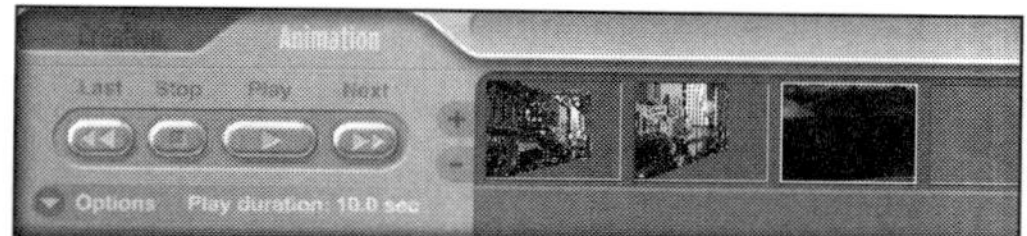

5.

Because this will be a Flash animation, set up your rendering parameters in the following manner: Choose File|Render Animation and set the image width to 320 pixels. When you press the Tab key to accept the size, the height field automatically changes to the correct parameter. Next, choose Multiple Frames from the Output Module pull-down menu. Accept the new parameters. Create a new folder to store these images in a central place.

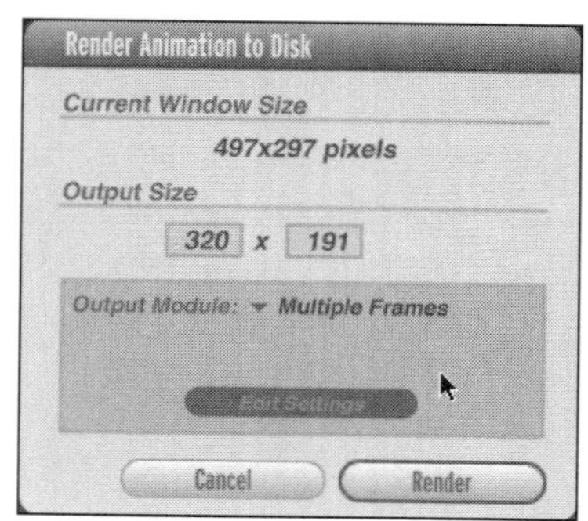

6.

Use the Store_Interior model you created at the beginning of the book and repeat the steps you just used to create a zoom in to the dress coat and coat rack. Leave space on the right side so you can place text over the image without covering the subject. Render this file into another new folder so they remain together.

7.

Use LiveMotion for this part of the project. When you open the program, a screen comes up, asking you to set the size of the workspace. Use 320 × 240 to provide extra room at the top and bottom of the screen. Now select File|Place Sequence, locate the Broadway Street animation you created, and click on Import All.

LiveMotion tutorials are provided on the Adobe Web site. They go over the basics of using the program and the timeline. Get familiar with them before continuing so you can understand the basic concepts in order to complete this project.

8.

Now, insert the store interior animation. If it isn't already open, use Command|Ctrl+T to open it. You'll see a bar to the right side of this screen, indicating the length (in frames) of your imported files. Scroll to the end of that bar and, approximately 15 frames prior to that, set an in point by clicking in the gray area just above the frame numbers. A triangle appears, showing that this is the new in point. Choose Place Sequence again and import the Store Interior animation files.

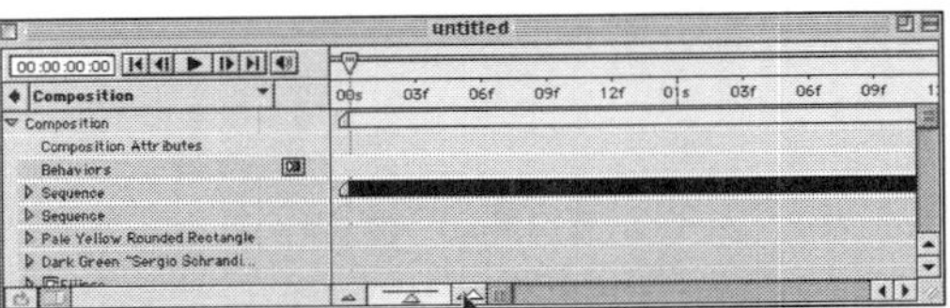

9.

Create an in point. You want to create a dissolve from the exterior shot to the interior, giving the effect that the viewer has entered the store. First, make sure the in point is set on the first frame of the store interior shot. This becomes your in point—the starting place for your dissolve.

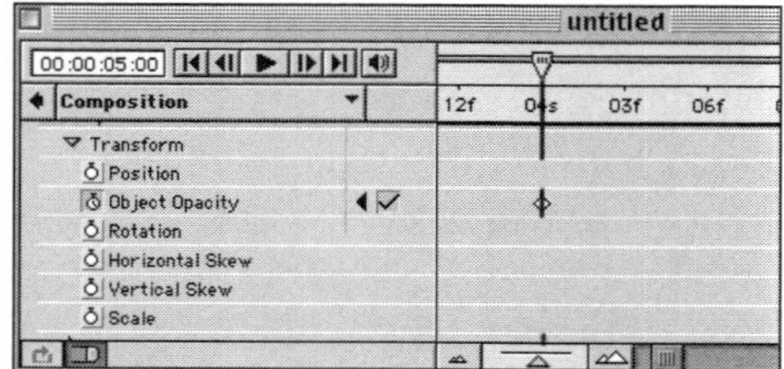

10.

Now set an out point. On the left side of the Timeline screen, select the store zoom-in footage and click on the little triangles to reveal the various options available. Here, you'll open the Transform options and choose Opacity. A diamond shape is inserted at your in point, indicating the location. Next move the marker to the right a few frames to select your out point (the place where the dissolve will end).

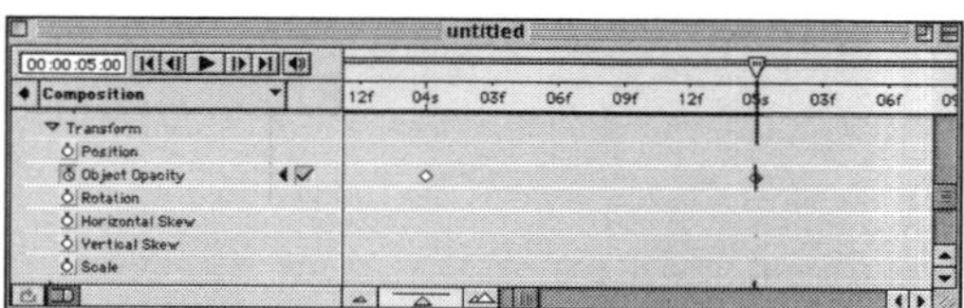

11.

Set the opacity. Under the Windows pull-down menu, select Opacity if it isn't already open, to reveal the selection screen. Either move the slider so the Opacity setting is 0, or type in a numeric value.

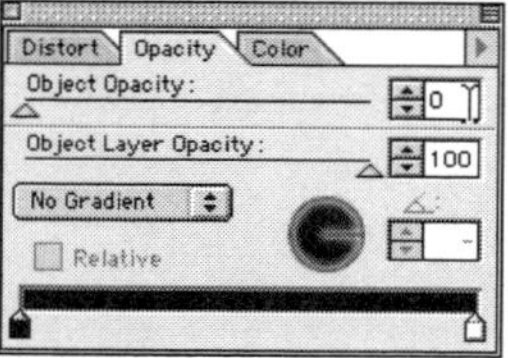

12.

Create an info screen. After the interior zoom-in stops, you want text to appear that describes the product. LiveMotion, Flash, Fireworks, and Director provide you with vector-drawing tools so you can create buttons or shapes. Place your frame marker on the final frame of the animation. Select the Box draw tool and create a box over the right side of the screen. Fill it with a color. Then use the Text tool to type in a description of the product.

13.

Now, you need to create a button. Using the Draw tools again, select and draw a shape at the bottom center of the screen. This becomes the purchase button. LiveMotion, Flash, Fireworks, and Director come with pre-built rollovers to simplify your creation of animated buttons. Select a style from the Styles palette.

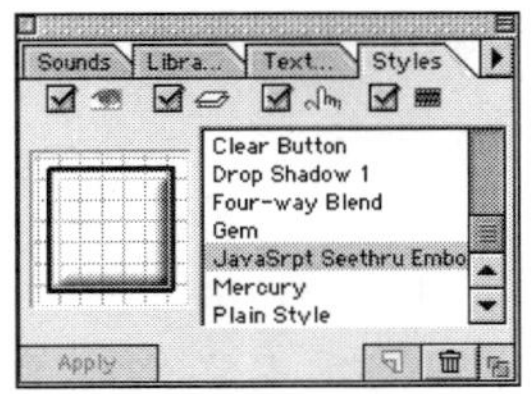

Review the LiveMotion tutorial files from the Adobe site to learn how to set a link for the button you just created.

14.

Now export your file. LiveMotion saves your file as both an html document and as a standalone .swf Flash file for importation and placement on your web page.

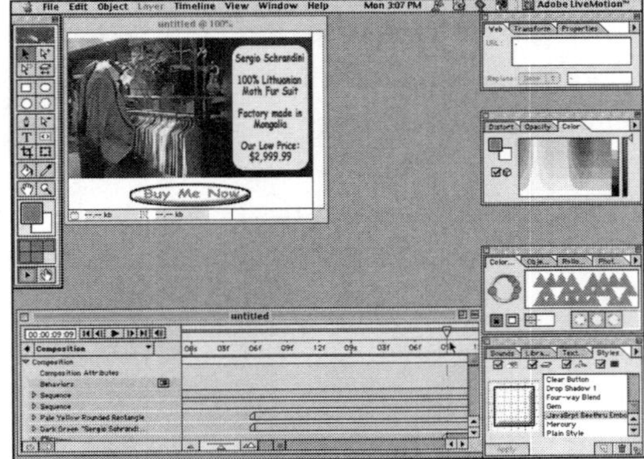

Project 4: Use Numerous Programs To Create A Print Ad

As mentioned, you can do final cleanup work in a 2D image manipulation program such as Photoshop, Photopaint, or Canvas. The final image in this section will be used for a Hearth & Home Network print ad, and you'll use various programs to build the image. You'll use Poser props, a Poser character, two Canoma models, and an image manipulation program.

1.

Create the background. Sex sells. Why else would you have an attractive model draped on a car in an advertisement? The producers at Hearth & Home have finally realized that they need to punch up the network's image. They also want an ad that will specifically be targeted to a male readership shopping for expensive trinkets. What better way to showcase the product than to display it in the hands of the kind of woman the customers wish they were buying for?

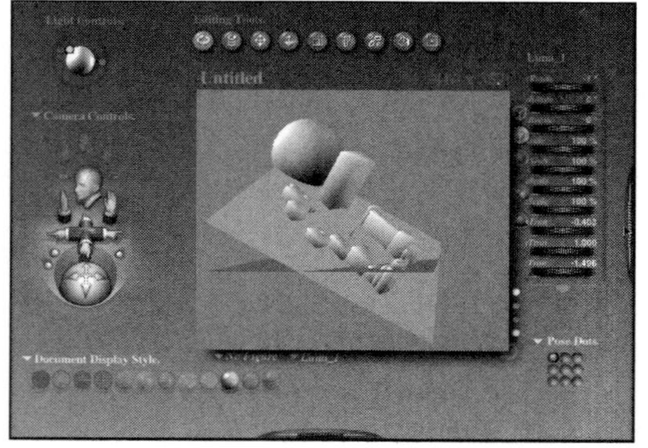

For the Bryce image, use the City.3dv file in the Chapter 9 folder on the FTP site.

2.

Now, you need to add models. Use a Poser model and create the basic pose. Import the Canoma product OBJ file and do the final tweaking of the Poser model to make her look as if she is holding the piece. Now render the image large enough that you can resize it to 300 ppi in your 2D image program and save it.

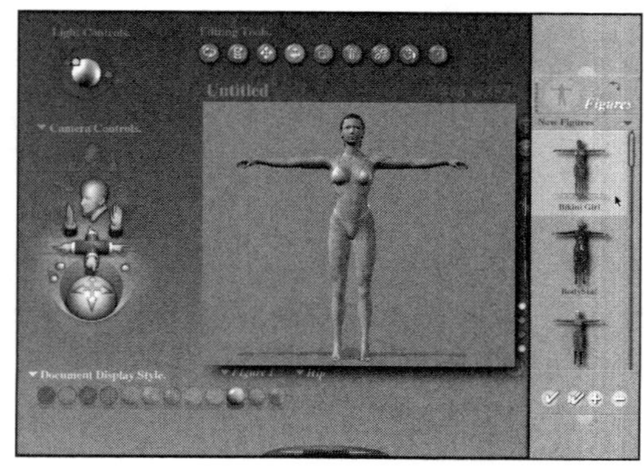

3.

If you need to clean up extraneous information that was mapped onto the Canoma model, use (in Photoshop nomenclature) the Lasso and Clone tools, replacing those areas with other portions of the image. You have created the logo, so bring it in on a new layer, position it, and add any effects you want.

4.

Save the layered image for later use. Remember that you want to retain continuity among all the various Hearth & Home Network pieces, so you might want to use this image on the Web site, in a multimedia presentation, or in another printed piece.

5.

Now finish the ad in this program, or import it into a program such as Canvas or Adobe Illustrator to do the final layout.

Project 5: Create An Animation Incorporating Poser And Bryce

You can use multiple software packages in a number of ways to create interesting and thought-provoking animations. In this project, you create a street scene using Bryce, Poser, and (of course) Canoma. You create a simple, static street shot with moving characters. As you become more proficient with the software packages, you'll be able to combine various animations. You could use the scene on the Web or in a multimedia presentation for the Chamber of Commerce.

Although you're using Poser 4 and Bryce 4 as secondary programs, you can import Canoma OBJ files into any 3D modeling application that accepts this format.

1.

Create the street scene. Open the file of the model you made in Chapters 2 and 8 using Broadway Street. If it wasn't saved as an OBJ, open it in Canoma, make sure it's mapped correctly, and export it in this format. To add interest, you could also do a fly-around animation or a push in (or zoom in or dolly in), but it would add some difficulty when you create the final animation in another program. So you'll create only a static backdrop this time.

2.

Now add an environment. Bring the OBJ into Bryce and create an environment. Your main concern here is to create a sky backdrop. Be careful here and in the next program to set the lights correctly so that all the shadows match up. Use the shadows on the Canoma image to judge the correct placement of the sun and lights. Resize the image to the desired resolution and then render and save it as an image file.

3.

Next, begin the animation process. Bring the new image into Poser (File|Import|Background Image). When Poser says the image size differs from that of the canvas, tell it to resize. Now add some characters, starting with a jaywalker in the foreground. Be careful and take the time to get the height ratio correct. You can use cars in the image as indicators.

4.

You are now ready to assign animation and paths. Add characters to the scene and either create your own keyframes for each one or use Poser's Walk Designer to assign a prebuilt animation. As you assign the walk cycles (the character animation frames) or add moving props, you must assign a starting point: Position the object and then go to the last frame and reassign a new position. This technique effectively creates a motion path for the characters and props.

You can see the finished three-second animation by downloading the StreetScene.mov or StreetScene.avi file from the Chapter 9 folder on the FTP site.

5.

With prebuilt movements from Poser's Walk Designer, a number (the animation frame total) appears in the upper-right corner of each menu selection. If you chose 30 frames and Poser is set for 30 fps, the walk cycle is one second. A 15 fps cycle delivers a two-second animation, 10 fps with a three-second animation, and so on.

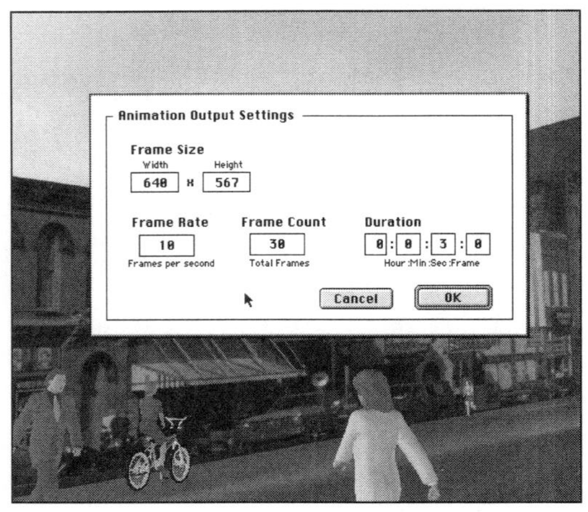

---

*If these walk cycles aren't too short, you can create new cycles within Poser, assigning the frame number to match the timing of the animation. You can save these files in numerous formats (notably BVH) and assign them to any organic model. You can use LifeForms by Credo Interactive (**www.charactermotion.com**) to create specialized animations.*

6.

There are various uses for this kind of animation. You can use it as the opening scene in a multimedia presentation for the Chamber of Commerce, dissolving to the name of the city or town, or you could use it as a transition between sections. To do this, import your QuickTime or AVI footage into Macromedia Director or Adobe Premiere to build the final presentation. You can save animations as streaming video for Web sites, or you can put it on your résumé reel.

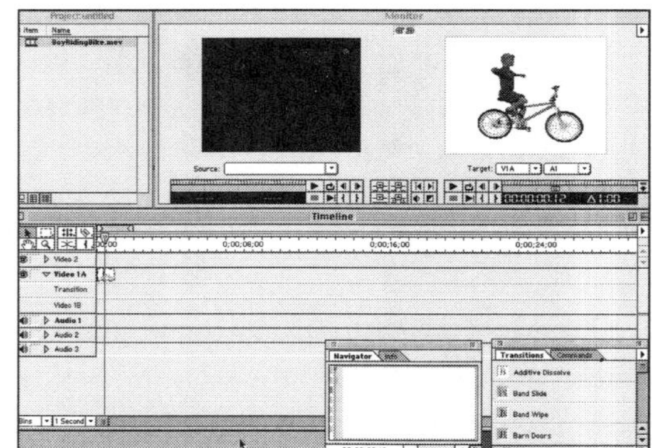

Chapter 10
Bring It All Together

Project 1: Create an interactive city

Canoma Worlds

It's time to bring everything together and explore the ultimate Canoma modeling experience: creating a truly interactive city environment that can be used in e-commerce. In this chapter, you'll use the techniques you've mastered from the previous chapters to create a city. You'll incorporate DEM files, modify elements in a 2D photo editing program, bring in static Poser figures, and finish in Bryce—including creating Web link hotspots in that program.

You can explore numerous sites on the Web where organizations and design schools are expanding the knowledge of how Canoma can be used in its most intricate form. Just choose a Web search engine and enter "Canoma".

Project 1: Create Asheville, NC In 3D

You'll use aerial photographs of Asheville, North Carolina, a model for an exciting project that will eventually bring Canoma's Web interactivity and e-commerce possibilities into a new realm. I suggest that you use the low-resolution files in this instance unless you have a lot of RAM on your computer and have assigned at least 200,000K to the programs you'll be using.

You'll find the files used in this project in the Chapter 10 folder on the Coriolis FTP site. Building the city takes about six hours because of the large number of primitives involved. The model itself, which is included on the FTP site, has more than 120 elements.

1.

Import Asheville_01.jpg and Asheville_02.jpg. Begin modeling with Asheville_01.jpg, the base shot from which you'll model all the other angles of Asheville. These aerials were taken at a high altitude, so run your Helper application and delete extraneous information to make your workflow more smooth, and to make matching the shots much easier when the time comes.

2.

The tall, boxy building near the center of the shot is perfect for your starting point. Using the Box primitive, create this building. Then add a Ground Plane, taking as much of the overall photograph as possible.

3.

The second building you'll create is the long one at the bottom right of the one you just created (you can see part of it in this illustration). As you piece this one together, use Stack and Align, and don't forget to use glue to keep the alignment correct. Start with the main part of the building, and then add the other elements to form the entire structure.

This building has a raised area that juts out. To avoid placing two Box primitives to create both parts of the building, first activate the main primitive and click on Align. Next, align the bottom front edges of the Box primitives, glue the corners of the new box to the main building, and then outline your modeling area. Your two primitives will now align correctly.

4.

Add a Ground Plane so that you have a base from which to work. You have to choose: Do you stretch the plane to fit the complete photograph, or do you create one that encompasses the area you'll be modeling first? If you do the latter, you can add any needed planes as you create additional buildings and elements.

5.

Throughout this project, you'll have ample time to use the Line tool to help retain correct perspective among primitives. The city has buildings that must be lined up as closely as possible. For example, row houses and multi-tiered storefronts don't lend themselves to a single Box primitive. The Line tool won't show up in the final rendering, so use it as often as you like.

6.

Begin working around the image, creating the larger structures first and then filling in the other buildings. Take time, and zooming a lot to make sure the primitives are correctly placed. When you're moving a corner into place, don't forget to use the Command (Mac) or Ctrl (PC) key to activate the Glue shortcut. This technique is helpful as you place more primitives into the scene.

7.

Another trick: Activate the Ground Plane before you place the base of the next building. If you're zoomed in on an area, the program places the primitive in the viewing area rather than in the center of the overall picture. In that way, you avoid unnecessary zooming in and out. The new primitive is placed on the plane, already attached.

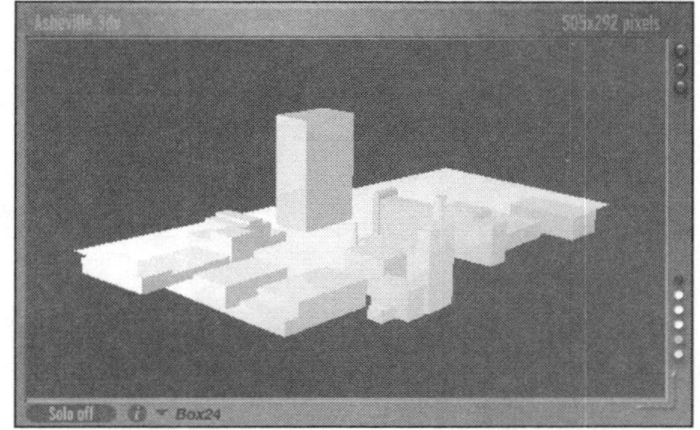

8.

Create the other buildings in Asheville. Perspective lines will help, so use them as often as needed. Point-To-Point glue is also useful. Because many buildings are the same size and shape as those you created, just duplicate and reposition the Box primitives. To help maintain the perspective ratio while moving the Box primitives into place, use the Line tool to lock in the dimensions of one or two of them. Take your time, use all the tricks and tools at your disposal to create this intricate city model.

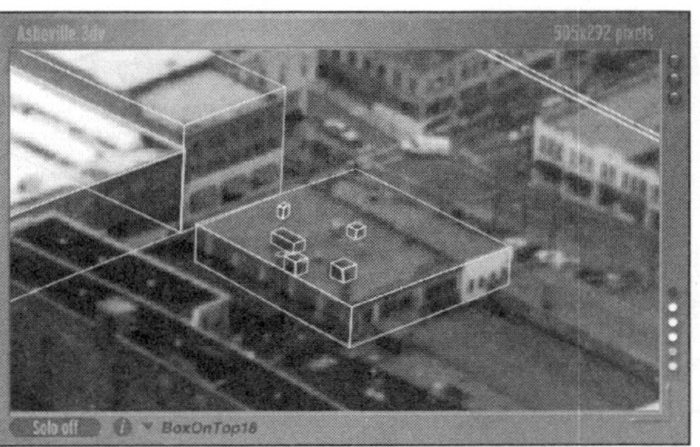

9.

A number of vehicles in the shot (refer to the preceding image) lend themselves to being modeled. They're small enough that Box primitives work, so model the cars and buses. These elements add dimensionality that goes beyond the norm, and they'll set you apart as a master Canoma modeler.

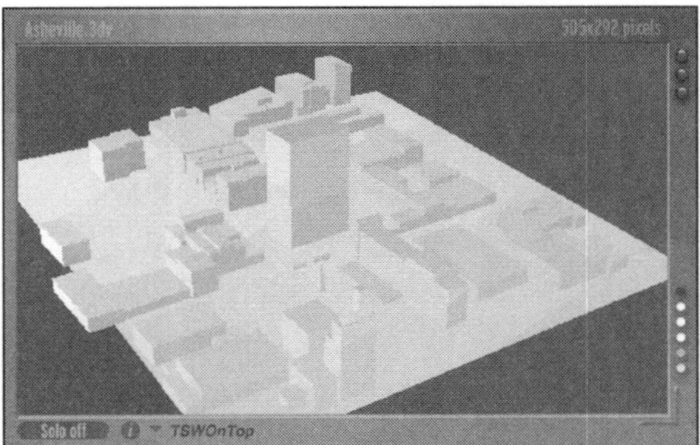

10.

While you're adding primitives to the scene, add more Ground Planes to your model. The Ground Planes will line up perfectly, and you can reposition and resize them as needed to act as bases for the various areas you're modeling. As you place buildings and go outside the boundaries of the original Ground Plane, the additional Ground Planes act as a strong base as you move into the next phases of creation.

11.

Near the top of the photograph, you see a row of odd-shaped buildings that veers off at a strange angle, and some have curves or angles that don't fit the standard primitives. To model these, use a Box primitive to create the row. Then use Horizontal Sweep to create the angle, gluing the points to align everything. To create the odd-shaped buildings, use Horizontal or Vertical Sweep. Also, use the Rotate 90 Degrees option as needed.

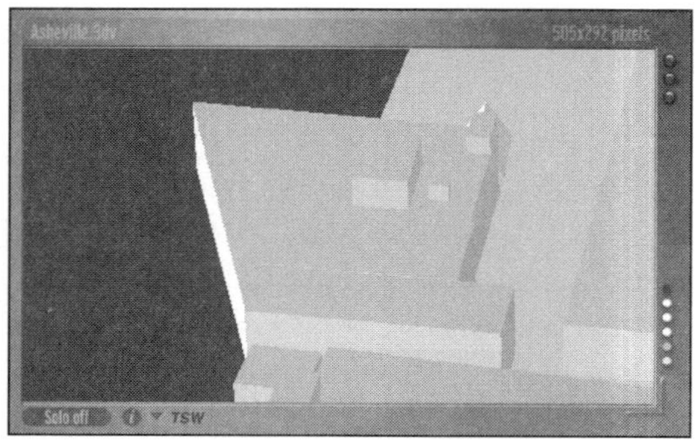

12.

As mentioned previously, you'll create Weblink hotspots in the final image. Some of these hotspots will send viewers to fictitious site sponsors, named Asheville Telephone Collective (ATCo) and International Internet Cooperative (IIC). You already designated the Helper application Canoma uses, so render your image, and then click on the Paint Brush icon to access it. Create billboards or banners on some building faces. If you don't want to create these, I included artwork you can import and place on the files.

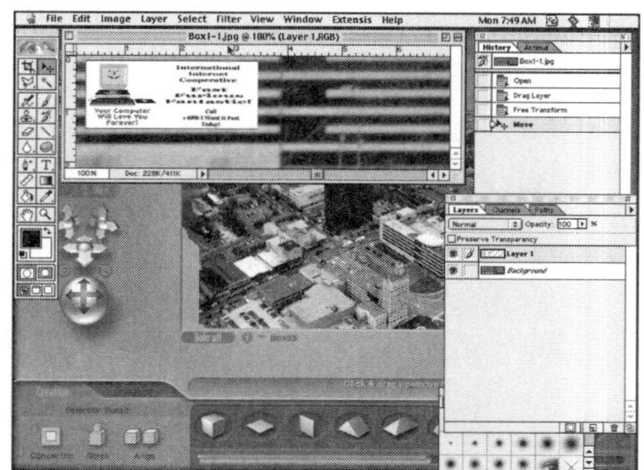

13.

After you finish the buildings, modifications, and other elements within the scene, choose Asheville_02.jpg by clicking on the down arrow in the Image window. Rotate the image you've created to fit it as closely as you can with this new image.

14.

You've been saving your Canoma file as you've gone along, but it's now time to save it in the various formats: MTS (MetaStream), OBJ (Wavefront), and PP2 (Poser Prop). You can also create a fly-around video.

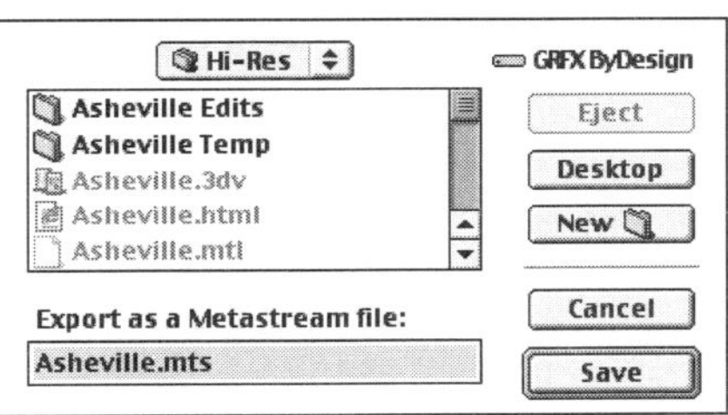

Importing The Files Into Bryce And Poser

From this point on, use Bryce and Poser to create your final Web-ready image. On the FTP site, you'll find demo versions of the programs provided by MetaCreations for use with this book. In the first step, you'll use Poser 4 to create animated files for sales presentations. You'll also build some basic models to use as static props inside Bryce.

*You can download demo versions of Poser 4 and Bryce 4 either from this book's FTP site or from MetaCreations' site at **www.metacreations.com**.*

15.

Now you use the PP2 or OBJ file. After you open Poser 4, choose File|Import|Poser Document/Prop. The PP2 file takes a while to load and may lock up your program or computer. We don't necessarily recommend using this format unless you save buildings as individual models that you import and place by yourself. The OBJ file imports more smoothly, so consider using it. Try both types and see which one you prefer.

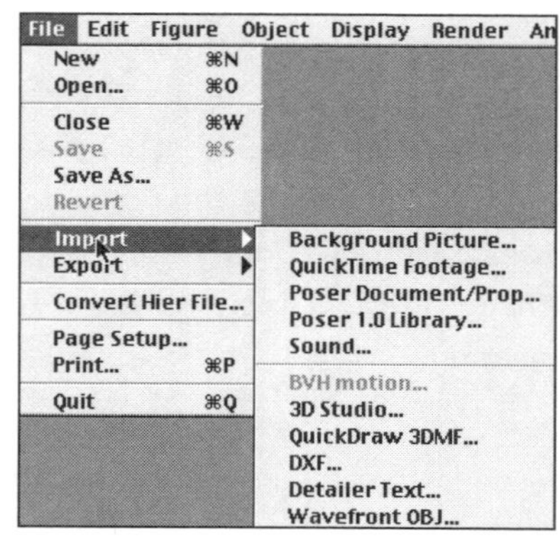

After the OBJ or PP2 file is imported, rendering it could take a little while. Be patient. It's best to take the time now to make sure that everything is mapped correctly than to go through the modeling process and then find out the textures aren't there.

16.

You'll find that Poser gives you numerous models to use as well as some new features that add to its usability. To enhance the appearance of the figures you'll use to populate the city, you can import a character and assign different clothes to it. Asheville is already imported, so spend some time creating various characters strolling through town.

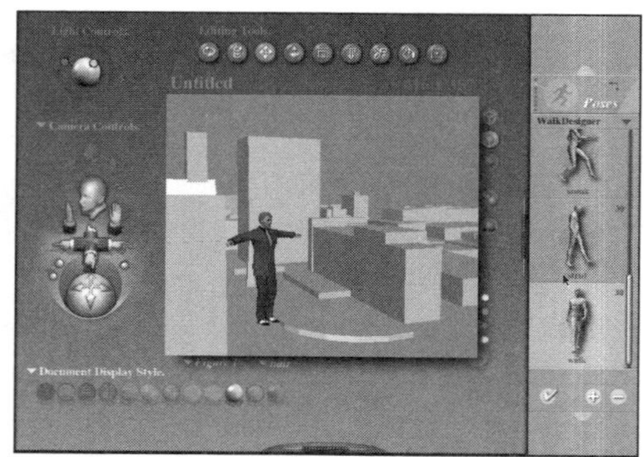

As you zoom in or scale the Asheville model, you need patience as you create figures. Resizing and positioning characters is tedious because of the way imported files update on the screen. The wire frame disappears and is replaced by a solid color, masking your resizing and placement efforts. Take your time; the results are worth it.

Animation Files

Now you create some Poser figures, pounding the pavement in search of great deals. You'll also focus on a model who will look up at your billboard ad, and you'll change camera angles to show the ad and character. You can use an animation (BVH) file included with Poser—walking, jogging, and so on—to assign to each model. Also, programs such as LifeForms 3.5 by Credo Interactive (**www.charactermotion.com**) allow you to create BVH files for importing into Poser and other programs.

17.

Here, you see just one such Poser pavement pounder.

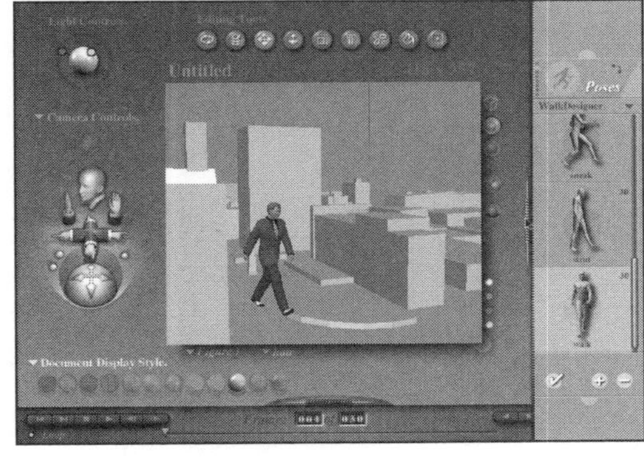

18.

Assign a time frame to the animation. I recommend 30 frames at 10 fps, producing a 3-second animation. Make sure that you're on the first frame and then position the characters where you want them to start their assigned action. Then click on Frame 30 and move the characters into place. Press the VCR-like start button on the Animation panel, and watch a rough draft of your work.

When you run this test animation, set up the program to do a Pencil test. You can select this option under the Render pull-down menu.

19.

Now place your central character in the scene. With Frame 1 selected, position your model in the initial pose and go to Frame 30. Select the head and then tilt and use the Camera control arrows to rotate it as necessary so that the figure looks up at one of the billboards you created. To make this character talk, you'll need a program that allows you to record audio. You'll also need a program such as Mimic (**www.lipsinc.com**) to create the speaking animation.

20.

With a few extra characters added in, the scene begins to come to life. Here, it's starting to look like a populated city.

21.

Now run a test of the animation. After the test runs, remove the Asheville city model, create some static poses in Poser, save the models as OBJ files, and quit the program. It's now time to move to Bryce.

Use Bryce For Web Creation

Bryce 4 is mainly a world-building program that allows you to generate original landscapes or import elements such as digital elevation map (DEM) files to render real-world 3D images. Because Asheville is a real place, you'll want to use the actual Asheville DEM files provided on the FTP site.

22.

After you open Bryce 4, delete the Ground Plane. Now import Asheville's plane. You need to have the two Asheville DEM files, the singular sheet, and the folder containing all the coordinate files. When you select the folder, one file from the folder will appear in the list of choices.

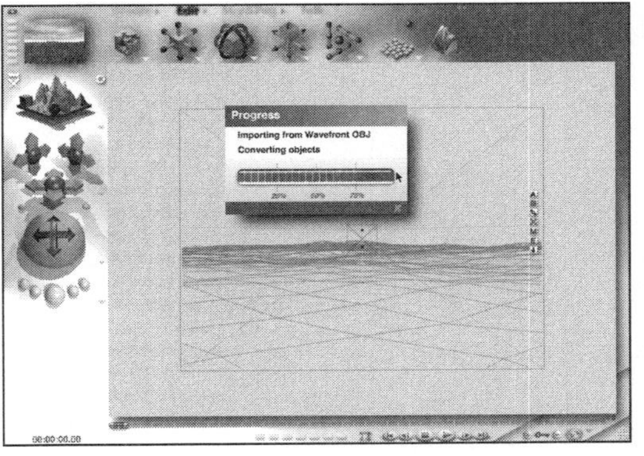

23.

Now create some geological activity. Click on Edit to select it, and then click on the downward-pointing arrow to the right of the first crosshair set. Resize the Asheville DEM plane on the X, Y, and Z coordinates to 1900. That sounds high, but you need to fill the screen with the new Ground Plane. Here, it's resized again, on only the Y axis to make the mountains stand out. Don't resize it too much—enough so that you can see the terrain clearly without having to zoom in much. Using the trackball, rotate the view so that you're looking straight to the horizon.

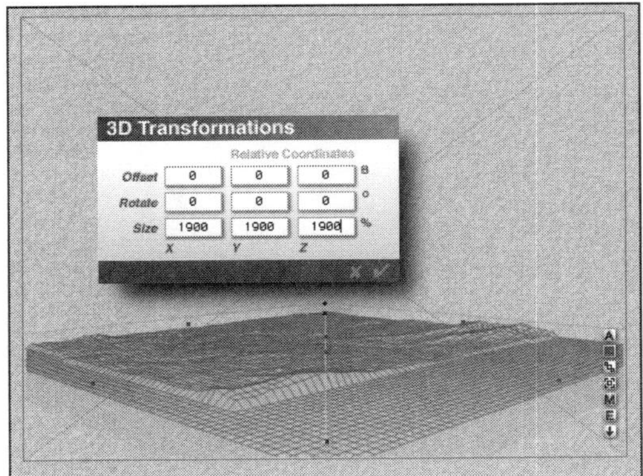

24.

Now import the Asheville OBJ file you created. You'll notice an anomaly: It seems that when a large number of primitives exist in a model, the model doesn't import exactly right. In the case of Asheville, the model is placed on two different levels.

25.

You need to Ungroup (click on the U button immediately next to the active model), and then click and drag the cursor over the high- and low-level elements, respectively.

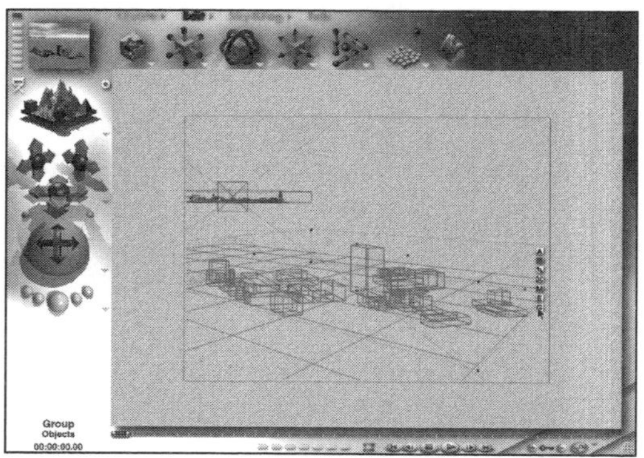

26.

The high portion of the model is also much smaller than the one on the ground. Use the trackball to rotate, and resize the higher elements to match the width, depth, and height of the one on the ground.

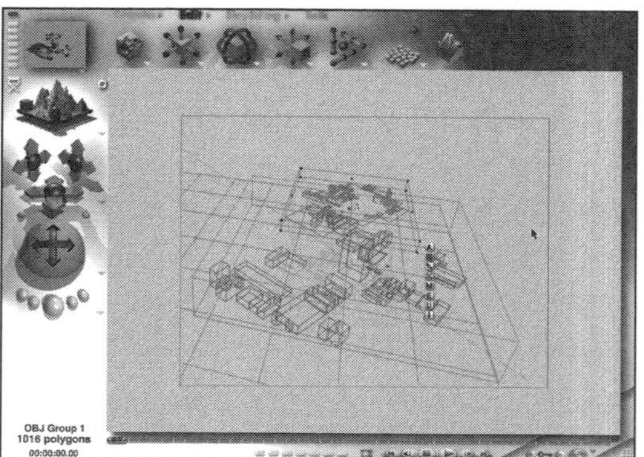

27.

Take some time and move the upper-level primitives back into place with the other primitive set (the lower level). After you're happy with the placement, select both groups and group them.

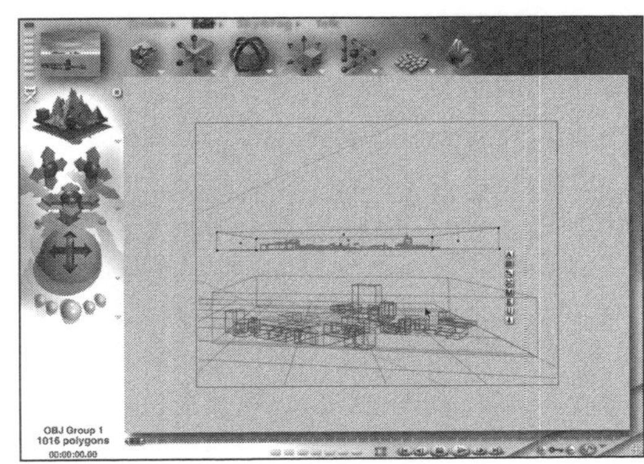

As an alternative to going through all the manipulation just outlined, if you have a program such as Poser 4, Ray Dream 5/5.5, Carrara, or Pixels:3D—or any 3D program that reads OBJ files—import the files into it and then resave. For Carrara and RD 5.5, group all elements before saving. This method has drawbacks; often, you must reload every image map associated with the scene—in this case, more than 250.

28.

To make sure that both elements are lined up correctly, render the image—Command|Ctrl+R—and you'll get a good feel of whether or not you need to reposition the elements. If you do, click the U button again and move a selected group.

29.

Notice that your revised building faces—those with the artwork you created—didn't import with the other files. This is easily corrected. Select Asheville, and click on the M button to go into the Materials Lab area. Click the first dot to the right of Diffuse. A Properties Modifier screen appears. To activate the Bitmap Editor, click on the second button in the row of two at the lower-left corner of this screen, and then click on the second button in the row of two at the upper-left corner. This action transports you to the Picture Editor, where you can import images to map onto your models.

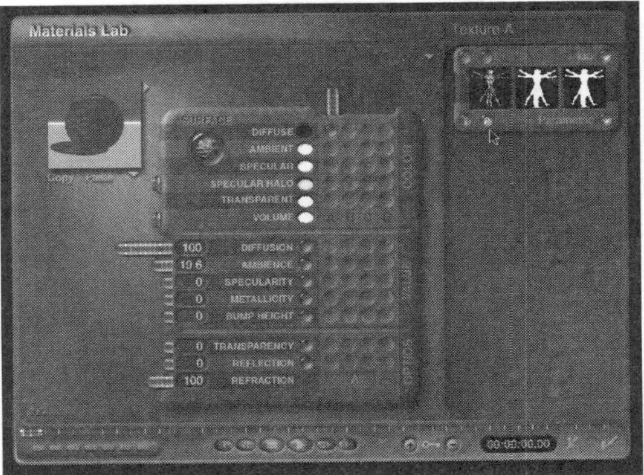

30.

The Picture Editor shows various textures assigned to the model, and it has three frames at the top of the screen where you can bring in new images. Click on the Load button for the first frame. Locate your modified image and select it. After importing, select Copy and then Paste to insert a copy of the image into the third window. To import other modified images, repeat the process. Then click on the checkmark at the lower right of the screen, click it again on the Materials Lab screen, and see your new images mapped onto your model.

31.

Remember those Poser OBJs you saved? Now import them into the scene. Because they're OBJs, they're imported with all the textures you assigned, and they're ready to be included. All that remains is for you to scale the figures to fit. It's an easy task as long as you don't accidentally ungroup the model. When the dimensions are right, place your figures where they work best, and save your file.

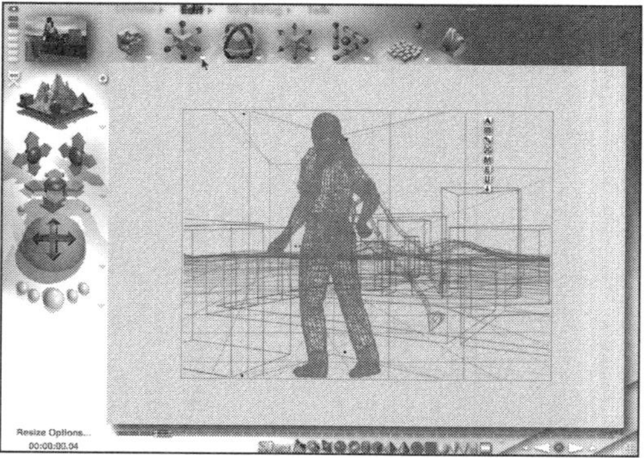

32.

To create a generic hot link in Bryce, select File|Export and select HTML from the pull-down menu. This action creates a JPEG image and an HTML page for use on the Web, and your entire image will act as a link button. You can upload the page to your site as is, or you can open the page in your Web editor to include it on your site.

33.

Now, assign your links. You could import the saved Canoma/Bryce/Poser JPEG file into your Web editor and create Web links there, but what's the fun of doing something you've already done over and over again? Isn't it more interesting to work in a new environment? Remember, you're the expert! You can assign links by clicking on specific portions of your model, in this case the front face of the ATCo building. A menu bar shows up, and the first button is labeled "A". Click on this, and then click on the Linking tab. At the bottom of the screen is a place for you to assign a link.

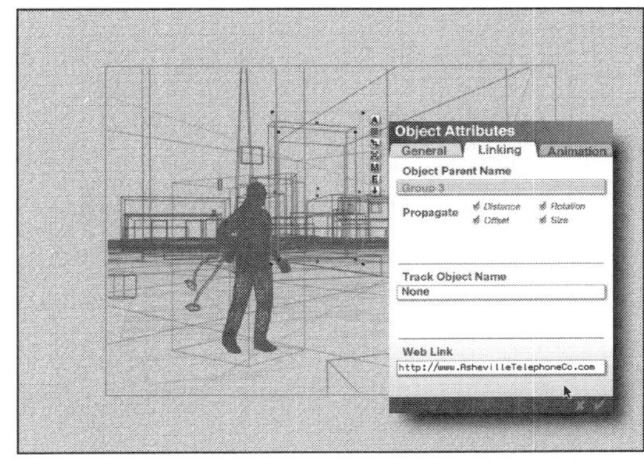

34.

Using this technique, you can assign a different Web link to literally each face of each building you've created as well as to the figures you imported. To express your sadomasochistic tendencies, ungroup a Poser figure you imported and assign a different link to each element of the model. Talk about driving your visitors crazy!

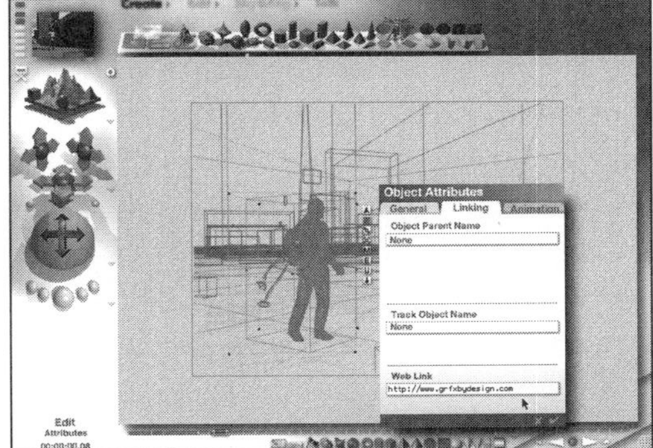

35.

Here the city is placed in its environment. What you see here will be the first frame of the zoom-in animation, with the textures placed on the OBJ city file and ready to have hot links assigned.

Taking It To Extremes

Creativity is the key to your success, so let's take your work to the next level. First, you'll create an animation that ends in a position that makes it appear as if hyperlinks are embedded in the file. Then, if you have QuickTime Pro, Adobe Premiere, or a similar video-editing program, you can combine elements to create a moving image that ends with a screen that becomes a gateway to other areas.

To create these animations, you'll use Adobe's GoLive! Web creation software. You can download a demo from the Adobe site at ***www.adobe.com****.*

36.

To create an animated link "fooler," start with the Bryce file you created, but remove the Poser characters. Create an animation—possibly starting from far away, flying over the ground to the city, and then stopping at the IIC billboard. After you create the flight path, render the animation and save it to import into Poser.

Read the Bryce 4 User Guide and become familiar with the material outlined in the "Animating Techniques" section. Bryce 4 F/X & Design by R. Shamms Mortier, published by The Coriolis Group, is another resource for learning ways to create animations and more.

37.

Import the animation file into Poser as a background image. Create a female character. After she's posed, move her out of the frame. At the point where the animation locks into place, bring your model back in. You want to make it appear that the camera's field of view is changing to reveal her. Now you can do more animation, such as turn her head or make her smile. Check how the animation looks, and then render again.

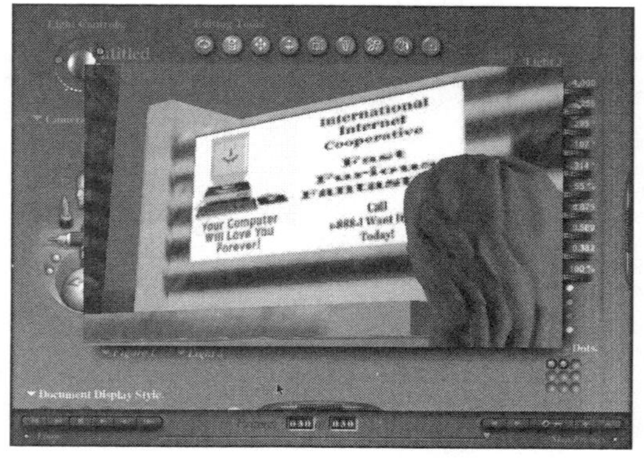

38.

As the animation ends, the female "model" has walked out of frame and a delivery person (obviously, another client of the advertiser) let's you know he's very satisfied with the product. The sign in the background is a hotlink.

39.

Open QuickTime Pro (or any other video-editing software), and resave the file in Streaming mode. Make sure Looping is turned off. Even if you keep the image small, you'll have a rather large animation file. It's one of the drawbacks of video on the Web.

40.

Sorensen Video is a great compression choice when saving your files. It produces small files which are easily downloaded via modem. This compression feature is available in virtually all the newer versions of programs such as QuickTime, RealMedia, Macromedia's Fireworks, and Flash. The more you can compress video files before the quality of the presentation becomes affected, the better. Experiment a bit to find out which compression technique is the right one for your project.

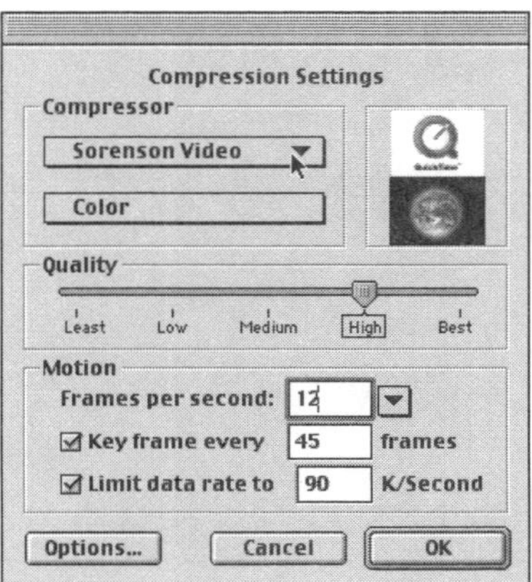

41.

Remember that 33.6K or 56K Internet connections are common, so download times for large files may be long. As cable modems and satellite connections become more common, this will change. Also, consider the amount of space your ISP provides. Don't create an incredible animation only to learn that you have no room left on your site. It's no problem, however, if you're creating an interactive CD-ROM or DVD.

42.

To assign hotspots, bring the streamed file into GoLive! 4. Place the video file onto your page and let it play. A great GoLive! feature is that it lets you edit QuickTime files directly. You can put together a complete QuickTime presentation without leaving GoLive! When you reach the end of the video, place your link frame over the billboard and assign the link. It's sleight-of-hand: By the time people realize a link is there, the video has already ended and your links were in place from the start.

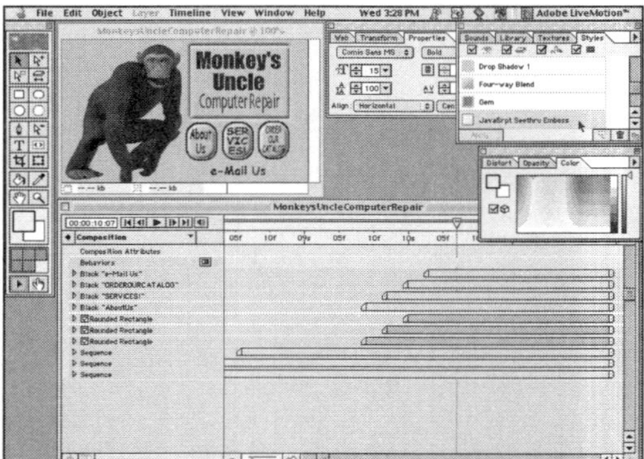

Create An Animated Link With LiveMotion

In Chapter 9, you created an animation with two Canoma files, added a dissolve and link to the file, and saved it as a Flash file. Now, here's something a little different.

43.

Here's another project, using Adobe LiveMotion, Poser, and Canoma to create an animated link screen for your site. The completed Flash animation, the LiveMotion file, and the JPEG series of files are all included in the Chapter 10 folder on the Coriolis FTP site.

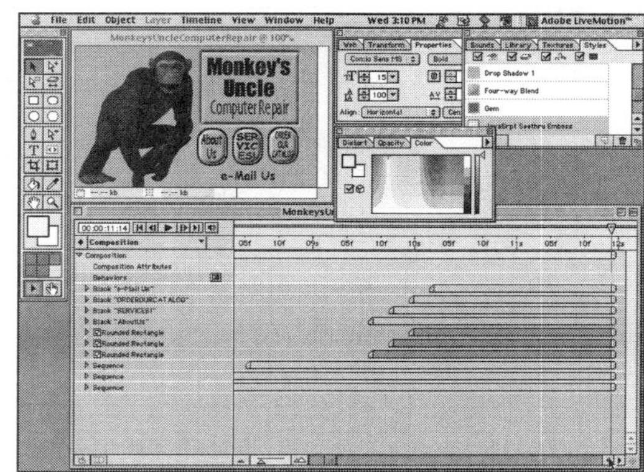

44.

You need to show the location. The first portion of the animation will consist of the modified Raleigh, NC model. Create a five-section keyframe, four-second animation that circles across the city, flies into the public square area, then zooms into the computer billboard on the side of the low building.

45.

You need to create only five keyframes so you keep the animation smooth, and not include *overkill* into the movie you're creating. A five frame set is perfect to assign specific spots in your animation to make the motion smooth.

46.

You want to save the animation (and the others you'll build) as a series of image files. If you're using Flash, Fireworks, or Director, you could import QuickTime MOVs or AVIs, but it's often easier to incorporate a series of static images that comprise the animation so you can have a little extra initial control over your files.

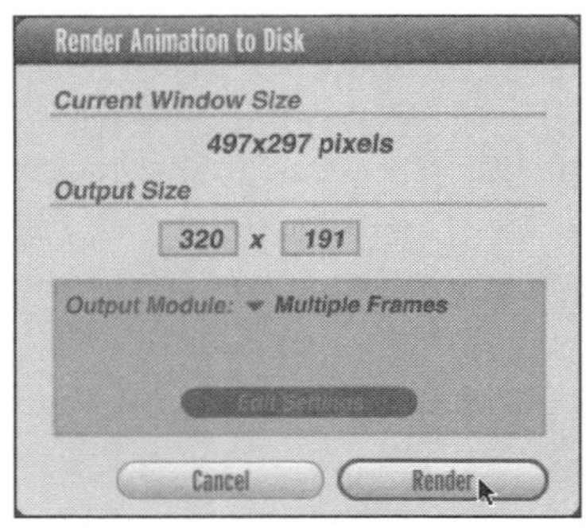

47.

By static image control, I mean that if you've assembled your animated file in LiveMotion or another application and the middle series of files doesn't work as a whole, you can delete those images and import only files you need. Alternatively, to add extra time prior to the start of or after the conclusion to the animation, you can import the first or last image file as many times as you like. You can also duplicate the end images within the program—it's far easier than trying to extend a self-contained video.

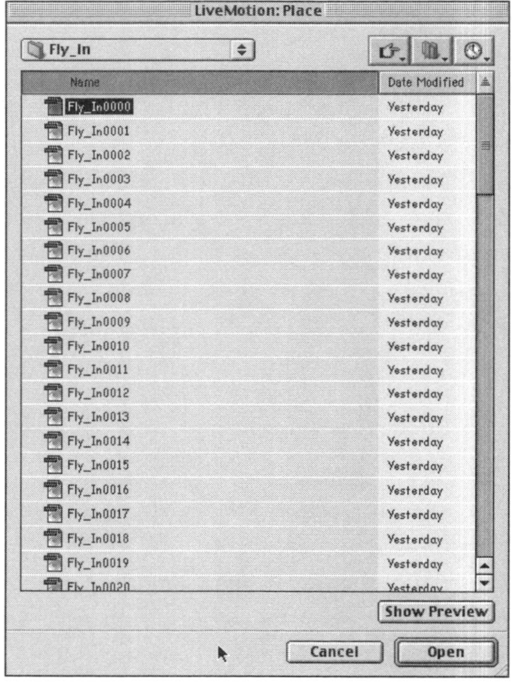

48.

For the next two steps, you'll want two different Background image files. One to use for the animated computer, the second to use with the Monkey (this company site is for Monkey's Uncle Computer Repairs). Create these in your preferred 2D image program.

49.

Now, build the Poser animations. Because of copyright issues, we can't provide you with the specific models used in this sequence, but you can purchase these characters at **www.zygote.com** or you can practice using any Poser characters. Refer to Chapter 8 and the Poser 3/4 User Manual to refresh yourself or learn how to create animations within the program.

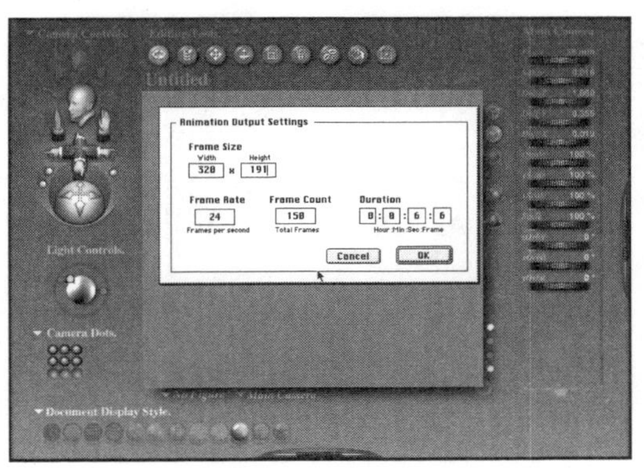

50.

As you did in Chapter 9, import your animation files into LiveMotion. Use File>Import Image Sequence and choose the folder or directory in which you housed your sequences. If you need to import single frames later, use File|Import Image.

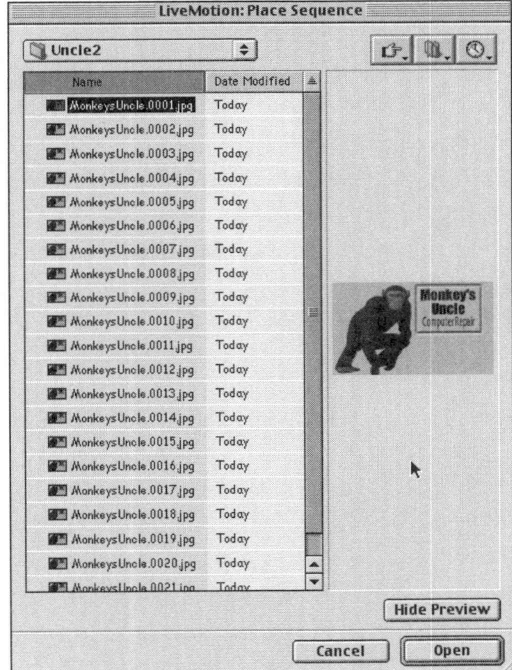

51.

Now, as you did in Chapter 9, build your animation using LiveMotion's Timeline screen. Place the image sequences, and then assign effects such as Pushes (where one image appears to push another off screen) or dissolves, squeezes (the video squeezes down to or expands from apparent nothingness), and more.

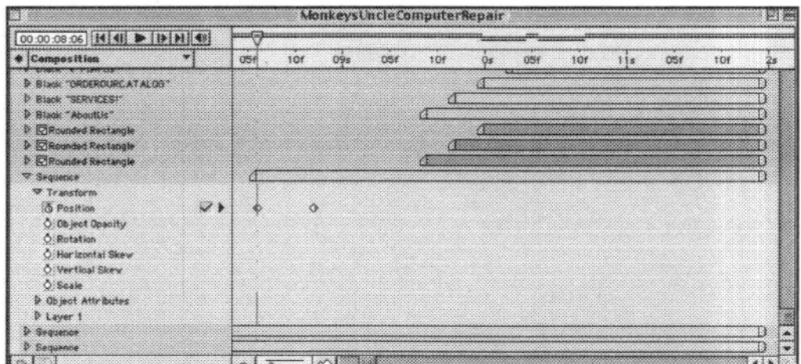

52.

Create the buttons and related text using the Vector Graphics tools, or import original buttons you've created in programs such as Adobe Illustrator or CorelDRAW. Then assign the Javascript Seethru Emboss attribute to the vector graphics. This will automaticaly create an animated effect for the buttons.

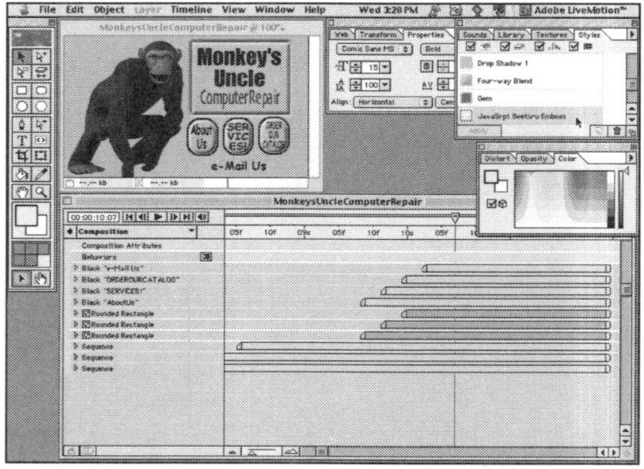

53.

Finally, add sound. Select the Rollover and Sound options from the Window pull-down menu, and assign a sound to each of the buttons when the mouse rolls over them. For detailed instructions, read the Adobe LiveMotion online tutorials at the Adobe Web site, or from the User Manuals for Flash, Fireworks, or Director. Export the file as a Flash animation. Select File|Export. LiveMotion and the Macromedia programs create both an swf (ShockWaveFlash) and an HTML file.

54.

For full interactivity, the file has been placed into a Web-design program. Hot links were added, as described previously (and you can easily add a Monkey's Uncle billboard hot link within the city). After completing this project, you're ready to create impressive interactive elements in your Canoma models to make your Web sites take on a new dimension.

Chapter 11
Canoma Creativity

Project 1: Another method to create an intricate model

Project 2: Finish the secondary buildings

Creative Complexities

Throughout this book, you've gained new ideas about how to use Canoma to create far more than architectural structures. You've learned how to work around the apparent shortcomings of the program to create objects that, on the surface, seem impossible to create. You've discovered how to combine Canoma models with other programs to expand your creative workflow. You've even created a model of a real city. Now it's time to create one more project, something that will serve to refresh your skills as well as explain how there are different ways to achieve the same results.

Project 1: Creating The Main Sports Arena

Let's return to Adelphia Stadium. In Chapter 8, you built this model; but now you'll build it again, this time with more detail.

1.

This aerial photograph was provided by the Tennessee Titans professional football team, which graciously gave permission to use it in this book. You can download this photograph from this book's FTP site.

2.

Now, zoom in on your starting point. You'll begin with the front entrance of the stadium. Zoom in on this area and take a look at what you'll need to construct it.

3.

Start with this part of the structure, which looks to me like scaffolding. Using a Box primitive, surround the image. Zoom in to make sure the primitive is positioned correctly.

4.

Now it's time to work on the other segments. With the primitive you just created still active, click on Align and place another Box primitive behind the first one. Form this one to the larger portion of the structure.

5.

Then click on the first primitive again, choose Align, and build the smaller entranceway. Again, select the first primitive and align and place the left side of the building.

6.

Glue the corners and edges to guarantee their positioning.

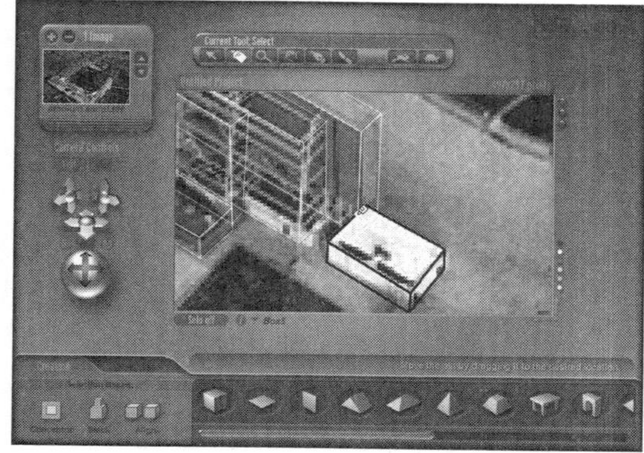

7.

Rotate the trackball to see a rough render of how the elements fit together.

8.

Now select the rearmost (largest) primitive, choose Align, and create the building at the right. As you can see in this picture, you'll place the left side of the primitive against the right side of the large one. Glue the two primitives together.

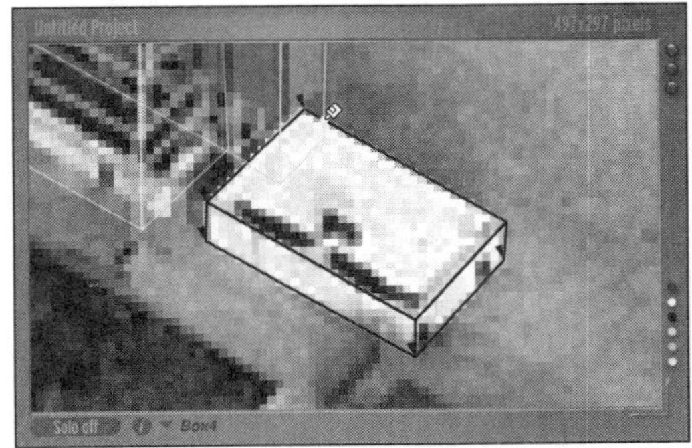

9.

Again select the largest primitive and choose Stack. Place and position a Box primitive. Glue the right rear corner of the new box to the larger one. When you're finished, click on the View button above the trackball. The model should look like the one shown here.

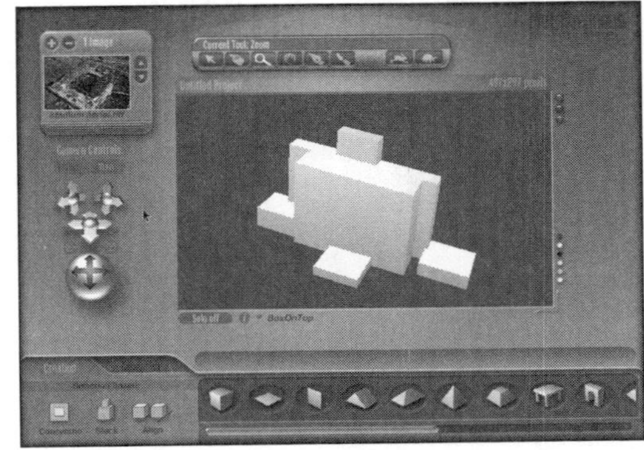

10.

To help you work with the other primitives, place a Ground Plane. Click on the primitive to place it. Now resize it to fit the area on which the stadium sits.

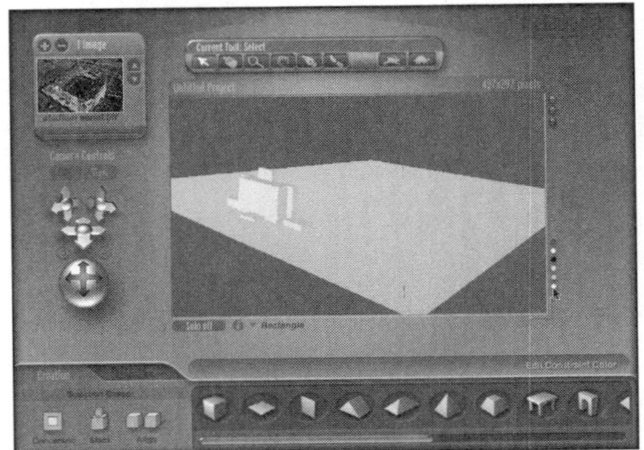

11.

To make sure everything is working the way you want it to, do a Quick Render. Rotate the model and zoom in on it to make sure everything is positioned correctly.

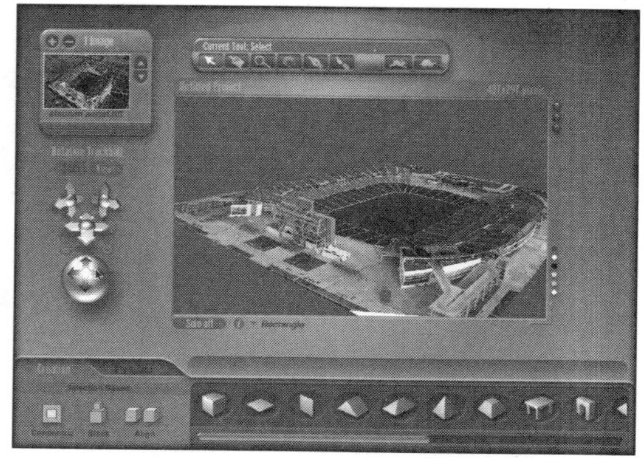

12.

Now it's time to work on the walkways. On the left side of the photograph, you'll see the three-story pedestrian walkway. Click on the Ground Plane, choose Stack, and model this portion of the complex.

13.

You still don't need anything except Box primitives. To build this section of the building, as well as the front corners of this portion, use the Ground Plane and the Stack option.

14.

Don't forget to glue the edges and corners to make sure everything aligns correctly. If you click on the View button at this point, the model should look like this.

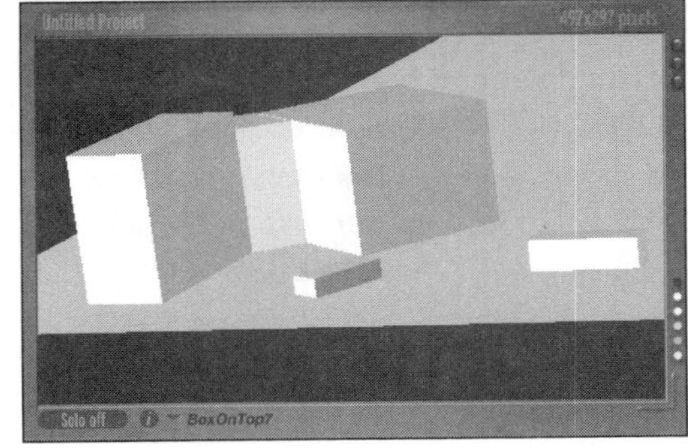

15.

When you're happy with what the left side of the stadium looks like, begin creating the right side. Start with the structure farthest away. Again, use the Box primitive to create this area.

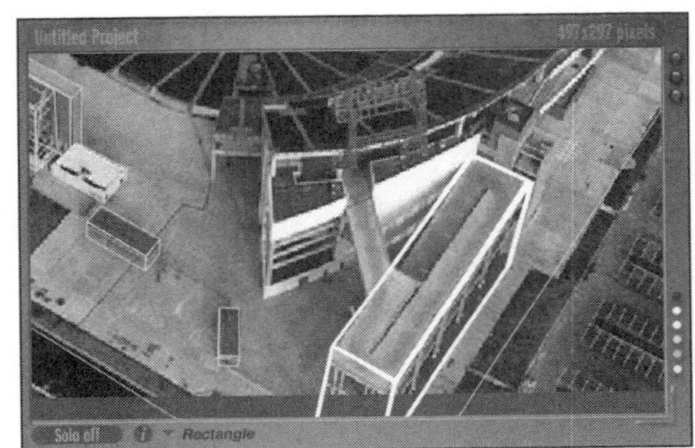

16.

Now it's time to use the Vertical Translation Sweep on the walkway. As before, select the Ground Plane, choose Stack, and position the sweep to outline the main portion of the building. Then select the Point tool and prepare to build the overhead walkway.

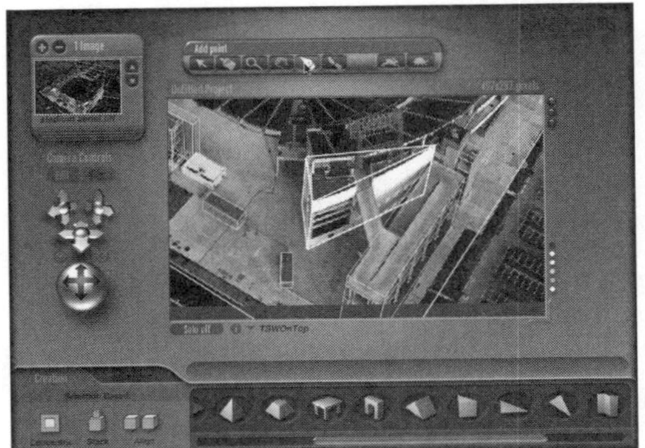

17.

Place some points along the top edge of the walkway's Translation Sweep. Start with two points to create the frontmost portion of the walkway, and then add two more points to outline the back portion. This part of the building also curves slightly. If you want to, you can add a couple more points to create the curve.

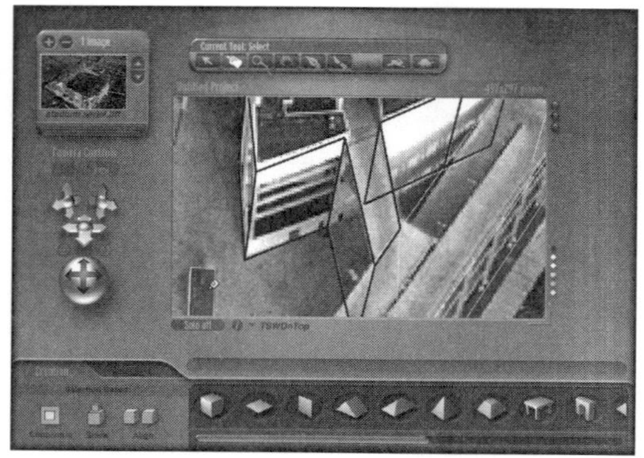

18.

Again, choose View and see how these two new primitives look. Your model should align like this. Notice the very slight curve in the structure.

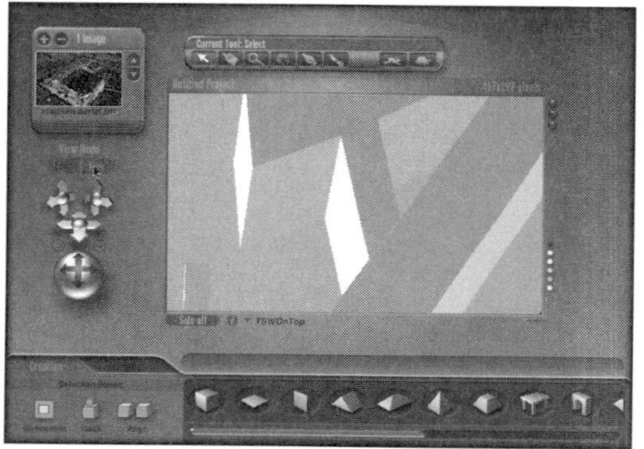

19.

You'll use two more Box primitives for this portion of the building: the small area jutting out just behind the portion you created, and the base of the playing field. Create the abutment first. Then place the box that will represent the playing field and the bottom portion of the seating area.

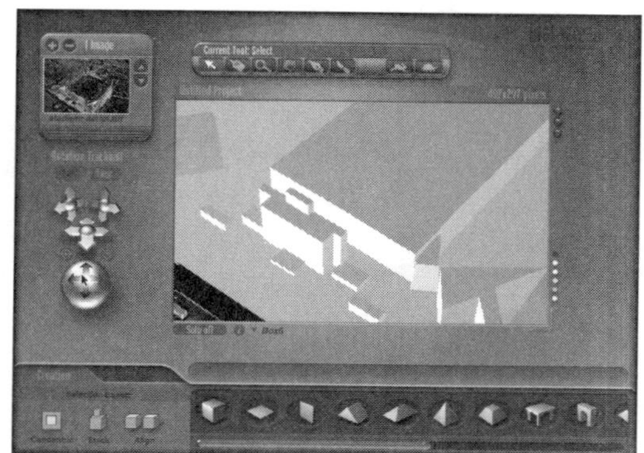

20.

Stretch the field primitive so that it extends the entire length of the structure. With this primitive still active, choose Stack and build the base of the scoreboard. To create the scoreboard itself, stack another Box primitive onto the first one.

21.

Now stack one more Box primitive onto the last one you created. At the risk of being repetitive, don't forget to glue the corners and edges so that everything sits correctly.

22.

Save your model again, and then click on the View button. The scoreboard area should look something like this, with well-aligned edges and plenty of pieces to give your model realistic detail.

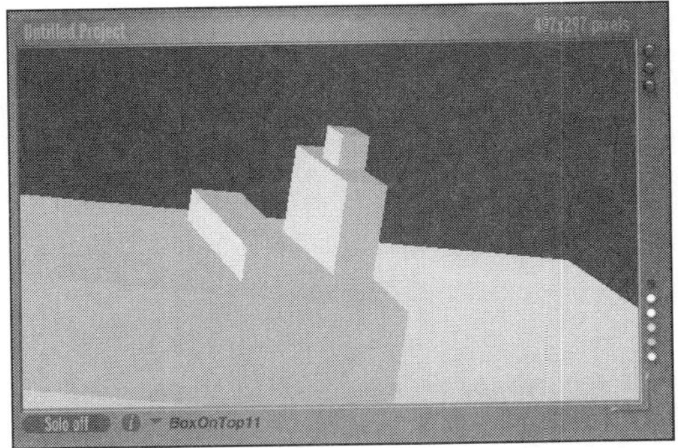

23.

It's a good idea to stop and zoom out, rotate around, and enjoy what you've built so far. By doing this periodically, you'll get a feel for how things are working together as well as how you'll create the next portions of the stadium.

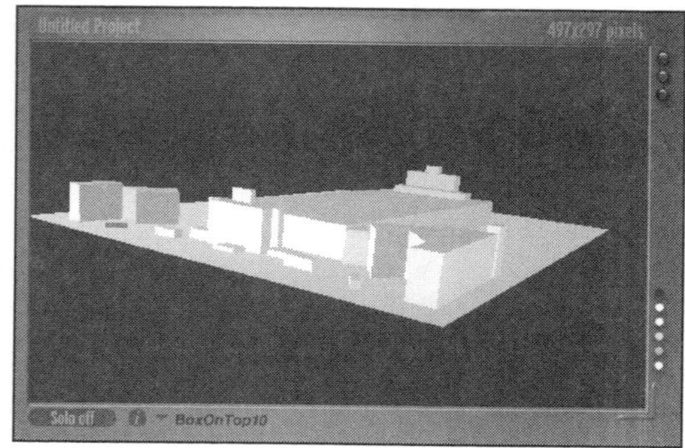

24.

Start creating the stands. As you work with Canoma, you'll probably come up with your own way of creating intricate or odd-shaped areas of a subject. To create the far left seating areas, I used the Horizontal Translation Sweep (HTS).

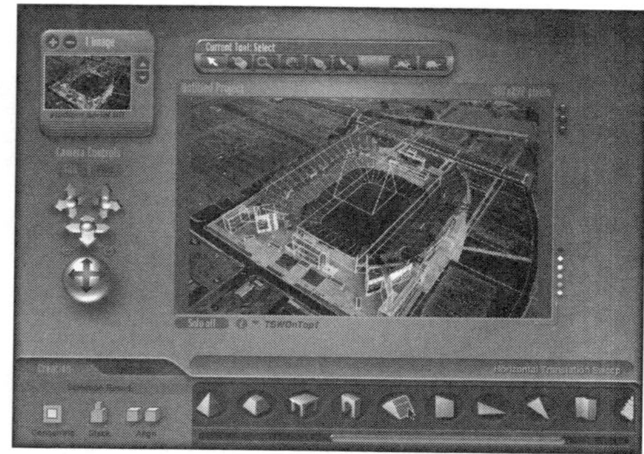

25.

To turn the Horizontal Translation Sweep in the correct direction, select Rotate 90 Degrees On The Y-Axis. Then begin placing it into position using the frontmost corner on the right and moving it into the center of the field.

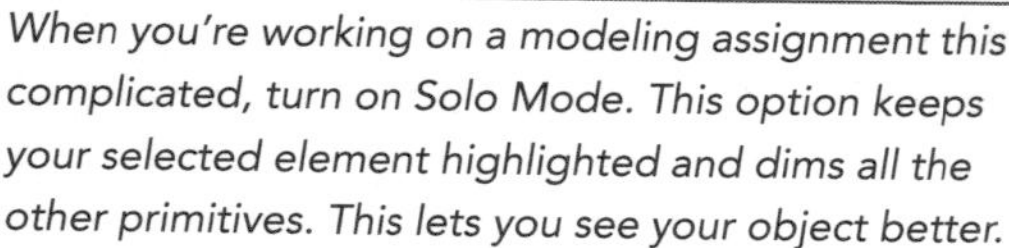
When you're working on a modeling assignment this complicated, turn on Solo Mode. This option keeps your selected element highlighted and dims all the other primitives. This lets you see your object better.

26.

If you select View after you've positioned the Horizontal Translation Sweep, you'll notice that the edge of the Box primitive and the middle of the HTS don't look right. Let's fix this. Use the Add Point tool and create a new edit point on the HTS. Position that point against the edge of the Box primitive and glue it.

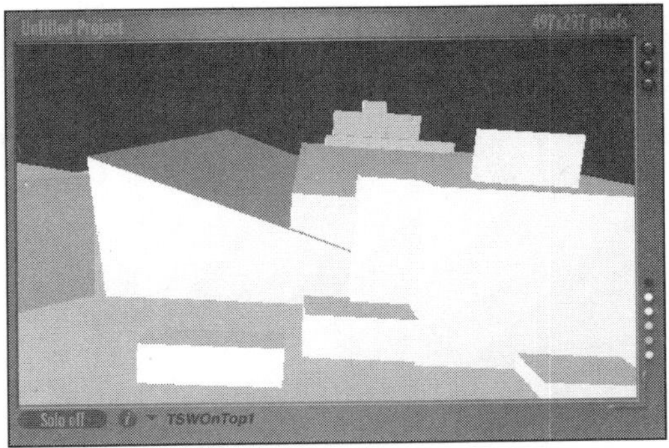

27.

To create the stands on the right side of the stadium, duplicate the HTS and move it around to the other side. You might need to do some minor tweaking of the primitive.

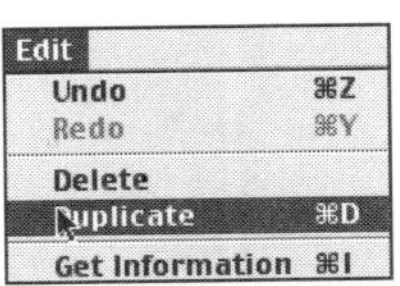

28.

If you select one of the rear corners of the primitive, it should rotate into position so that you don't have to do much work at all to create this side of the stands. This is one of the little-known tricks within Canoma.

29.

With the two Horizontal Translation Sweeps in position, make sure that the bottom edges of each sweep (the ones on the field) meet. You can glue their corners if you like.

30.

Again, save your model and notice how everything is coming together. Rotate around the image, zooming in to make sure all the edges align properly. Examine the elements closely to see where you need to make any modifications.

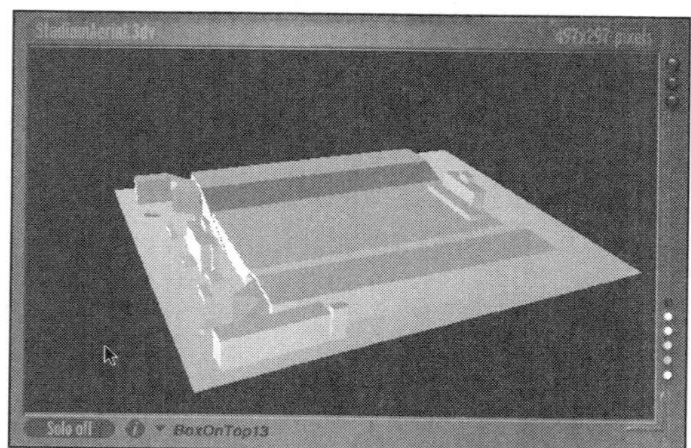

31.

Make all needed modifications, and then do a Quick Render or a Quality Render to get a feel for what Adelphia Stadium will look like when you finish.

32.

Only a few tasks remain. First, you need to create the rear edges of the stands. If you don't add them, the overall model will be incomplete. Use the Vertical Translation Sweep and follow the edges of the other primitives that touch it. Again, glue the corners to make sure the edges meet.

33.

Now you can create the lights. One option, shown here, is to stack a Box primitive on top of the HTS. If you prefer, you can also stack it on the Ground Plane, creating the girders that jut out from the sides of the stadium. It's up to you.

34.

If you choose to stack a Box primitive on the Ground Plane rather than on the HTS that forms the stands, this is what it will look like. If you're interested in creating realistic detail, it's best to do it this way, but again, it's up to you.

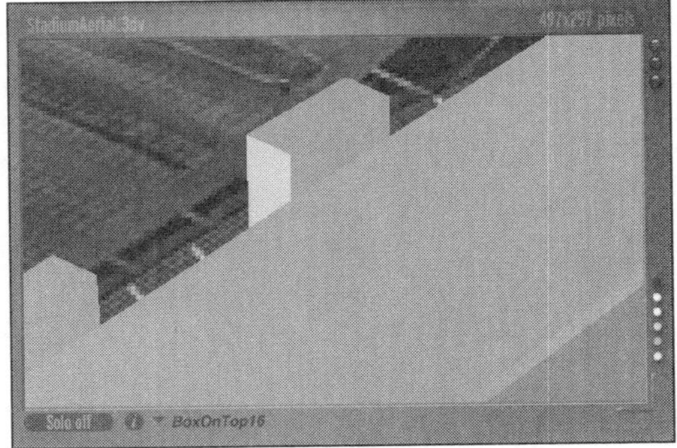

35.

Make sure that Mirror Texturing is turned on, and then do a Quality Render. This image contains numerous elements. It may not be as complex as the Chapter 10 project, but it will take time to map the photograph onto the primitives.

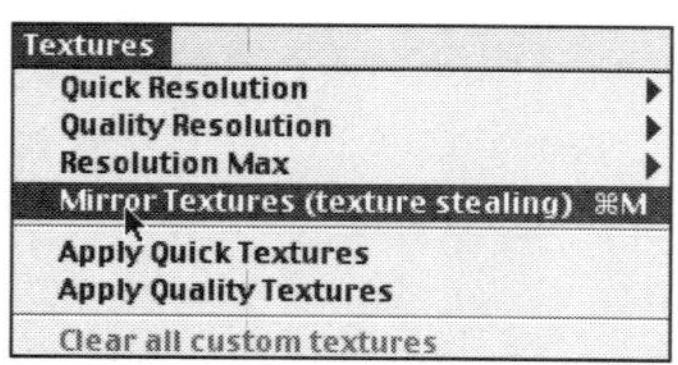

Project 2: Modeling The Other Buildings

Notice that other buildings dot the image. Some people would advise you to ignore these smaller structures because they aren't worth the trouble to build, but don't listen to them. The more modeling detail you put into your work, the more impressive your final product will be.

1.

To begin, click on the Ground Plane, select Stack, and place your structures, as shown in this first example.

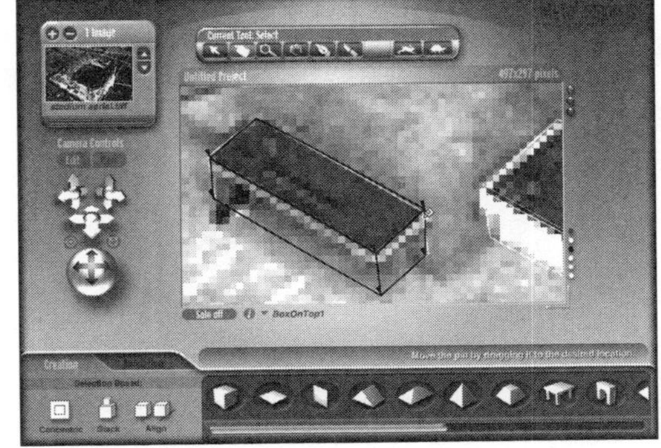

2.

Some of these smaller buildings are off-kilter from the other parts of the image. Don't worry about that. Just use a Box primitive for each one and surround the subject. As long as your stress indicator doesn't show unusually high stress areas, your model will look fine.

3.

To enjoy your handiwork, do another Quick Render (or, if you prefer, a Quality Render) at this point. The model's really coming along now with the extra touches you've added.

4.

Here's the final rendering of the football stadium. It's ready to be used on a Web site or to be placed into a scene using any of the other programs—both 3D and 2D—that we have discussed.

Index

B

C

D

E

F

G

H

I

X

Z